JACQUES DUBOIS
CROSIER PRIOR GENERAL
AT CLAIRLIEU
1778 - 1796

EMILE FONTAINE, O.S.C.
TRANSLATION BY MICHAEL COTONE, O.S.C.

Starting Afresh from
A Place of Light

A Crosier Jubilee Publication

Edited and Published by the Crosiers

- Crosier Generalate, Rome, Italy
- Crosier Province, Phoenix, AZ USA

For information on obtaining additional copies of this book or other Crosier publications, contact the Crosier Generalate via:

Website: www.oscgeneral.org

Email: infoosc@oscgeneral.org

Or write:

Crosier Generalate
via del Velabro 19
00186 Roma, Italia

Publication Number: ISBN 978-0-9799986-1-4

CONTENTS

Prior General Jacques Dubois, O.S.C.

INTRODUCTION

December 1996 marked the bicentennial anniversary of the death of Prior General Jacques Dubois, O.S.C., the last to hold that office between 1796 and 1853. This anniversary naturally also reminded the Crosiers of the four decades which followed, a period which nearly saw the extinction of their Order.

This translation is meant to acquaint those members of the Order who do not read French with these events of two centuries past and thus enable them to become more familiar with this part of their heritage. Reading Father Fontaine's account of Prior General Dubois and his contemporaries may also offer modern Crosiers a vantage point from which to reflect on their present circumstances, for the dogmas of the Enlightenment have yet to exhaust their claim on our culture, and those of emergent postmodernism may prove as seductive as what preceded them.

In preparing what follows, I have chosen to translate only those citations from the primary sources in the "annexes" to Father Fontaine's work which he quotes in the text. To translate these documents in toto would lessen their value as primary sources, and I have assumed that, as such, they will be of most interest to the professional historian, who will also have the skill to read them in the original, rather than to the casual reader, for whom my translation is intended. I have, on the other hand, included translations of the two articles by Father Fontaine which were published posthumously in the Order's historical journal, Clairlieu, in 1951 and 1952, and which carried his story into the decade after the death of Prior General Dubois [Note: these articles are included in this English language edition as Chapters Eight and Nine].

To provide the reader with some sense of the author's life and contributions to his Order's historiography, translations of a memorial article about him by Father Anton van Asseldonk, O.S.C., of a letter to him from Prior General Willem van Hees, O.S.C., which appeared in the 1947 edition of this book, and of the preface to it by Professor Leon E. Halkin of the University of Liège appear below.

In preparing the translation, I have enjoyed the generous assistance of Fathers Clemens Brasseur, O.S.C.; Pierre Winkelmolen, O.S.C.; Joseph Boly, O.S.C.; Albert Wieërs, O.S.C.; and Roger Janssen, O.S.C. To them and to the late Father Andre Ramaekers, O.S.C., who first proposed the project to me, I offer my sincere thanks. A special word of thanks is also owed Father Thomas Radaich and the people of St. Joseph's and St. Augustine's parishes in Grand Rapids and Cohasset, Minnesota, who have offered me not only a welcoming home and opportunities for ministry but also much encouragement and support in a scholarly endeavor which does not touch on them directly.

I dedicate this translation to all those sisters of Crosiers, especially my own, who, like Jeanne Josèphe Dubois Demany, have been a support and consolation to their brothers in times of trial.

Michael Cotone, O.S.C.
July 13, 1996

INTRODUCTION TO ENGLISH TRANSLATION

Jacques Dubois O.S.C. was the last Prior of Clairlieu. The French Revolution ended not only the age-old Crosier Priory at Huy. The French Revolution upended the historic form and traditioned rhythm of Crosier Religious Life that had been lived there. With the death of Prior General Jacques Dubois, an era of mass confusion and irresolution about religious life settled on the immediate horizon for Crosier Religious Life. Generally confreres were dispersed and disoriented. Monasteries were appropriated and suppressed. Properties secularized. Library holdings nationalized.

Confrere Emile Fontaine's book chronicles this important moment in Crosier History from the perspective of the struggles of Prior General Jacques Dubois to retain traditions and religious practices cherished and upheld for centuries in the Order. Fontaine's book, in many ways, serves more as a chronicle, almost a raw exhibit, of the historical documents available for this chapter in the Crosier Story. In that sense Fontaine's book is not an analytic history of the French Revolution. One really needs broader reading to position the chronicle Fontaine gives to make complete sense out of the events and hardships he narrates.

We might think of Eugen Rosenstock-Huessy's monumental *Out of Revolution: Autobiography of Western Man,* as a helpful backdrop and philosophical framework through which to read well the significance of what Fontaine chronicles. Philosopher Rosenstock-Huessy urges an understanding of history as more than naming dates, events, and heroic persons. In particular the French Revolution was a concerted effort: 'a passionate marriage of war and revolution', squarely positioned to do away with the *ancien regime*. According to Rosenstock-Hussey, the revolutions of humankind, "create new time-spans for our life on earth. They give man's soul a new relation between present, past, and future; and by doing so they give us time to start our life on earth all over again, with a new rhythm and a new faith."

Jacques Dubois, in Fontaine's analysis, suffers directly both from the ravages of Paris' revolutionary decrees and from his own confreres, the Clairlieu conventuals of Huy Priory itself. These revolutionary souls had a different relation to the past, present, and future than did Dubois. They had a very different role relationship to the contemporary signs of the times than did Prior Dubois. And they took concerted steps to undo the old rhythm and faith to which they had made profession.

The presentation of Dubois's story and publication of Fontaine's book in English falls at the end of a Crosier period in history we have named a 'Decade of Transformation'. The Jubilee Year 2010, committing all Crosier communities to 'Start Afresh from *A Place of Light*', consciously and conscientiously points with sorrow to the revolutionary demise of the old Clairlieu and the end point of that historic phase of Crosier history. It also points to a new rhythm and a new faith. This is not the place to layout in full the benefits gained and damages done to European Society, to western civilization, to Christian Religion, to Crosier self-understanding as a result of the French Revolution. It would be too daunting a task and too delicate a task to judge justly in such short space. But, generally speaking, most politically correct historians, at least until recently on this score, follow what is called a Tory view of history: history is forward progress and advocated evolution.

In my own unstudied perceptions of the French Revolution, most presumptions always fell on the side of how good and how important it was to undo and dismantle the traditionalist society of aristocratic privileged society. Thus, I recall – with not some little surprise – how, one occasion, Master General Lambert Graus voiced his regret for the French Revolution. He decried the massive destruction of scores of Crosier monasteries and the revolutionary loss of a living religious heritage, decided arbitrarily by rational fiat, as unfit for the human race and therefore also for Crosier members. Although Graus's perspective was actually the first I had ever heard voiced, naming so clearly an alternative assessment of the French Revolution's arguably dubious achievement, his balancing judgment certainly surfaced not from the point of view of a professional historian or a philosopher of history. Rather it was as the living successor of Prior General Jacques Dubois, now inhabiting the 'new time-spans for our life on earth' in the aftermath of that revolution. The life of the Order of the Holy Cross had almost died out in the aftermath of the "revolution of hope for humankind". That near demise Graus sincerely mourned.

When Rosenstock-Hussey calls living 'out of revolution' as marking our contemporary autobiography, he touches on the relevance of Fontaine's book for a more penetrating self-understanding of the our Crosier Story for contemporary members. A more dialectical weighing and adjudicating between the values and disvalues of the past, between the living and desiccated traditions of the past, as well as the treasured signs of the present times, affords contemporary post-Vatican II readers a different alternative to either revolution or absolute conservation. Certainly the Second Vatican Council's impact on the Crosier Constitutions reflects this dialectic: Unlike the revolutionary framework, the Constitutions of the Order of the Holy Cross "... certainly do not intend a break with the past." Nevertheless, living 'out of' the French Revolution, wherein religious life came to be redefined especially in light of specific usefulness to the social commonweal, has put forward the fitful struggle to rethink community life in terms of both tradition and evolution: "They [the Constitutions] try to set forth in a new way the traditions, which have always defined our community, and to carry this evolution toward ever new eras in the history of humanity and the Church." Indeed the contemporary Crosier autobiography and life project is significantly marked by the story of having passed through the fiery ordeal of the French Revolution.

The present publication of this book on Prior General Jacques Dubois in English provides a wider reading audience a significant resource in Crosier Order history. The translation was first commissioned by Master General Lambert Graus to enable contemporary Crosiers a perceptive insight into the story of the loss of the Crosier's foundational Priory at Clairlieu, Huy, as well as the valiant efforts made by Prior General Jacques Dubois to stay the execution of the order to expropriate the Monasteries and cultural-spiritual heritage of the Order.

The death of Dubois and the dismantling of the mother-house would seem to announce sure defeat of Dubois's bold efforts to save his beloved Clairlieu. Yet, still again in 2010, the Crosier Order dares assert its bold convictions for "Starting Afresh from *A Place of Light.*" Clairlieu, if it is always of God, blossoms to life in new, fresh ways.

Glen Lewandowski, O.S.C.
57th Prior General of the Order

Feast of Saint Agatha, 5 February 2010

In Memoriam
Father Emile Fontaine, O.S.C.

In the early hours of the morning of Wednesday, January 17, 1951, Father Emile Fontaine passed to his eternal rest at the monastery in Hannut. He was, from the first, an enthusiastic member of the Clairlieu Circle and a valued contributor to our journal.

Born on February 26, 1891, at Ciplet, in the province of Hesbaye, and to a family native to the region, Emile Fontaine left his village at the age of nine, when his father, a stone-dresser, moved the family to Hannut. Enrolled in that city's independent school, Emile's intellectual talents and great piety soon attracted the attention of its headmaster, Mr. Jacquemart.On May 3, 1903, when he participated, as an altar boy, in the laying of the cornerstone of the monastery which the Crosiers were establishing in Hannut, Emile had the premonition that this would one day be his second home.

The name of Emile Fontaine appears among the first students enrolled in the high school which the Crosiers of Hannut opened in 1904. During his third year of studies in the Greek and Latin program, he expressed a wish to become a Crosier and was, as a consequence, enabled to continue his studies in the humanities under private tutelage at the same school.

Emile was the first student from Hannut to enter the Order's novitiate at the monastery of St. Agatha (the Netherlands),

on September 6, 1910. In this new forum, the young semi-
narian soon displayed those qualities which were to mark his
whole life: a keen sense of responsibility, solid piety, affec-
tionate goodwill, a lively intelligence, a delicate and nuanced
sensibility, a distaste for any rough or coarse behavior, and a
naturally upright character which invited a similar response
from those around him. He would not have been a true native of Hesbaye, however, had he not also been possessed of
a jovial and happy disposition touched with a bit of playful-
ness.

Being thus by nature one of those upon whom life, in all its
difficulties, often inflicts suffering, Emile also had to endure
certain painful circumstances which made his monastery,
although he loved it deeply, a place of exile. Such was the
consequence of the war of 1914-1918: four very difficult
years, during which he lived in a foreign country without
news of his family and under the burden of a state of health
which forbade any possible military service.

In those years Emile was also ordained a priest--on June 17,
1916--and the next day celebrated his first Mass, without the
supportive presence of those whom he held most dear. His
feelings on this occasion are revealed by a single touching
incident. He had chosen not to have printed memorial cards
of his ordination and even declined an offer to have such
cards prepared for him. At the last, however, he yielded to a
classmate's urgings and, artist that he was, created a simple
design in India ink: a rich bouquet of flowers, among which
unfolded a single rose, its thorns barely concealed. The accompanying text reads: "In memory of my priestly ordination, received through the hands of His Grace, Monsignor
Arn. Diepen, Bishop of 's Hertogenbosch, June 17, 1916."
This is followed by a cross entwined by a plant and, "Grant

me, a God of mercy, to always celebrate the Sacred Mysteries worthily. The Friday within the Octave of Easter. Emile Fontaine."

In the first months of 1919, Father Fontaine was finally able to return to Hannut, where he was appointed a teacher at his old school. The next year he was elected prior of his community, which the Very Reverend M. Kronings, recently appointed superior of the first Crosier mission to the Belgian Congo, had guided for sixteen years. The new prior's dynamism was soon evident. While the press reported the rumor that the Crosier monastery in Hannut would be closed or had already been sold, its young prior published circulars announcing that it would open a boarding-school at the beginning of the new academic year and that a program in agricultural studies was being established.

Nothing escaped his concern, and the monastery church was its first beneficiary. Large numbers of people always filled it to hear his eloquent sermons. He also had a statue of the Little Flower, St. Therese of Lisieux, placed there, the first in the area, and after her canonization established a confraternity dedicated to her. When the church was later repainted, the polychrome color scheme was his creation.

The school, also enlarged, was still separate from the monastery. In 1927 Prior Fontaine connected the two buildings by a new one, which contained four spacious classrooms, a physics laboratory and a large dining room. He also founded an alumni association and a Marian sodality, of which he remained, even during the long years after his priorate, the enthusiastic director.

Unfortunately, in the midst of all this activity, he soon fell ill with double pneumonia. If, contrary to all medical expectations of the time, he survived it, he was never again to re-cover his previous energy. At the end of his third term as prior, he sought to return to the ranks of his confreres, but his successor, Prior Jaspers, appointed him subprior, an of-fice which he held until his death.

When the working group of historians and journal known as Clairlieu were founded at Hannut in 1941, Father Fontaine displayed such an outstanding love for his Order, both by his insightful remarks to our gatherings and by his first writings, which soon appeared in our journal, that one might have thought him a prior addressing a chapter or a novice master instructing his charges. Thus, no sooner had he left the pulpit than he took his seat in the historian's chair. Once seated, he astonished his class with the first fruits of his learning and research, viz., his biographical study, "Mgr. Jacques Dubois, Général des PP. Croisiers à Huy, 1778-1796," which occu-pied two issues of *Clairlieu* (1946 and 1947) and was ac-claimed as "a substantial contribution to the history of the Meuse region and... to the religious history of the late eight-eenth century." Several supplementary articles followed, to round out certain aspects of the history upon which his biog-raphy of Prior General Dubois had touched, viz., "Les Crois-iers de Liège en face de la suppression" *(Clairlieu* 7 [1949] 14-39), "Une première crise à Clair-Lieu au XVIIIᵉ siècle (1735-1752)" *(Clairlieu* 8 [1950] 3-30), and "Mgr. Jacques Dubois et la fin du Prieuré de Carignan" *(Clairlieu* 8 [1950] 46-66). The reader will find in this issue yet another article on this same period, which the author's unexpected death has made a posthumous publication.[1]

---

[1] In fact, two of Father Fontaine's articles were published after his death: "La Fin de Clairlieu" *(Clairlieu* 9 [1951] 6-42) and "Le Definitoire (1796-1803)" *(Clairlieu* 10 [1952] 28-36). Translations of them appear in the

Prior General Jacques Dubois, O.S.C.

On January 1, Hannut's subprior had, with his characteristic warmth, again offered to the community's prior its wishes for a happy new year. Shortly thereafter, however, his health began to fail rapidly. Only he seems to have perceived how grave was his illness, for he asked to receive the Church's last sacraments on the morning of January 15. He endured his illness until the early hours of January 17, when he came to his death with a calm and steadfast spirit. Urged by one of his confreres to pray with him, he replied that he no longer could. His energies soon faded and, in a last effort, his heart burst, leaving his soul free to be enwrapped in the eternal embrace of God. May he rest in peace.

Rev. Dr. Anton van Asseldonk, O.S.C.
17 June 1951
Hannut, Belgium

appendices. – Tr.

LETTER TO THE AUTHOR FROM MASTER GENERAL VAN HEES, O.S.C.

Your affection and love for the history of our Order have led you to devote many years to its study. Today we joyfully welcome the publication of your first major work, the biography of Msgr. Jacques Dubois which you promised us some years ago.

Thanks to your zealous pursuit of this research, numerous historical documents of inestimable value, many of whose very existence was hitherto unsuspected, have been saved from oblivion.

Kindly accept our abundant thanks for whatever pains your efforts have cost you. Your work will enable us to better understand those terrible years of the French Revolution, which so greatly threatened the very existence of our beloved Order.

May the noble figure of Msgr. Jacques Dubois shine forth once more, especially on the next generation of Crosiers. May your work encourage them to admire him and, more importantly, to imitate him *candide crescens in gratia.*

Devotedly yours in Christ Jesus,
Wm. van Hees, Mag. Gen. O.S.C.
1 November 1947

PREFACE

The Order of the Holy Cross, or of the Crosiers, was founded shortly after the beginning of the thirteenth century by Blessed Theodore of Celles, a canon of St. Lambert's in Liège.[2] The monastery of Clairlieu at Huy was the Order's cradle and the home of its priors general until the end of the French monarchy. During these centuries the Crosiers played a significant role in our country's spiritual life. Today, however, their memory has sunk into an undeserved oblivion, even in Wallonia, of which they were one of the glories. We therefore commend to you the present work by Father Emile Fontaine, O.S.C., a biography of Prior General Jacques Dubois, O.S.C., who was the Order's Prior General during the time of the Revolution.

It is appropriate that the first Walloon Crosier since the Order's revival has devoted his research to the last prior general at Clairlieu before the Revolution. Father Fontaine's book, however, is not merely a panegyric of Prior General Dubois: in a work of grander design and greater merit than that, the

---

[2] See Henricus van Rooijen, O.S.C., Theodorus van Celles. Een tijds- en levensbeeld (Cuyk, 1936). (Father van Rooijen's later books, "De Oorsprong van de Orde der Kruisbroeders of Kruisheren: De geschiedbronnen" [Clairlieu 19 (1961), 1-240] and The Church of the Holy Cross de Claro Loco and the True Origins of the Crosiers: A Spiritual Drama, ed. and trans. M. Cotone, O.S.C., [Denderleeuw, 1994], question this traditional version of his Order's origin and early history. – Tr.)

author has sought, with the help of monastic archives, to accurately trace the history of a major crisis.

We may venture that Prior General Dubois was neither a genius nor a saint. He did not labor under the weighty burdens of, for example, a Cardinal von Franckenburg or a Prince-Bishop de Mean.[3] Nevertheless, we cannot help feeling a certain respect for this religious, who stood athwart the currents of his time, nor help admiring the courageous old man who so squarely faced adversity day after day.

We may also venture that, had Prior General Dubois lived some years beyond 1796, the Crosiers would not have been so long absent from Wallonia. The old General was one of the combatants in the Revolution's religious history: one of those who lost, perhaps, but still a true champion of the Church's vitality. Prior General Dubois is, in and of himself, an interesting figure, but his biography can also serve as an introduction to the religious history of the eighteenth century, for his story is also the story of the Crosier Order and more. Except for the individual circumstances, this account reflects a much wider history.

Father Fontaine does not conceal the decline of religious life on the eve of the Revolution. The decline of ideals dried up recruitment. The reaction of religious communities left to their own devices and weakened by the ideas of the philosophies is described in great detail. The author's skillful use of various scattered source documents enables us to see how the" majority chapter," an institution of republican inspiration, encroached on the authority proper to the Order's supe-

---

[3] The former was the archbishop of Mechelen and cardinal primate of Belgium during the time of the Revolution; the latter was the last prince-bishop of Liège and was expelled from his city and see by the French in July of 1794. – Tr.

rior. He likewise enables us to see the insubordination of some of the Order's members and their complacency when confronted with the revolutionary governments. In the midst of so many intrigues and such spiritual turmoil, however, there is no trace of impiety: rather, oppression seems to have revealed nothing but numbed consciences.

Consequently, the work which I am honored to here introduce is more than a learned or pious biography. It is a substantial contribution to the history of the Meuse region and, in a broader sense, to the religious history of the late eighteenth century. Perhaps its author will also soon favor us with the other book which we await, namely, the story of his Order's rebirth when the torments of the Revolutionary era had passed.

Professor Leon E. Halkin
University of Liège

FOREWORD

The principal sources used in the preparation of this monograph are archival documents in the State Archives at Liège. Their great value is that they provide a complete dossier on the Crosiers of Huy during the era of the Revolution.

If the registers of letters and decrees provide us with the official texts of these documents (i.e., as they were issued, after the scissors of the Republic's censors had finished with them), the Crosier sources allow us to read them in their uncensored form. It is both quite interesting and highly informative to read the marginal notes, to see which words have been changed and which passages excised, and so determine what the secretary's pen actually recorded during the deliberations and votes of the five-member Central Administration which heard Prior General Dubois' case. The wealth of documentation is almost an outline of his eventful life, and is a portrait of his true moral stature. This material has been supplemented with:

- The Registers of the City Administration of Huy under the French Regime, years III, IV and V (twenty-four volumes); especially helpful were the Registers of Minutes of the Sessions of the Municipal Council and the Registers of Letters, both in the archives of the city of Huy.

- The account-book of Father Noiville, the subprior of

the Crosiers of Huy, from 9 Messidor, year IV (June 27, 1794) to 28 Brumaire, year V (November 19, 1796), which is in file 2 of the collection" Sources: Crosiers of Huy" in the State Archives at Liège.

- The Record of drugs and merchandise delivered to the Messieurs Crosiers of Huy by H. Delloye, from April 20, 1777 to January 3, 1790. This source, which was formerly the property of Clairlieu, was made available to me by the Dominican Fathers of la Sarte lez-Huy. It is cited in the text as "Record of drugs."

- The record Pro luminario alba,4 also in "Sources: Crosiers of Huy" in the State Archives at Liège.

The significance of the archival sources which I have used justifies, I believe, my less frequent citations of printed sources. When reference is made to the latter, it is done so in the notes to the text with the pertinent information. Archival documents have been accurately transcribed and are printed in the Annexes. The order in which they appear there has been determined by the chronology of the narrative.

Professor Leon E. Halkin of the University of Liège has been kind enough to review my work and grace it with a preface. I take this opportunity to extend to him my sincere thanks.

The ways in which my confreres, Fathers A. Ramaekers and M. Colson, both members of the Clairlieu Circle, have assisted me are too numerous to mention. I am equally conscious of the assistance of Father Bussé, who has prepared the indices of personal and place names.

During the preparation of this text, help and suggestions

---

[4] Father Fontaine explains this record "pertaining to white lighting" in his second chapter; see page 16 and the accompanying note 4. – Tr.

were provided at various times by the following individuals out of their kindness and interest in my work: Mr. Jean Puraye, Licentiate in the history of art and architecture; Mr. Emil Dantinne, Archivist of the city of Huy; Mr. Etienne Helin, assistant at the University of Liège; Mrs. Marie Georges Goldenberg, Licentiate in historical sciences; and Mr. Emil Nondonfaz, former secretary of the city of Liège, who died in November 1944, as a result of mistreatment suffered in the concentration camp at Buchenwald. Finally, I must note that the ever-obliging Mr. Ivan Delatte, curator of the State Archives in Liège, provided me with a veritable flood of precious pieces of information. My very sincere thanks to all who helped, counseled or encouraged me during the course of my work.

Emile Fontaine, O.S.C.
Hannut
21 December 1946
150th anniversary of the death of Prior General Dubois

CHAPTER ONE
PRIOR OF KOLEN

Jacques Gisbert Joseph Dubois was born at Liège on December 19, 1730, and baptized the same day at Notre Dame aux Fonts. His baptismal sponsors were his grandfather, Jacques du Bois, and Catherine Vandewane.[5] His parents, Jean François du Bois and Jeanne Cologne (the widow of Denis Dupont), had been married on May 6, 1727, in the church' of St. Thomas.[6]

Of the ten children born to this couple between 1728 and 1744, Jacques was the third child and eldest son.[7] The family belonged to the parish of St. Thomas.[8] We have no clear information about its social status nor about the upbringing, education and vocation of its future Crosier. When his parents came to choose a school for him, they would have

---

[5] City Archives Of Liège, Notre Dame aux Fonts, Register 29, fol. 136. My thanks to the former secretary of the city of Liège, Mr. Emile Nondonfaz, for this information.

[6] City Archives of Liège, Marriage records of St. Thomas, Register 284, fol. 23vo.

[7] See Annexe 1 (E. Fontaine, O.S.C., Mgr. Jacques Dubois, General des PP. Croisiers à Huy, 1778-1796 [Diest, 1947], 125.)

[8] Among Jeanne Cologne's relatives was Father Egide Joseph Bertho, who was godfather to Catherine Jeanne Dubois.

1

found that, except for the bishop's seminary, the local Latin schools were operated by the Jesuits: that in the upper city by the English Jesuits and the other, on the site of the school of the Hieronymites[9] and now part of the University of Liège, by the Walloon Jesuits. English Jesuits and the other, on the site of the school of the Hieronymites[10] and now part of the University of Liège, by the Walloon Jesuits.

Young Dubois probably attended the latter. The time he spent there may well have led to his entrance into the Crosier Order, for his school was practically next door to its monastery in Liège. In those days the Crosiers owned a strip of land along the bank of Meuse and their buildings fronted on the street whose name records their presence in Liège. Did young Dubois often go to pray in the church of the *Creuhis*, as the people of Liège called them? We have no way of knowing, but in time his vocation brought him to their church and monastery.

Jacques Dubois made his religious profession in 1751. His superiors must have taken note of his piety and intelligence, for he had scarcely been ordained to the priesthood in 1755 when he was appointed professor of philosophy and theol-

---

[9] One of several congregations established in Italy and Spain during the fourteenth century. They initially Jived according to the rule of life which St. Jerome had composed for the women who had settled in Bethlehem with him, and were known as the Hermits of St. Jerome; they afterwards gave up their hermitic way of life and adopted the Rule of St. Augustine. – Tr.

[10] One of several congregations established in Italy and Spain during the fourteenth century. They initially Jived according to the rule of life which St. Jerome had composed for the women who had settled in Bethlehem with him, and were known as the Hermits of St. Jerome; they afterwards gave up their hermitic way of life and adopted the Rule of St. Augustine. – Tr.

ogy.[11] The young professor began his career in collaboration with his mentor, Prior Henri Seulen.[12] but his knowledge and speaking ability soon earned him a reputation of his own.[13] He carried out his new assignment so conscientiously that his reputation quickly spread beyond his monastery and caught the attention of the Crosiers at Kolen-Kerniel, who elected him their prior in 1763.[14]

Martin Aubée, one of the artists later commissioned to adorn the Kolen monastery, has given us a portrait of the young prior, in which Dubois appears healthy and robust in the full vigor of his young manhood. His face is both pleasant and firm; the wide forehead and expressive eyes suggest a serious yet engaging personality. The pen in his right hand and another in the inkwell beside him seem to foreshadow the *fortiter in re* and *suaviter in modo* which characterized his eventful career.[15]

As soon as the young new prior of Kolen had assumed his

---

[11] C. R. Hermans, *Annales Canonicorum Regularium S. Augustini Ordinis S. Crucis* ('S Hertogenbosch, 1858), 3:589-590.

[12] This learned theologian and brilliant controversialist was prior of the monastery in Liège from 1746 to 1771. (See Hermans, *Annales*, 1(2):143, and P. van den Bosch, *O.S.C.*, "Thomas van Kempen en de Kruisheren," *Archiefvoor de geschiedenis van de katholieke Kerk in Nederland* 13 [1971] 301-302. – Tr.)

[13] Hermans, Annales, 3:589.

[14] J. Daris, *Notices historiques sur les eglises du diocese de Liège* (Liège, 1868), 1:412. The township of Kolen-Kerniel was in the province of Limburg, about six miles from Tongeren. The Crosiers had established their monastery of Mariae Laudes at Kolen in 1438.

[15] Hermans, *Annales*, 1 (2): 167. The portrait now hangs in the Crosier monastery at Maaseik. Aubée was born at Liège in 1729, studied under Coelers and Berthon, and died at Paris in 1806. His signature appears on numerous portraits, genre-scenes and decorative panels of the period. See J. Helbig's article in the *Biographie Nationale* 16, cols. 51-54.

duties, he turned his attention to the status of studies in the community, not surprisingly for someone who had begun his career as a teacher. The program of theological studies which Prior General Werner d'Audace had established at Kolen in 1721 had long since fallen into desuetude.[16] In 1767, at the first general chapter after his election, Dubois made such a strong case on behalf of his community that the chapter decided to re-establish the program which had existed at Kolen forty years earlier and appointed Father Jean Baptiste Ghysens to teach it.[17]

Prior Dubois was as concerned for the physical state of his monastery as for its intellectual life. Fire had destroyed the church of *Mariae Laudes* in 1750, and Prior Mathias Francken (1747-1760) and his procurator, Father Humblet, had rebuilt it on the ruins. Dubois now invited the woodworkers of the time to adorn its choir and chancel with wainscoting and commissioned Martin Aubée to decorate the choir stalls with scenes from the story of St. Odilia,[18] but he is most often associated with the construction and decoration of the sacristy. The quality and richness of its furnishings make it a true work of art in itself and much more than an annex to the

---

[16] Hermans, *Annales*, 3:431. (Father Fontaine cited the texts of the relicts of the general chapters as found in Hermans. I have in each case added a reference to them as found in the critical edition prepared by the late Father A. van de Pasch, O.S.C., *De Definities der generale Kapittels van de Orde van het H. Kruis, 1410-1786* [Brussels, 1969]. Here the reference is to van de Pasch, *Definities*, 520. – Tr.) In 1721, the instructor assigned to teach at Kolen had been Father Dieudonné. LeCaen, its subprior, who had been born at Hodeige and educated at Louvain. After his election as prior of Maaseik three years later (in 1724), he established a similar program there, and Kolen's was suppressed. During the next eighteen years, Le Caen was assigned to teach at Hohenbusch and Huy, successively.

[17] Van de Pasch, Definities, 542.

[18] Daris, Notices sur les eglises, 1:411.

church. Its fine paneling and the arrangement of its furnishings testify to the skill and taste of Liège's eighteenth-century woodworkers. Art historians consider its harmonious ensemble of vesting table, cabinets and paneling one of the finest achievements of the artists of the Meuse area, even without Aubée's paintings.[19] The *carmina gratulatoria* which the Kolen Crosiers often composed to honor their priors give us an idea of the care which Dubois lavished on his community,[20] but which did not keep him from being involved with the well-being of the whole Order, as the following incident will make clear. For many centuries, charitable confraternities of both clergy and laity had relieved human misery in the Princedom of Liège through a number of hospices which operated in various ways and at various levels of society. In the sixteenth century, Prince-Bishop Erard de la Marck had planned to revise the Princedom's legislation governing such institutions, but had died before he was able to do so. Subsequent prince-bishops, such as Ernst of Bavaria and Georges Louis de Berghes, had been similarly concerned. When Prince-Bishop Charles Louis de Velbruck took the matter up in the last half of the eighteenth century, he decided to establish a general hospice at Liège.

To do so and to fund its work, Prince-Bishop de Velbruck decided to suppress several religious houses in the city, including that of the Crosiers, and to turn their incomes to the

---

[19] Count Joseph de Borchgrave d'Altena, *Decors anciens d'inteneurs mosans* (Liège, n.d.), 1:53 and 75; and H. van Lieshout, O.S.C., "Lutgardis herinneringen in't klooster Kolen," Gudrun 16 (1934-1935) nos. 9-10,243.
[20] See Annexe 2 (Fontaine, Jacques Dubois, 126-128) for an example of these applausus in honor of Prior Dubois, which allows one to catch something of the character of his administration at Kolen. A partial translation is provided.

support of his new hospice.[21] Even if we applaud the Prince-Bishop's initiative, we must decry his means. That he could think of doing such a thing is wholly understandable in the context of the times: Prance was pouring out writings critical of religious life, French freemasonry was busily disseminating pamphlets which attacked both religious and secular clergy, and Emperor Joseph II was ordering governmental intervention in various spiritual matters. Religion was everywhere in retreat.

This critical time called for solid and trustworthy religious leadership, but the old prior of Liège, Henri Seulen, had died not long before[22] and his successor, Joseph Namur, had also passed away after only three years in office. In the meanwhile, the Crosiers of Liège had become lax in their religious life and became more so under Namur's successor, Jacob Zéguers.

Thus, when Prince-Bishop de Velbruck asked them to cede him their monastery and its possessions for the support of his new hospice, they agreed. (We can see in this transaction, witnessed by the Notary Apostolic Hénault on March 11, 1775,[23] signs of the coming secularization and indemnification of religious.) Twelve Crosiers of Liège signed the document, but three of them (Heuskin, Devenne and Bertho) protested, stating "that they did not wish to be released from the obedience which they owed the General of their Order and that they had signed only because of the pressure to which

---

[21] In 1773, he had requested and received permission from Pope Clement XIV to absorb the Priory of St. Leonard; see J. Daris, *Histoire du Diocese et de la Principauté de Liège (1724-1852)* (Liège, 1868), 1:265.

[22] On September 29, 1771, after a long and painful illness; see Hermans, *Annales*, 3:544.

[23] Hermans, Annales, 3:551-552.

the constant importuning and vigorous pleas of the vicar general, his secretary, and their own prior had subjected them. That is why", they added, "they considered their signatures null and void, and declared their express wish to live and die in that selfsame monastery. For these reasons, they begged the Pope to grant them this grace."[24]

Despite the resistance, the Prince-Bishop continued to press for the monastery's absorption into his general hospice. Around the same time and shortly before the meeting of the diocesan synod, his vicar general assigned to Lambert Meyers, O.S.C.--a Crosier of Liège, a definitor, and Prior of Mount Orient,[25]--the task of explaining the Prince-Bishop's intentions to Prior General Lambert Fisen. The latter neither protested nor agreed, only remarked that, "if Rome permits it, let Rome's will be done."[26] That, at least, is how this rather unusual episcopal emissary reported the discussion. But the reply of the Prior General leads one to suspect that he had said little and heard much: clearly the wisest thing to do under the circumstances.

Wanting more information and some good advice about this disturbing business, Fisen turned to the Prior of Kolen. The latter was well aware of how some were ready to take advantage of the General's advanced age (he had just turned seventy-eight), and decided to rescue the monastery at Liège. Because three of its members opposed its suppression, Dubois knew that to do so would require papal approval, and

---

[24] Hermans, *Annales*, 3:553.

[25] This title derives from the former Crosier monastery at Osterburg (mons oriens) in Westphalia. After the monastery's suppression, the title "Prior of Mount Orient" seems to have become an honorary one occasionally conferred on Crosier professors of theology.

[26] Hermans, *Annales*, 3:555.

so advised Fisen to write the Congregation for Bishops and Regular Clergy in Rome and request that suppression be denied. This Fisen did on March 17, 1775, arguing that secularization would have ill effects on these religious and that the precedent so established would have no effect but to encourage those princes who wished to suppress monasteries.[27] Even as he encouraged the appeal of his Prior General to Rome, Dubois was having recourse to the Aulic Council in Vienna,[28] before which he argued that the Order's existence, goods and privileges had been approved by the emperors.[29]

When the Congregation in Rome learned what was afoot, it naturally and immediately became involved. Although the papal nuncio in Cologne, Caprara, prepared a report which supported de Velbruck's plan,[30] the Aulic Council a month later directed the Prince-Bishop to reply to the charges brought by the Prior General and forbade him to proceed with his plans until it had rendered a decision.[31] De Velbruck retreated into diplomatic silence, but there seems to have been another sort of intrigue going on, one aimed at neutral-

---

[27] E. Marechal, "Le village et la paroisse de Hodeige," Bulletin Societe d'Art et d'Histoire du diocese de Liège 15 (Liège, 1906) 2nd part, 256. The princes to whom he alluded were de Velbruck and Emperor Joseph II, who some years later suppressed a hundred and sixty-six monasteries at a single stroke of the pen. The Dutch Estates General were merely following his example when they declared their intent to suppress the monasteries of Maastricht; see Daris, Histoire de la Principaute, 1 :331 and 333.

[28] The council of the court of the Austro-German or Hapsburg Empire. – Tr.

[29] Marechal, "Le village et la paroisse," 256.

[30] This report seems to have been mostly the work of Meyers, which is not entirely surprising, since the Order's Belgian leadership had commissioned him to deal with the higher clergy of Liège on their behalf.

[31] Hermans, Annales, 3:564.

izing the Council's veto. On January 16, those Crosiers in Liège who favored de Velbruck's plans sent the Council a document requesting suppression of their monastery and claiming they were no longer able to support themselves.[32] (Why these Crosiers so desired their own suppression remains a mystery.) When the Prior General learned of this, he circulated a letter to the definitors and all the priors of his Order sometime around the end of January 1776.[33] Since the authorities had indicated that they would be satisfied with a consultation of this sort, Fisen's letter asked the definitors and priors whether or not they approved the suppression of the monastery at Liège. Meyers made no reply. When the Prior General pressed him,[34] he offered the evasive response, three days later, that only the Prior General and the Prior of Kolen were to blame for this affair.[35] In the meantime, de Velbruck had sent another letter to the Council in an attempt to thoroughly discredit Fisen and his advocate at Kolen,[36] and had taken the liberty of beginning a complete inventory of the monastery in Liège.[37]

Deeply hurt, Fisen turned defense of the case completely over to Dubois. Backed by the delegation of his Prior General, the Prior of Kolen struck a heavy blow. On March 22, 1776, he sent to the imperial court in Vienna a long petition, and in it he did not hesitate to reveal Meyers' role in everything which had transpired. "Who could believe," he exclaimed, "that a loyal definitor would participate in the subversion of his Or-

---

[32] Hermans, Annales, 3:563.
[33] Hermans, Annales, 3:561.
[34] Ibid.
[35] Hermans, Annales, 3:561-562.
[36] E. Marechal, "Le village et la paroisse," 256-257; see also Annexe 3 (Fontaine, Jacques Dubois, 128).
[37] Hermans, Annales, 3:566

der?" and concluded with a request for "a declaration of insufficient grounds, so that the Nunciature will drop the pending suit."[38] In the meanwhile, de Velbruck had, with the help of the Papal Nuncio Bellisomi, sent Rome some new information, but this was really little more than a panegyric of the Prince-Bishop of Liège and all his enterprises.[39] We do not know if Meyers had some part in this last effort, but five days later the Prior General sent him a notarized letter which stripped him of his authority to deal with the higher clergy in Liège and replaced him.[40]

The whole affair now began to emerge from the confusion into which it had wandered. In May, Cardinal Caraffa[41] instructed the nuncio to make a canonical visitation of the monastery in Liège: the latter declined, "because the Bishop did not wish" him to comply![42] This blatant interference brought the matter to a head. In December 1777, the Holy See decided in favor of the Crosiers. "Rome has turned down those rebels in Liège," Dubois wrote when he received news of his success, "and has also decided that there will be an apostolic visitation, to reform and punish them. The authors of all the trouble are to be removed from the monastery, and the Prince-Bishop will be instructed to keep silent hereafter and to forego any more attempts at suppression, since his alleged motives are insufficient."[43] The sanctions which were

---

[38] Hermans, Annales, 3:565-566.

[39] E. Marechal, "Le village et la paroisse," 257.

[40] He was replaced by Canon Jacquet of the collegial church of St. Martin, who was entrusted with all Meyers' privileges and authority.

[41] . Prefect of the Congregation of Bishops and Regulars, to which General Pisen and Dubois had appealed.

[42] E. Marechal, "Le village et la paroisse," 258.

[43] From Dubois' letter of December 29, 1777, to Prior Oeyen of Venlo; Hermans, *Annales,* 3:566.

subsequently imposed followed the Papal Bull quite closely. Zéguers was forced to resign,[44] and Augustin Heuskin, one of the three resisters and former prior of the Crosier monastery in Paris, was put in charge.[45]

The month after this unhappy affair ended, Prior General Fisen died on January 4, 1778, in the mother house at Huy, after a term of office which had been as long as it had been productive.[46] His death came at a time when the virtues of obedience to the Order and respect for authority were in decline. Always opposed to intrigue and wishing to insure that his death would not provide an occasion for it, Fisen had, four years earlier, taken steps to prevent any possible confusion arising from a delay in promptly replacing him.[47] His adjustment of the election procedure respected law and tradition, but must have also given some indication of who was best suited to succeed him. The sorry business in Liège, which was only the most recent manifestation of the Order's internal troubles, clearly suggested who was the most likely candidate for his office. Many houses and priors were un-

---

[44] Zeguers first retired at Tihange, near Huy, and later settled in the suburb of Amercoeur at Liège. He formally surrendered his office only upon completion of a proceeding held on June 12, 1780, and in consideration of a pension of 1,000 Br. florins. The records are in the files "Crosiers of Liège" in the State Archives at Liège.

[45] E. Marechal, "Le village et la paroisse," 259-260.

[46] Fisen's health became a concern to members of his community on April 20, but they did not stop hoping for his recovery until the following December (see the Record of drugs for 1777-1791, 17). His death seems to have resulted from a combination of age (he was eighty-one) and exhaustion. He had held office for thirty-seven years, longer than any of the Order's previous general superiors. The Annales inform us that this "watchful shepherd" (see page 13, note 2) had made a visitation of each of his Order's monasteries at least four times.

[47] Hermans, Annales, 3:548-550.

happy about breaches of discipline and wanted to see the Order's leadership in strong and worthy hands. So it was that, on February 17, 1778, Jacques Dubois was elected Prior General of the Order of the Holy Cross and Prior of the monastery of Clairlieu.[48]

---

[48] The Order's masters general were at that time elected by the majority vote of the four sitting definitors, the four men who had held that office under the previous prior general, and the conventuals of Huy. The latter had voice in this election because the office of prior general included that of prior of Huy. There was no investiture of a new general other than the announcement of his election: upon election and his acceptance of it, he became by right of succession both prior of Clairlieu and the head of his Order.

Chapter Two
48th Prior General

What, then, was the situation of the Order of the Holy Cross when Jacques Dubois took up the perilous task of guiding its destiny?

In the centuries since its founding at Huy in the early thirteenth century,[49] the Order had experienced diverse fortunes. From its earliest days, its members seem to have devoted themselves to divine worship, charity to travelers in their hospices,[50] preaching the Cross and praying the choral Office. Vowed to the common life set out in the Rule of St.

---

[49] . The late Henricus van Rooijen, O.S.C., has raised serious questions about the traditional account of his Order's foundation and earliest history, and has proposed a novel but plausible alternative.See his "De Oorsprong van de Orde der Kruisbroeders of Kruisheren. De Geschiedbronnen," *Qairlieu*19 (1961) 1-240 and The *Church of the Holy Cross* de Claro Loco *and the True Origins of the Crosiers*(Denderleeuw, 1994). – Tr.

[50] The late Piet van den Bosch, O.S.C., has proposed that the Crosiers were in fact founded as an order of hospitalers. See his "De orde van de Kruisheren in het verleden een hospitaalorde?" *Handelingen van het XLle congres van de Federatie van de Kringen voor Oudheidkeit en Geschiedenis van Belgie* (Mechelen, 1970) and *Sie teilten mit Jedermann* (Cologne, 1978; English translation, The *Crosiers: They Share with Everyone* [Collegeville, MN: The Liturgical Press, 1992]). – Tr.

Augustine and detailed by their own constitutions, the Crosiers lived in monasteries governed by local priors. The whole Order, which had become exempt in 1318,[51] was under the direction of a superior called the prior general, who resided in the Order's mother house, Clairlieu, near the city of Huy.

The Order had quickly spread from its Belgian birthplace to France, England, Germany and the Netherlands. During the fourteenth century and into the first years of the fifteenth, its religious observance had suffered from a certain laxity. A reformation begun in 1410 under Prior General Libertus Janssen did not completely permeate the Order until the second half of that century, when the Crosiers achieved a new level of growth. They had established only forty monasteries during their first two centuries but added thirty-four foundations between 1422 and 1499. Their renewal during this century left them well-prepared for the religious strife in that which followed, but the sixteenth century also halted the expansion which their renewal had engendered: they founded only one new monastery during the 1500s, while more than twenty-five of their older houses were suppressed. Not until the middle of the next century, in 1639 and 1645, did they attempt to recoup their losses, but these efforts resulted in only two new foundations, the last before the French Revolution. History thus places the Crosiers' greatest splendor in the late fifteenth century.

The ordeal of the sixteenth century also lessened the authority of the Order's leaders. During that century, the priors general saw all the English monasteries suppressed and those in

---

[51] See A. Ramaekers, O.S.C., "De Privileges der Kruisheerenorde vanafhaar onstaan tot aan het concilie van Trent," *Clairlieu* 1:1 and 2 (1943) 29-36, for an informative review of this.

the Netherlands and Germany come under severe and disastrous trial. Their greatest success in the midst of such trials was to maintain a religious discipline and obedience which kept the harmful ideas of Protestantism at bay. Nine of the ten men who led the Order in sixteenth century displayed such force of character, perseverance and moral authority that the Crosiers emerged from the travail of the Reformation battered but victorious and, at century's end, even enjoyed a new vigor. Around this time, too, they opened their doors to humanism and not long afterwards found themselves ready to establish two new monasteries, at Wegberg in the Rhineland and at Uden in the Netherlands. But this was more of a conclusion than a beginning, for the period of stagnation which followed would last until the Revolution. Still, on the threshold of the seventeenth century, the Order showed unmistakable signs of a return to its early austerity, the leaven which had produced such marvelous expansion during its first two centuries.

But at precisely this point something else intervened, viz., the renewal begun by the Council of Trent, which conditioned every further development in religious life. The Crosiers, however, seem to have been unable to participate fully in the renewal of religious life which the Council initiated. The sixteenth and especially the seventeenth centuries saw an unparalleled flowering of new religious congregations with entirely new missions reflecting the needs of the time: education, foreign missions and the spiritual renewal of the people. Some older orders, like the Dominicans, Carmelites and Hieronymites, realized that they could redirect their energies into these new apostolic activities and that to do so would assure their survival, for the new challenges offered by their life and work would attract candidates.

Weakened by the prolonged ordeal of the sixteenth century, the Crosiers were able to make only modest efforts at these sorts of changes, although there is every indication that they wished to. During the seventeenth century they made real efforts to adjust their constitutions and align them with the reforms called for at Trent. That these revised constitutions, approved in 1660, added nothing to the Crosiers' traditional life and work suggests that concern about the losses which they had endured in the previous century outweighed their desire to become involved in the new missionary and educational efforts. Nevertheless, they did open six Latin schools in these years,[52] and those of their German priors who enjoyed the privilege of the care of souls continued that work locally.[53] They also produced a remarkable number of mystical writers, chroniclers and humanists, notably moralists, during the seventeenth century,[54] but all the activity of these individuals took place in relative isolation, at the margin of the new institutions which were springing up.

---

[52] At Briiggen (1606), Venlo (1624), St. Agatha (1630), Helenenburg (1633), Maaseik (1644) and Diilken (exact year unknown). That at Tournai had been established in the fifteenth century, and those at Liège and Wickrath in the sixteenth (in 1538 and ca. 1560, respectively). The Crosiers in Dus seldorf had intended to open a school, too, but were prevented from doing so by the local Jesuits. The Crosiers in Wegberg operated a parish school from 1656, and those in Uden opened their Latin school in 1743. See van den Bosch, The *Crosiers*, 99-100. – Tr.

[53] Other monasteries, such as Ehrenstein, Pedernach and Helenenburg in the Rhineland and Virton in Belgium, had hospices connected with them. The needy were also cared for at Cologne, Dusseldorf and Schwarzenbroich; the monastery at Roermond also operated a hospice. (See van den Bosch, The *Crosiers*, 39-59 and 67-76, for a complete list of monasteries which operated hospices, and 100-102 for a summary of the Crosiers' work in parishes and chaplaincies. – Tr.)

[54] See van den Bosch, The *Crosiers*, 95-98 and 103. – Tr.

The seventeenth century also saw the beginnings of a new decline within the Order. Since western Christianity's great fourteenth-century schism and especially since the sixteenth century,[55] the Order's French province had more or less gone its own way.[56] That and the suppression of the English monasteries by Henry VIII had shifted the Crosiers' center of gravity eastward and given predominance to their Dutch and German provinces. These, too, were showing tendencies toward autonomy. Prior General Renerus Augustinus Neerius (1619-1648) opposed such tendencies but was unable to eradicate the seeds of discontent and laxity. The waves of Fébronianism and illuminism[57] which swept Germany and

---

[55] Hermans, *Annales,* 1(2):6 and 25.

[56] The use of "province" here and elsewhere in the text is something of a misnomer, since it refers to a geographical rather than a juridical entity. Like the constitutions of others of the Church's older orders, those of the Crosiers make no provision for the existence of provinces. Although neither the constitutions of 1248 nor the revisions of 1660 speak of provinces, the Crosiers in the regions of the Meuse and Rhine sometimes utilized a kind of provincial government and even held provincial chap ters. (For the French Crosiers and their growing divergence from the rest of their Order, see 1. Michael Hayden, "The Crosiers in England and France," *Clairlieu* 22 [1964] 91-109; "The French Crosiers in the 17th and 18th Centuries," *Qairlieu* 27 [1969] 3-46; and "From Inspiration to Mediocrity: The Early Modern Crosiers of Paris," *Crosier Heritage* 17 [November, 1985] 8-18. – Tr.).

[57] The former derives from the ideas of John Nicholas van Espen (1701-1790), auxiliary bishop of Treves, which were published at Frankfurt in 1763 under the pseudonym Febronius. Van Espen argued that papal claims to primacy were an usurpation of powers properly belonging to the bishops and the Church as a whole, that the popes were merely the first among equals, and that the Church had conferred primacy on the bishop of Rome as an administrative measure and could transfer it to any oth er bishop. The popes therefore could not claim infallibility nor the right to receive appeals from the whole Church. Primacy, he argued, resided with general councils; and papal power could and should be limited, in cases of abuse, by general councils, national synods or secular princes. Illuminism

whose influence the Rhineland monasteries could not escape only compounded the problem. During the last two decades of the century, the monasteries of the Rhine and Meuse provinces ceased to hold provincial chapters, although they had done so regularly in previous years and had produced solid measures. This unhealthy situation was exacerbated by a seventeen-year hiatus (1698-1715) in the meeting of general chapters: throughout this period, the city of Huy, where such chapters were obliged to be held, was under blockade by French and Dutch armies alternately.[58] All this greatly complicated the malaise from which the Order was suffering, and by the last quarter of the eighteenth century, the effects were obvious.

Alarmed by the Order's descent into lethargy and spiritual weakness,[59] the general chapter of 1736, which met under Prior General Reynders, tried to infuse its confreres with a new vitality[60] by re-establishing a single program of philosophy and theology *(studium generale)* for the Rhine and Meuse

---

has its roots in ancient gnosticism's claim to a knowledge which is secret and mys terious, based on direct revelation and reserved to a gifted elite. In the seventeenth and eighteenth centuries, such beliefs were combined with claims of the emerging Enlightenment about the powers of hu man reason to promote the belief that all past culture, religion and government were unworthy of natu ral, enlightened mankind and so had to be changed or abolished. – Tr.

[58] French troops had burned Huy in 1689 and withdrawn only because of the 1697 Treaty of Ryswick. When the War of the Spanish Succession broke out in 1700, they again appeared before the city, but were dislodged by the Count of Malborough in 1701. The latter maintained a Dutch garrison in Huy until 1718. See T. Gorissen, *Histoire de la ville et du chateau de Huy, d'apres Laurent Melart* (Huy, 1839) 423-427 and 428-431.

[59] *ut otium et socordia eliminetur*: Hermans, Annales, 3:445 (van de Pasch, Definities, 531).

[60] *ut Ordo noster reflorescat*: ibid.

provinces, but the attempt was stymied by the local authorities.[61] Reynders, who was known among his confreres as someone who led them toward higher goals,[62] died during the first year of the War of the Austrian Succession (1740-1748), after which the incursions of the opposing armies again prevented the meeting of general chapters. Thus, the turmoil of the eighteenth century, when the ideas of the philosophes made common cause with Josephinism[63] against the Church and against authority and religious life, only served to dangerously increase the Crosiers' difficulties.

Like his predecessor, Prior General Lambert Fisen was a "watchful shepherd"[64] who saw that the Order's troubling decline required what had been best expressed by a sixteenth-century general chapter: "new times... require different remedies."[65] His primary goals were to reaffirm his authority as prior general, to end his confreres' readiness to have recourse to the papal nuncio in Cologne and, above all, to renew them in the practice of their regular life. His belief that these goals would be best achieved through a revision of

---

[61] Master General Fisen eventually succeeded in establishing these programs at Hohenbusch and Cologne in 1749; see Hermans, *Annales*, 3:453 (van de Pasch, *Definities*, 535-536).

[62] *manuductor ad altiora*: Hermans, *Annales*, 1(2):127.

[63] So called because it embodied the views of the Hapsburg Emperor Joseph II (1765-1790), who deemed the church to be that department of state which governed the moral life of his people. As head of state, he claimed to be head of the national church as well, and so free to appoint bishops and other clergy as he saw fit and, in the interests of efficiency and economy, to redraw diocesan and parish boundaries, regulate the practice of liturgy and popular devotions, and even suppress monasteries and convents which served no "useful" purpose. – Tr.

[64] *vigil pastor*: Hermans, Annales, 1(2):142.

[65] *temporum novitas ... alia requirit remedia*: Hermans, *Annales*, 3:45 (van de Pasch, *Definities*, 373).

the constitutions led to a fifteen-year struggle. Wearied by his confreres' vacillation and resistance, Fisen finally promulgated the new constitutions in 1765 and simply imposed them. Because his action violated both law and custom, the constitutions were not formally binding. When the dispute was brought to Rome for judgment, Fisen lost and had to fall back on enforcement of the old constitutions. By.1769, his efforts to dissipate the clouds looming over his Order had utterly failed.[66]

Because an attempt to reform the constitutions in the previous century had provoked a crisis which had lasted twenty-five years, we ought not be surprised to learn that the eighteenth-century crisis threatened to be as long. The latter, however, was far more serious and far more acute, for it was rooted in that century's utopianism. The devastation which would follow its weakening of the Order's central authority was not far off. We will not pursue the details of the crisis.[67] However, because the tendencies to self-destruction revealed by the Crosiers of Liège some seven years later clearly show how slippery the downward slope had become.

If Fisen had left his successor a weighty heritage, Dubois' election at this critical juncture in his Order's history reveals a changed outlook among its leaders: their sense of present and approaching danger must have been what convinced them to entrust this *homme fort* with the office of prior gen-

---

[66] See Hermans, *Annales, 3:494-520.*

[67] Father Fontaine returned to this topic in a later study, and others have contributed to our knowledge of it, too. See E. Fontaine, O.S.C., "Une premiere crise a Clairlieu au xvme siecle, 17351752," Clairlieu 8 (1950) 3-30; L. Heere, O.S.C., "Dokumenten uit de statutenstrijd van 1765," Clairlieu 18 (1960) 71-80; and A. van de Pasch, O.S.C., "Kapittelbesluiten van het Kruisherenklooster te Keulen 1679-1789," Clairlieu 33 (1975) 31-58. – Tr

eral. They knew that the Prior of Kolen believed in the provisions of the old constitutions, and their choosing him to succeed Fisen is evidence of their wish for a prior general who, with them, would foster respect for discipline and love of the Order. But this was not true of all: not only would the French province, whose long separation from its confreres was slowly destroying it, resist any efforts at renewal, so would about a third of the German monasteries. On the eve of Dubois' election, then, a dangerous crack was visible in the Order's foundations. The Revolution was coming, and Clairlieu would soon reveal how shaky its own sense of discipline and regular life had become. The history of the mother house would come to an abrupt end, and its collapse be the most dramatic example of the climate of the time. Without losing the integrity of their faith and morals, yet blind to the real drama of the Revolution, the Crosiers of Clairlieu surrendered themselves to ambitions born of their times. They twisted the aims of their Prior and Prior General, muffled his voice and impeded his efforts and care. Against such a somber background will we sketch the figure of Prior General Dubois, backlit by a halo of misfortune.

But let us first complete our portrait of the Order and its mother house in the eighteenth century. When Dubois became its Prior General, the Order had nine monasteries in Belgium, five in the Netherlands, eighteen in Germany, and twelve in France.[68] There were, however, no more than forty-

---

[68] At Huy, Liège, Kolen, Maaseik, Dinant, Tournai, Namur, Suxy and Virton in Belgium; at Maastricht, Roermond, Venlo, Uden and St. Agatha (near Cuijk) in the Netherlands; at Aachen, Ehrenstein, Hohenbusch, Brüggen, Beyenburg, Marienfrede, Helenenberg, Schwarzenbroich, Wegberg, Diilken, Glindfeld, Emmerich, Brandenburg, Cologne, Wickrath, Dusseldorf, Duisberg and Bentlagen in Germany; and at Toulouse, Chaulnes, Caen, Buzan<;ais, Salviac, St.-Georges (near Trediar), VergerSte.-Croix, Mail St-

seven Crosiers in the French monasteries, and all of them would be suppressed by the government in the next year. Nor were all the Order's monasteries were of equal importance, although they were all comfortably well-off[69] and did reckon the mother house at Huy their center of gravity.

Clairlieu itself was a worthy residence for the dynasty of priors general. Situated on a wide stone terrace cut into the thick greenery of the hill of la Sarte (on an axis which followed the flank of the hill), its buildings formed a large quadrangle, some what wider on the side where the east-oriented church raised its lofty bell-tower above the right bank of the Meuse. The wide courtyards, long terraces, and vineyards of the complex alternated with tall oaks and high walls to produce an atmosphere of solitude.

The nearly six centuries of Clairlieu's existence and its prominence as the Order's mother house had endowed it with a long, rich list of landed properties, rents, mills, houses, quarries, lead-mines, forests, cleared lands, meadows, vineyards, hopfields and ponds, and with rents paid in silver, grain, vine-plants and other goods. Its known holdings amounted to 2,257 acres. Eighty-eight parcels of land worked by three hundred and fifty-six tenants (sixty-nine of them

---

Antoine (near Warode), Ste.-Marguerite, Lannoy, Yvoy-Carignan and Paris in France. Of the French monasteries, the last three seem to have resisted suppression the longest. Until the period under discussion, Crosier monasteries were called priories, at least in the French-speaking parts of the Order. The constitutions prescribed that priors be elected for life, that their election be presided over by the prior general or his delegate, and that they be confirmed in their election by the prior general. They were allowed to wear a ring *(ius annuli)* as a mark of office. See *Nova Statuta Ordinis sanctae Crucis* (Maastricht, 1765),59, accesorium: reflexio III, resp.

[69] Except those at Duisburg and Beyenburg, whose financial situations were very precarious.

from Huy itself) were tributary to the monastery.[70] The administration of all this property was the task of the monastery's procurator and two lawyers, one for the forests, the other for rents. The monastery's domestic staff consisted of twenty-three to twenty-five individuals, ten of whom were employed in the vineyards.[71]

Such was Clairlieu at Huy when Jacques Dubois was invested with supreme juridical power over his Order. In those days the Prior General resided in a private Quarter adjoining the monastery[72] and enjoyed a separate income.[73] He was served by a valet[74] and received an allowance of wine,[75] the income from twenty to forty "beasts of wool," and a small tithe of lambs from every lessee in return for the renewal of the lease.[76] He also held the benefice of the *luminarium album*[77]

---

[70] File 2 of the Sources: Crosiers of Huy in the State Archives of Liège. I propose to offer a complete account of these in a subsequent study entitled, "The End of Clairlieu" (it appears as Chapter Eight in this English translation. – Tr.).

[71] These details will be clarified by what follows.

[72] This had been rebuilt during the time of Master General Mathias Goffin (1711-1720). We do not know if these apartments were outside the cloister, but the presence of two porters at Clairlieu, one for the monastery and another for the general's Quarter, makes me think they were.

[73] The eighteenth-century Crosiers apparently found nothing anomalous about the prior general and the monastery having separate incomes.

[74] Record of drugs, 176. There is also reference to the general's domestic (ibid., 84), who was probably his valet. For an idea of how contemporary dignitaries surrounded themselves with domestic servants, see T. Gobert, Rues de Liège, 2:466, 2. The dean of the Cathedral of St. Lambert in Liège, for example, enjoyed the services of a chamberlain, two valets, a coachman, a cook and a domestic servant.

[75] A survival of the medieval practice under which a man presented his feudal lord with something from the property which he had bought or rented and was able to pass on to his heirs.

[76] File 2 of the Sources: Crosiers of Huy in the State Archives at Liège, con-

and the bestowal of several beguinages.[78] For his travels, he enjoyed the use of a coach, two horses and a coachman, who also served as his porter.[79] His office also gave him owner-ship of a country house at Lamalle, a kind of small chateau with a garden and arbor, on the left bank of the Meuse about five miles from Huy.[80] The high honor in which the Prior General was held during the final years of the French monar-chy was reflected in the practice of having all the members of the monastery go in procession to welcome him at the gate with holy water and incense upon his return from a long journey.[81]

---

tracts and official documents.

[77] 4. An income drawn from contributions made toward the annual cost of the white beeswax used in candles. The beneficiary could use only the bal-ance left in the account after the purchase of "white lighting." The primary sources of income were those who leased land from the monastery and contributed to the benefice when accounts were settled. The monastery's procurator recorded these and, each November, presented the record, with a note of the surplus remaining in the account, to the prior general, the subprior, and two or three (usually older) members of the monastery for their signatures. The record of the *pro luminario alba* from Dubois' time is in the State Archives at Liège. The largest surplus recorded was 1,029 flo-rins in 1784. The last signatures in it are from 1791, although contribu-tions totaling 288 florins are recorded for 1792, the year of the French invasion of Belgium.

[78] Three are known, viz., Pasquette-Dehasque, Catherine Tille of Liège, and Mottet.

[79] 6. Record of drugs, 22, 82 and 83. Since Huy had no public or rental transportation at the time, private carriages and boats were the only means available; see Rene Dubois, *Huy sous la revolution et l'Empire* (Huy, 1889), 46.

[80] The course of the narrative will confirm this and the point made in the next sentence.

[81] The same sort of reception seems to have been accorded a general visita-tor (see Hermans, Annales, 1(2):93). When I consulted Dom Adrian No-cent, O.S.B., on this point, he kindly explained to me that it seems to have

Finally, to make what follows more clear, we can provide a list of the Crosiers who were members of the monastery of Clairlieu in 1778:[82]

#	Surname/Name	Birth Place	Age	Position	Professed
1	DUBOIS, Jacques Gisbert Joseph	Liège	48	Prior / Prior General	1751
2	De Noiville, Jean Paul	Namur	45	subprior	1755
3	HANSOTTE, Louis Antoine	Huy	47	elected prior at Carignan in 1780; returned to Huy in1790	1751

been a very old and widespread custom observed among the Benedictines for superiors who held the pontificalia. The 1639 edition of the Cassinese ceremonial (Ritus servandus, de visitatione, cap. XXI) describes it thus: "When the abbot arrives for visitation, he is offered a cross to reverence. Incense and holy water are prepared. The abbot takes the holy water and sprinkles the monks; he then puts incense into the censer and is himself incensed by the superior of the monastery." According to the 1896 edition of the Cassinese ritual, the abbot visitator is always received in the same way: "While the visitator is escorted to the choir and to a faldstuhl before the altar, the cantors intone Fidelis servus et prudens. Vested in a cope, the superior takes his place at the epistle side of the altar, facing the choir, and chants a prayer" (Ritus monastici ad usum congregation is cesinensis.,cap. III). At Beuron and in all other Benedictine congregations in Belgium, abbots are received in this same way, viz., with holy water, incense, a cross to be reverenced, organ, bells, antiphons, etc.; see the Ritus monastici congregation is Buronensis O.S.B. (Tournai, 1895).
[82] This has been developed from information provided by a document compiled at the time of Clairlieu's suppression in 1796 (State Archives, Liège) and supplemented with information from the Record of drugs.

#	Surname/Name	Birth Place	Age	Position	Professed
4	VANDERKAM, Philippe	Gembloux	??	elected prior at Virton in 1770 returned to Huy in 1787	??
5	WALTHERY, Joseph François	?	??	former secretary of M. G. Fisen	??
6	VANSPAUWEN, Henri	?	??		??
7	ANCIAUX, Jean Joseph	?	??	procurator until 1785; elected prior at Kolen in 1787	??
8	L'HOEST, Henri	Waremme	39		1763
9	TILLE, Lambert Theodore	Liège	32		1767
10	GERMEAU, F. Martin	Grandville	36	elected prior at Suxy in 1781	1770
11	HAUTPAS, Jean François Joseph	?	??		??
12	WARNOTTE, Pierre Lambert	Henricourt	27	procurator from 1785 on	1774
13	DENEUMOULIN, Christophe	Tongeren	24		1774
14	DEMET, Henri	Liège	24		1774
15	HAYWEGHEN, Lambert	Looz	27		1774

#	Surname/Name	Birth Place	Age	Position	Professed
16	TILMAN, Jacques Joseph	Trognée	28		1776
17	JEROSME, Jean François	Avennes	25	sacristan	1778
18	LONCIN, Pierre Philippe Bernard	Villers- le- Temple	21		1778
19	LACROIX, Jean Joseph	?	23	elected prior at Virton in 1787	??
20	HEUSQUET, Walthère	Roclenge	55	converse brother	1756
21	Henri	?	??	converse brother	??
22	Theodore	?	??	converse brother	??
23	Augustin	?	??	converse brother	??
24	LAVAILLARDE, Lambert	Liège	??	converse brother	??

Such was the fine young community of which Jacques Dubois would henceforth be prior. Over it and the nearly forty other monasteries of his Order he would enjoy full, supreme power and its accompanying privileges.[83] Despite the omi-

---

[83] Crosier masters general received the privilege of the pontificalia on July 10, 1630, from Pope Urban VIII. Thereafter they were allowed to bless altars and liturgical vessels and to confer the clerical tonsure and minor orders on members of their Order, both at Huy and in all monasteries under their jurisdiction. To tonsure and ordain in monasteries other than Clairlieu they of course had to obtain the permission of the local ordinary.

nous signs looming over the beginning of his generalship, he chose as his motto a phrase of high optimism, *candide crescens in gratia.*

As if to announce and symbolize his program of renewal, General Dubois undertook the physical renovation of his own monastery, which was showing signs of deterioration. Orders for pints of pigment and linseed oil, packets of putty and white lead, pots of red lead and lacquer, red goats-hair brushes and whitewash brushes, sealers and gold-leaf flooded forth in such abundance[84] that one can only conclude that the renovation was done with great care and diligence. It included the country house at Lamalle,[85] and even the carriage of the Prior General regained its pristine whiteness, with newly vermillioned wheels.[86]

But this first burst of activity may have overtaxed him: about three months after his election, General Dubois needed to see his doctor.[87] Whatever the problem was, it soon passed, but there were many other unhappy matters to preoccupy him.

Precisely when the depressing business with the Crosiers of Liège might have seemed to have at last been settled, it reappeared. Prince-Bishop de Velbruck had not yet given up the idea of absorbing their monastery into his hospice, and had written to Cardinal Palavicini, the Secretary of State, asking his protection.[88] A similar approach, directly to that office, had proven quite successful when Rome had earlier refused

---

See Hermans, *Annales,* 3:186-190.

[84] Record of drugs for 1778-1779, passim.

[85] Record of drugs for 1778-1779, 60 and 86.

[86] Record of drugs for 1778-1779, 34, 35 and 36.

[87] On April 13, 1778; see Record of drugs, 17.

[88] Marechal, "Le village et la paroisse," 258.

to agree to his absorption of the monastery of St. Leonard.[89] But this time his exaggeration of the problems which he claimed his general hospice would solve merely led Rome to conclude that this was an instance in which the champion of a good cause had mistakenly taken up arms.[90] On July 4, the Pope replied that he could not agree to the monastery's suppression but hoped that the zealous bishop would find the resources to erect his charitable institution.[91]

Undeterred, de Velbruck took another tack, this time through the city council of Liège,[92] which agreed, on January 17, 1779, to the absorption of the monastery into his hospice. But Dubois forbade it, and probably advised Rome of this latest maneuver.

The Congregation for Bishops and Regular Clergy now insisted that its decree of December 5, 1777, be executed, viz., that there be an apostolic visitation of the monastery. Despite the many set-backs which he had already suffered, the Prince-Bishop would have none of it. Rome then agreed that the visitation could be made by the nuncio, but accompanied by two diocesan priests who enjoyed de Velbruck's confidence rather than by two Crosier priors. This was unacceptable to Dubois, however, for it played right into his opponents' hands: he refused to agree. The next proposal was for the nuncio's auditor and the dean of Ste. Croix to make the visitation. Dubois was no happier with this proposal than its

---

[89] Daris, Notices sur les eglises, 14:208.
[90] See Annexe 5 (Fontaine, Jacques Dubois, 129) for the text of de Velbruck's letter.
[91] Marechal, "Le village et la paroisse," 258.
[92] . The text of the document is in Annexe 6 (Fontaine, Jacques Dubois, 129-130).

predecessor, and decided to make the visitation himself.[93] He also wrote to the Congregation and asked that it allow no visitation except his own, but that was denied. When the nuncio's auditor and the dean of Ste. Croix, Count Liberati and Jamar de Montfort, arrived at the monastery on August 20, 1780, to begin the visitation, however, they found Dubois already there and adamantly refusing to admit them.[94] The Prior General had concluded that the difficulties of his monastery had been exploited quite enough, and had decided to restore order himself.

His boldness and vigor met with unexpected success: peace and good order promptly returned to the Crosier monastery in Liège and, that same day, its members withdrew their consent to its suppression.[95] The Prior General then quickly submitted a second appeal to the Congregation against a visitation by the nunciature. On August 31, Count Liberati, who had stayed on in Liège, asked the Crosiers to meet with him and the dean of Ste. Croix, but their General's heated rebuke had awakened them, or perhaps had infused them with something of his firmness, and they declined. In the end, the Pope sided with Dubois: the Prince-Bishop's request was firmly and finally denied in January 1783.[96]

One might think that this protracted business would have absorbed all Dubois' attention and effort, but it was not the only claim on them: there were many things to preoccupy him in the difficult years immediately after his election.

On March 12, 1778, he had to preside over the election of

---

[93] Marechal, tiLe village et la paroisse," 259.
[94] Ibid.
[95] Ibid.
[96] Ibid.

his successor at Kolen, Andre Vlasseloir. A month later, on April 13, he became ill and had to content himself with merely confirming the election the next day of Joseph Leurs as the new prior of Maastricht. The next summer saw the completion, on August 29, of the reconstruction of Clairlieu's south wing, which Prior General Fisen had begun in 1777.[97] Whatever satisfaction Dubois might have had from this was tempered by the unexpected closing of the Namur monastery on October 14.[98] The suppression of France's monasteries the next year reduced the Order's French-speaking monasteries to eight.[99]

Amid these misfortunes came the time to convoke a general chapter. Despite his poor health,[100] Dubois presided over its sessions, which met at Clairlieu on May 2-4, 1779.[101] Its relict[102] reveals how the climate within the Order had changed since his election. Revision of the constitutions was again on the agenda, but each provision and each change was handled in strict accord with the Order's traditional practice. With a

---

[97] R. Dubois, Huy jadis (Huy, n.d.), 2nd fascicle, 112.

[98] F. Danhaive, "Le Croisiers de Namur,1f Guetteur WaUon 8 (1931) 34.

[99] . Huy, Liège, Tournai, Dinant, Suxy, Virton, Yvoy-Carignan and Lannoy. The monastery at Dinant was also in jeopardy, however; what the mischief-making chapter of St. Aubin had been to the Crosiers of Namur, the collegial chapter of Dinant was to those in their city. See E. Gerard, IfHistoire de la ville de Dinant, If Petite Encyclopedie: La Province de Namur (1936), 130-132. (An inquiry to the Clairlieu Circle about this comment produced only the observation that these two chapters were "bodies of the diocesan clergy who had probably offered negative comments about the Crosier monasteries in their cities, and so were at the root of their suppression. – Tr.)

[100] The prescription of January 30 was refilled on April 15, 1779; Record of drugs, 49.

[101] Hermans, Annales, 3:567 (van de Pasch, Definities, 545).

[102] Hermans, Annales, 3:567-570 (van de Pasch, Definities, 545-547).

prudent eye to the future, the chapter declared that the authority which the constitutions gave the Prior General and his definitors to direct and assign *(ordinandi et statuendi)* the members of the Order were inviolable. Dubois also asked for and received a chapter resolution stating that, during the six years until the next chapter, he might assemble the definitors every three months or whenever he wished to have their advice and help *(tempore Reverendo bene viso... pro consilio aut auxilio).*[103] A second resolution vehemently denounced those Crosiers who were for some reason embarrassed by wearing their habits *(vestes et Ordinem quodammodo erubescentes)* and had taken to dressing as diocesan clergy when outside their monasteries; priors were instructed to take firm measures against this abuse by word and example *(verba et exempla).* A final resolution affirmed that, if the Prior General or his appointed delegate did not preside at the election of a prior, the election would automatically be rendered null and void.[104] If these chapter resolutions reflect certain signs of the times, they also show that the foundation of Dubois' efforts at renewal was the solid and hallowed tradition of his Order's

---

[103] This resolution permitting regular meetings of the definitors at Huy was based on a similar provision from the previous century. That such a measure was adopted in the eighteenth century gives clear witness to the nature of the times.

[104] Abuses of proper election procedure seem to have been the exception. Besides the priors mentioned in the previous paragraph, several others were confirmed in office between 1778 and 1785: Theodore van Herdt at Aachen on May 9, 1779; Louis Hansotte, a conventual of Huy, at Carignan on July 14, 1780; F. Martin Germeau, also a conventual of Huy, at Suxy on October 19, 1781; Joseph Hendricks at Cologne on June 21, 1782; and Adrianus Smits at Uden on May 27, 1783. Three priors were confirmed in 1784: Conrad Ohoven at Wickrath on June 14, Jacob Dujardin at Lannoy on September 6, and Joseph Andre at Helenenberg on November 4. On August 20, 1785, A. Haupts was confirmed as prior at Hohenbusch. See Hermans, *Annales,* 3:575-577.

constitutions.

Now we must continue our account of his activities up to the final settlement of the business concerning the monastery in Liège. With the help of the diocesan officialis of Liège, Dubois finally succeeded, on July 27, 1779, in replacing Hubert Reynders as prior of the Wegberg monastery, in the Rhineland, with Jacob Hoogen.[105] Reynders had been relieved of his office some time before because of malfeasance, but had been contesting his dismissal since 1771.[106] Around this same time, in response to a request from the mayor, aldermen and clergy of Dülken for help in rebuilding their city's Crosier monastery and church, Dubois asked the district governor for the necessary subsidies.[107] It was his intent to give over part of the next year (1780) to formal visitations of the German monasteries and, despite the recurrence of health problems in May,[108] he did manage to visit those at Aachen and Beyenburg. In the latter he found serious problems which not even his intervention could completely resolve.[109] Not long after, Emperor Joseph II began to interfere in the

---

[105] For the career of this Crosier, see W. Zimmermann, "Jakob Hoogen (1742-1805), Prior des Kreuzherrenklosters und Pfarrer in Wegberg, der fiihrende AufkHirer und Padagoge am Neiderrhein," Rhein. Vierteljahrsbl. 19 (1954) 227-248; and R. Haaß, "Jakob Hoogen," Clairlieu 10 (1952) 54-62 and "Prior Jakob Hoogen, ein fUhrender Kopf der Aufklarung am Niederrhein," Annalen des historischen Vereinsfiir dem Niederrhein 128 (1956) 210-225. – Tr.

[106] Hermans, Annales, 3:572.

[107] The project must have come to a successful conclusion, because some years later the Diilken Crosiers found themselves able to cover all the expenses. See R. Haaß, Die Kreuzherren in den Rheinlanden, Rheinisches Archiv, Veroffentlichungen des Instituts fUr geschichtliche Landeskunde der Rheinlande an der Universitat Bonn (Bonn, 1932), 153-154.

[108] Record of drugs, May 24.

[109] Haaß, Die Kreuzherren, 113 and 56.

internal affairs of the religious houses in his realm and, in an edict of November 28, 1781, forbade them to elect foreign-born superiors. Less than a year and a half later, on March 17, 1783, he suppressed three hundred religious houses in the Austrian Netherlands, including the Crosier monasteries at Brandenburg, Roermond and Tournai.[110] But Dubois also had to deal with troubles at home. In May 1783, Brother Lambert of Clairlieu took to the road,[111] and during this already somber spring, the Prior General also had to attend to the sensitive matter of the secularization, for reasons we do not know, of one of the priests of his community, Jean François Joseph Hautpas.[112] Such, in brief, were the other cares

---

[110] A letter of March 12, 1782, from Prior van Cruchten of Roermond to the prior of St. Agatha shows how overwhelmed he was by this decree and allows us to understand the extent of the difficulties the Order faced when confronted with the Emperor's usurpations; see Hermans, Annales, 1(2): 164. The monastery fought a valiant but hopeless battle to save itself until the autumn of 1784, when it was implacably suppressed; see L. Heere, O.S.C., "Het Roermondse Kruisherenklooster," Publications de la societe his. et arch. de Ie Limbourg 76 (1942) 32. Brandenburg's death-sentence was made all the more painful by the fact that its community had just begun to enlarge the monastery; see Haaß, Die Kreuzherren, 169. The Crosiers of Maastricht were the next to be threatened. Soon after the debacle begun by Joseph II, the Dutch Estates General imitated his example and declared their intent to sup press the sixteen monasteries within their jurisdiction; see Daris, Histoire de la Principaute, 1 :333.

[111] Dubois, Huy Jadis, 112. The Record of drugs last mentions him on April 25. The informa tion available to us suggests that this was Brother Lambert Lavaillarde and that he went to the monastery at Hohenbusch in the Rhineland. Soon after Clairlieu's suppression, in 1798, Lambert Lavaillarde sought to claim a pension at Huy, but the local minister of finance refused to issue one, noting "that he had left the monastery at Huy about fourteen years earlier and had since been living in the monastery at Hohenbusch. n See Annexe 93 (Fontaine, Jacques Dubois, 203-204).

[112] In 1773 Hautpas had defended a series of theological theses before Master General Fisen; see Hermans, Annales, 1(2):135. He was at Huy in December 1779, when he and his confreres signed a legal document. The

and responsibilities which impinged on the Prior General during his struggle to save the monastery in Liège, a struggle which truly ended only in January of 1783.

During much of this time, especially over one three-month period, Dubois was not at all well. Around November 2, 1782, he contracted an illness which manifested itself in a severe rash resistant to all efforts at medication. The disease must have had a recurrent cause

During much of this time, especially over one three-month period, Dubois was not at all well. Around November 2, 1782, he contracted an illness which manifested itself in a severe rash resistant to all efforts at medication. The disease must have had a recurrent cause, for he suffered from it intermittently for about five and a half years, until June of 1788. During bouts of it he was medicated with "decoctions, fomentations and powders" and had to avoid the least chill, lest it provoke serious complications.[113]

Late in the year of his victory at Liège, the Beyenburg monastery began to show signs of an unhappy laxity in its life and discipline. To remedy the situation, Dubois transferred there

---

documents attesting to his secularization were signed by all the priests of Clairlieu's chapter. (See the four documents in Annexe 7 [Fontaine, Jacques Dubois, 130-131].) After Oc tober 31, 1788, he became principal of the Guillemite school in Liège; see Bulletin de la Societe d'Art et d'Histoire du diocese de Liège 13:175, note 2. (The Guillemites were an order of hermits founded in Tuscany in the twelfth century by two followers of William de Maleval. They observed the Benedictine Rule and their own constitutions, and were to die out in the eighteenth century. – Tr.)

[113] The Record of drugs informs us that the pharmacist Delloy prepared forty-two prescriptions for the Master General between November 2, 1782, and June 12, 1788. Their dates reveal that the symptoms most often appeared in the spring and fall and that, between bouts, the General enjoyed normal health.

two observant Crosiers from Hohenbusch.[114] Some six months later, the papal nuncio directed him to make a visitation of Kolen for what seemed to be similar reasons. Dubois did so on July 25-28, 1785, but soon discovered that the complaints which had prompted his visit were fabrications. When he found that religious life was being observed in Kolen as it had been only a few years earlier, Dubois handed the uncomprehending "informer" over to the care of the Cellite Brothers at Hasselt.[115]

The Order's constitutions required that a general chapter meet in 1786, and Dubois issued the letter of convocation on March 6,[116] summoning his confreres to gather at Clairlieu on May 14. This would be the Order's last such assembly until 1853. Our information also suggests that only a minority of the authorized delegates were able to attend. The political situation had become extremely volatile, making travel unsafe for some,[117] and for others, attendance was simply impossible. Archbishop Maximilian Franz of Cologne, for example, was engaged in a dispute with Rome and formally forbade the prior of the monastery in his city to obey the General's summons.[118] The presence of an insuffi-

---

[114] Hermans, Annales, 1(2):160 and 3:573.

[115] He seems to have recovered some five years later, for he was able to return to the monastery at Kolen on April 7, 1790; see Daris, Notices sur les eglises, 412. (The Cellite Brothers, who still exist in Belgium, operate institutions which specialize in the treatment of depression and other psychological ills. – Tr.).

[116] Hermans, Annales, 3:577.

[117] Even the Princedom of Liège showed signs of an active and bold opposition to Prince-Bishop Hoensbroeck in the dispute surrounding the J eux de Spa. (These" games at Spa," a town in the neighborhood of Liège, were the beginnings of the revolutionary movement in the territory governed from Liège and the precursor of the French Revolution. – Tr.)

[118] Haaß, Die Kreuzherren, 90.

cient number of delegates would provide a plausible explanation of why we have no relict of this chapter's decisions. The necrology prepared for it[119] contains the names of eighty-four Crosiers who had died since the preceding chapter, six years earlier, including that of Prior Heuskin of Liège. That and the number of monasteries suppressed during these years further testify to the Order's decline.

The Crosiers of Liège chose Mathieu Billard to succeed Heuskin, and the Prior General confirmed his election on June 27, 1786, while the city was in considerable turmoil over and rebellion against the edicts of its Prince-Bishop. The Emulation Circle, of which Billard was an active member,[120] soon came to be dominated by agitators thoroughly imbued with the maxims of the philosophes and the revolutionaries. In the next months, urgent and repeated appeals must have gone from Clairlieu to Crosiers of Liège in an effort to recall them to their religious duty, because in August 1787, Dubois deemed it necessary to remove Billard from office. The latter angrily rejected his dismissal and brought his case before the local civil court, whose magistrate was one of those fomenting change and which, on August 15, ruled in his favor.[121] But the Prior General did not give in: standing by his decision, he put François Bertho (one of the three Crosiers of Liège who had so energetically resisted their monastery's suppression in 1775) in charge of the monastery at the end of that month:[122] his vigorous leadership would justify Dubois' confidence in him.

---

[119] Van de Pasch, Definities, 547-549. – Tr.

[120] Daris, Histoire de Za Principaute, 313. (Well-known in the history of Liège, the Emulation Circle was a society which sympathized with and promoted the ideology behind the Revolution. – Tr.)

[121] Hermans, Annales, 3:580.

[122] Ibid.

Although much of the first decade of Dubois' generalship was absorbed by struggles against the growing clouds of decadence, its end was lit by a small spark of life, like a candle which flares brightly before it sputters out. On April 3, 1788, the Crosiers in Emmerich, under Jacob Driessen, accepted the task of teaching in the local school, which had belonged to the now-suppressed Jesuits and was well-known for its programs in philosophy and the sciences.[123] Theirs was a bold gesture. If clouds had long been gathering on the horizon, the rumble of distant thunder was growing: the Revolution was at hand.

---

[123] Hermans, Annales, 3:104.

CHAPTER THREE
REVOLUTION

The sources of the political and religious turmoil which engulfed the end of the eighteenth century were philosophical and social currents which arose at its beginning and of which France was the fountainhead. Awash with the atheistic principles and skeptical tirades of the philosophes, she dreamed of replacing the *ancien regime* and royal absolutism with the inalienable rights of man and the sovereignty of the people. Belgium, closely bound to her by language and geography, soon imbibed the same ideas. But the flood had other sources. If we look no further than those countries of particular interest to this study, we see that the Netherlands had risen against its Stadhouder[124] in 1787 because of pressures from the "French party", and that papal nunciatures and religious institutions in Germany had been shaken by the schismatic tendencies of many German bishops in support of Emperor Joseph.[125] In the early months of 1789, the tide of

---

[124] The chief magistrate of what was then a republic called the United Provinces of the Netherlands. – Tr.

[125] The tendencies reflected in the Punctuations of Ems. (These twenty-three points, issued by the prince-bishops of Cologne, Mainz and Trier in 1786, demanded certain "rights" for bishops vis-avis Rome, such as revoca-

revolutionary fervor had swept up people all across Europe.

The Revolution's flood soon overwhelmed every barrier which might have ameliorated this victory of political rights and freedoms, and if the Revolution deemed the Church, with its hierarchy, liturgy, faithful and religious communities, its greatest barrier, it would also make the Church its first victim. Like other foresighted men, Dubois probably sensed the approaching catastrophe, but if he were given to melancholy reflection about the rumblings on the horizon, his decision seems to have been to keep a close eye on all parts of his Order and be guided only by his duty. Everything he did in the face of the heavy blows which followed reflects two concerns: to root out the schismatic tendencies afflicting the monasteries far from Clairlieu and, after his return to Belgium, to care for the mother house itself.

Early in the summer of 1789, the people of Liège agitated for a provisional government and secularization of the Princedom. This growing rebellion against the authority of the prince-bishop did not cause Dubois to cancel the canonical visitations which he had planned. Although he had been sick for some months,[126] he had decided to make the most pressing of them. We know that his plan was to go to St. Agatha in the Netherlands, where, despite the opposition of its procurator, the community was engaged in a building project;[127]

---

tion of the exemption from episcopal authority enjoyed by religious orders, the grant in perpetuity of episcopal faculties which had to be renewed every five years, permission of the local ordinary for the issuance of papal decrees in his diocese, and a new form of the bishops loath of office. – Tr.)

[126] The Register of drugs informs us that a prescription of October 9, 1788, was refilled eight times between then and December 16 of the next year. This record ends on January 3, 1790, and so provides no further clues to Dubois's health and disposition.

[127] Hermans, Annates, 3:581.

thence to Beyenburg, where matters regarding the discipline of certain Crosiers required his attention;[128] from there to Cologne, where he planned to speak with the prior whom Archbishop Franz had forbidden to participate in the previous general chapter;[129] and finally to Ehrenstein, where division and confusion had reigned since the same Archbishop had illegally deprived those Crosiers of their exemption.[130]

Dubois concluded his visitation of St. Agatha on July 13. Because our records show that he did not visit the three German communities until September of 1789, he seems to have returned to Belgium in the meanwhile. That certainly is plausible, since the Revolution began in Paris the day after he concluded his visitation of St. Agatha. He must have seen that its echoes would resound through the Princedom of Liège, which was closely bound to France. If he went directly from St. Agatha to Belgium, he would have reached Clairlieu before August 18, when Bassenge[131] lit the torch of revolution in Liège with his "Note to the Citizens".

Huy was the second of the Princedom's "fair cities" and so had to wait to see what results the revolution's success would enjoy. On August 19, the heads of Liège's revolutionary government, Fabry and Chestret, sent the people of Huy a message about their city's "blessed revolution" and urged them to follow its example. Some leading citizens soon gathered at city hall, removed Burgomasters Bejar and Warnant and replaced them with "patriots".[132] But not everyone in Huy ral-

---

[128] Haaß, Die Kreuzherren, 57.

[129] Haaß, Die Kreuzherren, 90.

[130] Haaß, Die Kreuzherren, 189.

[131] Jean Nicolas Bassange, and Fabry and Chestret, who are mentioned in the next paragraph, were leading proponents of revolutionary ideas in Belgium. – Tr.

[132] L. Grandmaison, Souvenirs de Huy, fin du XVIIF siecle (Liège, 1891),

lied to the Revolution's cause; sixty of the Prince-Bishop's supporters signed and forwarded to Liège a letter declaring their support for and loyalty to their ruler.[133] In Liège, however, the Revolution ruled, and Prince-Bishop Hoensbroeck fled to Trier. On August 27, the Court of Wetzlar[134] ordered the rebels in Liège to lay down their arms, cease all revolutionary activities, and restore their Prince-Bishop. Prussian troops were sent into the city to enforce the order.

Dubois must have used the interval of calm which followed to resume his visitations. In September he was in Cologne, but Archbishop Franz, entranced with the Punctuations of Ems, formally forbade him to make visitation of the city's Crosiers.[135] Dubois immediately went on to Beyenburg, where he removed Matthias Mercken, O.S.C., from his position as pastor, transferred him to Düsseldorf and replaced him with Father Steeradt from Wickrath.[136] Turning south to Ehrenstein, he met with the same interference he had encountered in Cologne: the Archbishop had already taken steps to block his visitation of these Crosiers, too.[137] It must have been a bitter disappointment for him to have to forego his intended settling of the disputes which seemed to be spreading in direct proportion to the separation of these Crosiers from his jurisdiction. On his way back to Clairlieu, he probably stopped at the monastery in Liège to retrieve any correspondence which he might have received from abroad

---

78.
[133] Daris, Histoire de ta Principaute, 2:153.
[134] The imperial court of justice in Vienna, with connections to the imperial Chamber of Deputies of Wetzlar, which is mentioned below. – Tr.
[135] Haaß, Die Kreuzherren, 90.
[136] Haaß, Die Kreuzherren, 57.
[137] Haaß, Die Kreuzherren, 189.

(since 1786 all such mail had arrived through Liège). [138]

There he would have soon learned that King Frederick William's Prussian and Protestant soldiery was doing nothing to restore the Prince-Bishop. They did little of anything, in fact, save exercise an arbitrary tyranny while they were garrisoned in the Princedom's various cities. The Crosiers at Huy had a painful taste of that tyranny on December 15, 1789, when General Schliffen sent them a hundred and fifty soldiers to house. (He garrisoned his force of five hundred among the principal signatories of the letter supporting the Prince-Bishop.)[139] On April 16, 1790, the Imperial Chamber of Wetzlar reassigned the task of restoring order in the Princedom of Liège to Austrian troops and to those of the Archbishop-Elector in Cologne. The Austrians entered Liège on January 22, 1791, the traditional government was restored at Huy two days later, and on February 13, the Prince-Bishop re-entered his city to the deafening boom of artillery and the ringing of bells.

The next year was relatively calm, but the Revolution's second act in Liège would be far more somber. France declared war on Austria, and marched her armies toward Belgium.[140] After some initial reverses under Lafayette,[141] the French re-

---

[138] Hermans, Annates, 3:570 (van de Pasch, Definities, 547).

[139] Daris, Histoire de Za Principaute, 2: 154. This indicates that Dubois, and perhaps other members of his monastery, had been among the sixty citizens of Huy who remained loyal to their Prince-Bishop.

[140] Because, at the time, the Austrian Netherlands lay to the northeast of France in what is mod ern Belgium. These territories also flanked, to the northwest and southeast, the princedom governed by the bishops of Liège. – Tr.

[141] The same aristocrat-turned-revolutionary who had participated in the American war of inde pendence and who some of his countrymen hoped might become a French George Washington. – Tr.

sumed the offensive under Dumouriez.[142] On November 6, 1792, they won the battle of Jemappes, near Mons, and immediately invaded Belgium. The Prince-Bishop and many other ecclesiastics fled on November 27, carrying with them the most precious of their churches' possessions. [143]

The French invasion threatened to cut Dubois off from his imperiled monasteries in Germany for a long time. To prevent his road east from being blocked by the French advance, which was now pushing into the district between the Sambre and the Meuse, Dubois and Father Pierre Warnotte, Clairlieu's procurator, set out by river. Warnotte accompanied his Prior General because Dubois had had his monastery's valuables packed into a single trunk and, "with everyone's approval", taken it with him. Our sources reveal that the subprior, Jean de Noiville, had placed certain records into a "chest", that the sacristan, Father Jérosme, had added to it Clairlieu's most valuable silver objects, and that this chest was then nailed firmly shut.[144] Sometime around the end of October 1792, and about a month before the Prince-Bishop's flight, Dubois and his procurator embarked on the Meuse, heading north.

Dumouriez's forces entered Brussels on November 14 and reached Liège two weeks later; the Austrians were driven back across the Meuse. On December 15, the National Convention[145] began the plundering of Belgium with an order to its

---

[142] Charles Fran90is Dumouriez (1739-1823) was a professional soldier with Jacobin sympathies appointed to command French forces in this campaign. Victorious at Valmy and Jemappes, he was de feated at Neerwinden in 1793 and afterwards defected to France's opponents. – Tr.
[143] Daris, Histoire de Za Principaute, 2:375.
[144] Archives, city of Huy, Register 403,29.
[145] This third incarnation of France's revolutionary constitutional and legis-

generals that the properties of all religious houses were to be placed "under the protection of the Republic". French officials entered Clairlieu on December 31 to make an inventory of its possessions, a task completed two days later.[146] As in Liège, French troops were quartered in Huy's religious houses. Matters were in such disarray throughout the city that a revolutionary named Bouquette mounted the pulpit of Huy's collegial church and scandalously harangued the people.[147]

The French laid siege to Maastricht during the night of February 25, 1793, but were defeated at Aldenhoven on March 1 by Clairfayt,[148] who drove them back into Brabant. Four days later, the Austrians advanced to Liège and liberated the Princedom. To reward his victorious armies, the Duke of Saxe-Coburg set out to raise an enormous bonus, of which Huy's contribution was set at 10,000 florins. To ease the burden on the already hard-pressed populace, the task of raising this sum was given to the city's clergy, especially the Crosiers.[149] Heavy sanctions were also imposed on those who had been primarily responsible for the revolutionary upheaval: young Bouquette, for example, was executed in

---

lative assemblies was that which passed judgment on King Louis XVI, wrote the constitution for the first French republic (1792-1799), and governed the country from 1792 to 1795. – Tr.

[146] Grandmaison, Souvenirs de Huy, 59.

[147] Daris, Histoire de Za Principaute, 2:414.

[148] Charles Joseph de Croix, Baron von Clerfayt, was an Austrian field marshal who had acquired a distinguished record in the Seven Years' and Turkish Wars before commanding the Austrian forces in this conflict. To his victories in 1792 and at Aldenhoven, he would add his defeat of Dumouriez at Neerwinden later this same month and of Jourdan at Mainz in 1795. – Tr.

[149] Archives, city of Huy, Register 403, 29.

Huy's city square on March 25.[150] The Prince-Bishop of Liège returned to his city on April 21 at 6:00 in the evening.

We do not have enough information to determine when Dubois returned to the Princedom, so we cannot say whether or not he returned to Clairlieu after the French retreat in the spring of 1793. I believe that he did not, but rather used the following cessation of hostilities to continue the visitations which had been interrupted in the summer of 1789. Several points may be adduced to support this. The French withdrawal from Liège in the spring of 1793 and the beginning of the Reign of Terror in Paris not long after must have made it seem quite unlikely that the French offensive would be renewed any time soon. On the other hand, Dubois must have known that the situations in two of his German monasteries had become critical: a growing division between the older and younger members at Ehrenstein had worsened the situation which had existed there in 1790, and the extravagances of Matthias Biergans at Schwarzenbroich, who had rebelled against the authority of the Prior General in 1792, had triggered certain abuses.[151] Because war had made the convocation of the general chapter scheduled for 1792 impossible, Dubois must have wanted to convince the German priors how critical it was for them to remain in union with Clairlieu. The most telling argument in favor of a year-long stay abroad, however, is that Dubois seems to have returned to Huy only in October 1793. On November 1, Willem Wynants, the procurator of St. Agatha, wrote to inform the Prior General of the death of his prior, F. Loverix, on October 24. Dubois' reply was written at Clairlieu and begins, "I received

---

[150] Grandmaison, Souvenirs de Huy, 4.
[151] Haaß, Die Kreuzherren, 189, 103-104.

46

your letter upon my return from my vacation,"[152] which both hints at a recent return and reveals something of his wry sense of humor: his journey had been a long and arduous one. Since, despite the momentary peace, another French invasion could not be completely discounted, Dubois believed that leaving the chest containing the Order's valuables in the care of the Maastricht Crosiers had been a wise one.[153] On his way home, he had probably again stopped in Liège, to install Prior P. Fossoul, the successor of François Bertho, who had died around this time.

One's image of Prior General Dubois during these last years preceding the Revolution's victory is of a man who exhausts himself by rushing from place to place to douse one fire after another, even as the sparks ignite more blazes than he extinguishes. To the evils which had hitherto marred the face of his Order was now added an agonizing laxity in monastic discipline. While Dubois had been preoccupied with reform elsewhere, the circumstances and bad luck which had caused his prolonged absence from his own monastery seems to have had a perilous impact on the Crosiers of Clairlieu. The dissemination by Belgium's French invaders of ideas about unbounded freedom and equality had infected the ancient monastery, as he must have soon realized. When the French had been driven from the Princedom, he and many others earnestly begged Huy's municipal government to return the money which had been collected for the "war tax" imposed by the "people's government" and paid by the Crosiers. Some members of his monastery might not have openly criticized his action but they certainly did wholly disapprove

---

[152] Hermans, *Annales*, 3:588; see also Annexe 8 (Fontaine, *Jacques Dubois*, 131-132).
[153] Archives, city of Huy, Register 403, 45.

of it, either.[154] Here we might also note that the records of the *luminarium album*, which had been regularly counter-signed by the Crosiers of Huy each year until 1791 now cease. In other words, things no longer ran so smoothly at Clairlieu: the passage of the French republicans had sown trouble. In Germany, too, the decline of discipline which had disrupted some monasteries now also appeared in those of Dülken, Düsseldorf and Marienfrede.[155] In some cases, these disruptions were such that the King of Prussia and the Elector of the Palatinate wrote to the Prior General to insist that he remove the local priors and restore order.[156]

In June 1794, the French again invaded Belgium. Jourdan[157] advanced toward Charleroi, which he captured on June 25, and on July 6 won the famous battle of Fleurus. Advancing rapidly down the Meuse, he besieged and devastated Namur. On July 20, his troops entered Huy. Four days later, Prince-Bishop de Mean fled his city, never to return.

This sudden turn of events must have stymied Dubois' plans to remedy the difficulties which his Order was facing, but the

---

[154] As is revealed by an anonymous letter in the pertinent file of the State Archives at Liège. We will look at this letter more closely in chapter six.

[155] Haaß, Die Kreuzherren, 41.

[156] An undated letter in the State Archives, Liège; see also Annexe 19 (Fontaine, Jacques Dubois, 141-142). Reference by date alone to something in the file on Dubois means that the detail cited is from a document which has been or will be described more fully.

[157] Jean Baptiste Jourdan (1762-1833) had retired from the military after service in the French West Indies, but took up arms anew in support of the Revolution. He had defeated the Austrians the year before his victory at Fleurus, which led to the French occupation of Belgium. His career included two terms in the legislature of the first French republic, commands under Napoleon in Italy and Spain, appointment as a marshal of France and the grant of the titles of "count" and "peer of France" under the restored monarchy. – Tr.

invader's lightning advance had not caught him completely off-guard. To forestall his loss of all freedom of movement, he and two of his confreres, Pierre Warnotte and Henri Demet, took ship on July 7 and came safely to Maastricht. There Warnotte and Demet were probably to retrieve the precious trunk with the Order's records and valuables and take it to St. Agatha,[158] while Dubois made his way into the Rhineland. All this seems to have been done in accord with a prearranged plan in which speed was of the utmost importance: Dubois was to do what he had to do as quickly as possible and thus shorten an absence which, if it were again prolonged, might prove fatal to his monastery.

Whatever the plan, it was frustrated by the furious pace of the French advance. Thinking they would go on to Roermond,[159] Warnotte and Demet found their way already blocked: the retreat of the imperial forces and their hot pursuit by the French caused all entry to the Netherlands to be denied. Unable to wait for the border to open because of the flood of refugees which the French army was driving before it, the two Crosiers took to the road once more. Unable to go south or west, they turned east and followed their General into the Rhineland, although that was a blind alley which took them farther and farther away from both their destination and their starting-point. When they were at last reunited, the three Crosiers decided to make for the monastery at Brüggen, north and east of Roermond, and hired carriages for the journey.[160]

---

[158] Hermans, Annales, 1(2):166. It was probably safer to store these valuables in the Netherlands than in war-torn Germany.

[159] Ibid.

[160] Ibid. These were little more than wagons enclosed by sealed canvas and fitted with padded benches. Because most roads were hardly more than

Dubois and his companions reached Briiggen around mid-July, from where they had planned to go to Düsseldorf, Dubois' original destination. They were delayed there for a time because Prior A. Haupts of Hohenbusch had died of a stroke and the Prior General had to preside over the election of his successor, Conrad Ohoven, on July 19. The new prior's first official duty was to lock his monastery's valuables into valises for transport,[161] so rapid had the retreat of the anti-French forces become. Four days later, Dubois went to Wickrath for the election of a prior to replace Ohoven.[162] Only then were he and his companions free to set out for Düsseldorf, on the right bank of the Rhine.[163] We have no information about Dubois' visitation of Düsseldorf other than that it involved matters of discipline. His arrival there, however, brought him to Prussian territory just in time: Jourdan's pursuit of Saxe-Coburg soon reached Cologne[164]

---

cart-tracks following the contours of the area's mountainous terrain, these wagons usually moved at whatever pace was comfortable for the horses which drew them. When it rained, they sank to their axles in mud; when it was dry, they raised a cloud of dust which blinded their passengers. Toll-houses were frequent and the food in them poor fare: very dark and not very good bread and no vegetables. A traveler had to knock on many doors before he found lodging, and then only at an exorbitant price. See R. Paillot, "Le journal d 'un emigre," La Revue General (November, 1907) 600 and ff.

[161] Hermans, Annales, 1(2):165.
[162] Ibid.
[163] Crossing the Rhine at this time was so dangerous that, after his return to Huy in 1796, Canon H. Barette of the city's collegial church swore under oath before the local magistrates that the emigres had crossed the river only at the risk of their lives (Archives, city of Huy, Register 402, 171). The Rhine is slightly less than five hundred yards wide at Dusseldorf; for a description of the dangers which the emigres faced, see Paillot's article in La Revue General (October 1907), 492-493.
[164] Haaß, Die Kreuzherren, 91.

and, steadily sweeping all of the Rhine's left bank clear of opposition, arrived on the heights above Wickrath.[165]

In the meanwhile Dubois had probably gone up the river to Ehrenstein. After Prior Herschel had died earlier that year, the Archbishop of Cologne had taken the liberty of simply appointing his successor, a very young man named Philippe Collig. Six Ehrenstein Crosiers had rejected the Archbishop's claim to be able to do this and refused to obey an illegally appointed prior.[166] What resulted was probably one of the situations called to Dubois' attention shortly before the French invasion of Belgium.

The Prior General had also planned to travel down the Rhine to visit the Crosiers at Emmerich,[167] but in this case, too, military developments confounded his good intentions. Steadily driving the imperial forces in rout before them, the French had laid siege to Emmerich, bombarded and captured it.[168]

On October 5, Jourdan's armies came in sight of Düsseldorf and, during the night of October 6-7, began to fire upon the city.[169] Dubois was probably no longer there: its regent had ordered the evacuation of all foreigners on September 23.[170] The measure proved to be a wise one. The winter of 1794-95 was so bitterly cold that canals and rivers froze solid, becoming roads which enabled the French army and its artillery to

---

[165] Ibid.
[166] Ibid.
[167] Hermans, Annales, 1(2):165-166.
[168] Haaß, Die Kreuzherren, 165.
[169] See Paillot's article in La Revue General (October 1907), 86.
[170] Paillot, "Le journal d 'un emigre," 608.

cross the Rhine.[171]

Dubois had meanwhile gone east to the Crosier monastery at Beyenburg.[172] His visit may have been very brief, for during the winter these Crosiers were reduced to such straits that their prior had to send them out to forage for food.[173] On the other hand, since he, Warnotte and Demet are recorded as being there on May 15, 1795, he may have stayed on, wanting to help his unfortunate confreres with whatever means at his disposal. In any case, while he was at Beyenburg, Prior Joseph Leurs of Maastricht joined his entourage.[174]

The Treaty of Basel (April 5, 1795) ceded the whole left bank of the Rhine to France. Like most of his exiled compatriots, Dubois must have been thunderstruck by the news, for it meant that his return would be indefinitely delayed and implied the very real danger of a French invasion of the right bank. But the new situation also meant that he could go north, toward Clèves, to attend to the plight of those monasteries which had preoccupied him since he left Huy.[175] Accompanied by his three confreres and two porters and contenting himself with an ordinary mount,[176] he set out for Duisburg.[177] Ignoring his fatigue and age (he was nearly sixty-five), he soon pushed on to Marienfrede and made the visitation of that monastery which had been so long and unfortu-

---

[171] Haaß, *Die Kreuzherren*, 130.
[172] Hermans, *Annales*, 1(2):167.
[173] Haaß, *Die Kreuzherren*, 58.
[174] With four horses and two domestic servants; see Hermans, *Annales*, 1(2):167.
[175] State Archives, Liège; see page 32 and note 3.
[176] Because he had to cross the mountains on terrible roads and pass through bandit-infested forests. (Letter from Kiekens to Poswick, July 17, 1796.)
[177] Archives, city of Huy, Register 403,39.

nately delayed. From there he came at last to Emmerich, at the northern edge of the Order's territorial extension, where his intervention was also needed:[178] difficulties had arisen in the school when the Crosiers withdrew from certain possessions to which they held title and which had passed to the Franciscans.[179]

Although we can trace the stages of Dubois' difficult and dangerous outbound journey and the unfortunate course of events which continually thwarted his efforts, information about his homeward journey is less precise. We know that, before leaving the area of Clèves, he entrusted the trunk containing the valuables of Clairlieu to the care of the Crosiers at Duisburg.[180] He may have gone back up the Rhine by boat, but it seems more likely that he and his companions returned as they had come, on horseback. We have reason to think that they did not bother going to Beyenburg, but simply followed the Rhine to Düsseldorf, which would have considerably shortened their journey had Dubois wished to return to Ehrenstein. My suggestion is that he did, because "for the sake of a prioral installation, he had to uphold a procedure which was terminated only by the decision of August 5 last".[181] This allusion to a prioral installation, disputed and then settled, seems to reflect something of the situation one might find in a monastery which had been disrupted by a prioral crisis five years earlier. By August 5, then, Dubois was again in western Prussia and was probably looking forward to being able to go back down river, so as to be opposite Cologne on the date which French authorities had

---

[178] Ibid.
[179] Haaß, Die Kreuzherren, 165.
[180] Archives, city of Huy, Register 403, 39.
[181] Archives, city of Huy, Register 403, 31.

set for the distribution of re-entry permits.[182] We may also assume that, after his long exile, he was eager to return home.

When the frontier finally opened, however, Dubois would have been greeted with a tale of the woes which had befallen his monasteries on the river's left bank. He must have already heard that the Crosiers of Düsseldorf had been burdened with such a weighty tax that they had had to mortgage two of their farms to raise the necessary money.[183] Those at Cologne, whom he would have visited when he crossed the Rhine, had suffered a similar fate: Jourdan's soldiers had seized a number of their valuable manuscripts and sent them back to France as booty.[184] Those at Schwarzenbroich, about a dozen miles southwest, had also had to sell a farm to meet the war tax. When more money was demanded, they seem to have had to take out large loans. In the end, all of them had to cross the river in search of refuge at Schinrath.[185]

As Dubois passed through the war-torn areas, he would have heard the same sad refrain about his Rhineland monasteries. The Crosiers at Maaseik and most of those at Maastricht had had to flee to Germany, the latter under the guidance of their

---

[182] This is supported by the fact that Dubois was in one of the first groups to be repatriated to the former Princedom of Liège. Re-entry permits were issued only at the request of the interested parties, and the Representatives of the People reserved the right to decide each case separately, according to information furnished by the Central Administration. See Daris, Histoire de la Principaute, 3:49. (Representatives or Commissioners of the People were members of the National Convention sent out with France's armies; they were empowered to intervene in any local civil or military matters. – Tr.)

[183] Haaß, Die Kreuzherren, 130.

[184] Haaß, Die Kreuzherren, 91.

[185] Hermans, Annales, 1(2):167.

prior.[186] Those at Wickrath had suffered so much from the passage of the regular troops and the predatory mob which followed in their wake that they, too, had at last been forced to take refuge beyond the Rhine; only Prior John P. Claessen and Father Matthias Schunk had remained behind. A tax of 6,600 pounds had been levied on the monastery, which could pay only a third of it, and the contents of its wine cellar confiscated and sold at Düsseldorf.[187] The Crosiers at Aachen had been required to provide garrison space for the notorious soldiery of Liège, whose demands for money had become so exorbitant that the monastery was forced to sell its silverware and had afterwards been reduced to near destitution.[188] Soldiers had also plundered the large and valuable library of the Crosiers at Helenenburg, packing its contents up and shipping them off to Paris the day after the monastery's new church had been consecrated.[189] The other monasteries in the path of the conquerors--Hohenbusch, Wegberg, Dülken and Briiggen--had had to endure the same sorts of exactions and pillage, and three of the thirteen Crosiers at Briiggen had succumbed to the lure of secularization and the pensions offered by the republicans in the conquered territories.[190]

Sooner or later, all this sad news must have reached the ears of Prior General Dubois, who was already weary and ailing after his long journey. All that was needed to make the disaster complete was news of what had befallen the Belgian

---

[186] Hermans, Annales, 1(2):167. Three of them, however, found the city gates closed and so had to remain behind.

[187] Haaß, Die Kreuzherren, 214.

[188] Haaß, Die Kreuzherren, 114.

[189] August 28, 1794; see Haaß, Die Kreuzherren, 199. 5. Hermans, Annales, 1(2):166.

[190] Hermans, *Annales*, 1 (2):166.

monasteries, which had been the first to suffer from the deployment of the Revolution's armies. Dubois must have wondered how those seven monasteries had survived their trial and must have especially wondered what bitter cup awaited him in Huy, at Clairlieu itself.

CHAPTER FOUR
HUY AND CLAIRLIEU UNDER THE REVOLUTION

With the dismantling of Huy's castle and redoubts,[191] the city had ceased to be a military center. The resulting lack of barracks meant that the burden of housing and supplying the French troops who entered Huy on July 20, 1794, fell on its people and especially on its religious houses.[192] During the first days of the occupation, thousands of French soldiers swarmed through Clairlieu. The Crosiers welcomed them without hesitation, and even greeted them with eagerness and generosity. Filled with the spirit of good fellowship, they also permitted their visitors to enter their extensive cellars and see the abundant supplies which issued there from. Impressed by this display of such obvious goodwill, a group of French officers made so bold as to "stay to dinner" for over six weeks. At some point, the wine seems to have run out and, because of hospitality's requirements toward guests of such exalted rank, the Crosiers broke into the cellar of the

---

[191] As part of the Treaty of Anvers in 1715; see Gorissen, Histoire de la ville de Huy, 431.
[192] R. Dubois, Huy sous la Republique et l'Empire (Huy, 1889), 187.

Prior General, which "contained some barrels of wine and some full bottles". After seeing to the needs of their guests, they shared the surplus out among themselves. They treated the Quarters of the Prior General with a certain lack of respect, too: after they broke into his private rooms, certain pieces of his furniture somehow found their way into the rooms of certain of his confreres.[193]

Such, according to one contemporary account,[194] was the behavior of the Crosiers of Huy while the French were quartered in their monastery. They seem to have been of a singularly confused, even equivocal, state of mind in the period after the invasion and during the upheaval which it caused. The turmoil which followed did not in any way lessen their confusion.

Because Clairlieu's long agony now becomes inseparable from the Revolution's history in Huy, we must begin by sketching the calamities which befell the city in 1794 and 1795.

In the name of Citizen Laurent, General Lecourbe took up residence in the Abbey of Neufmoustier, from which he immediately levied on the city a tax of 150,000 pounds, which was to be paid in cash within five days:[195] "The clergy are to pay two thirds, with the chapter of the collegial church and the Crosiers responsible for 50,000 pounds; payment of the

---

[193] They would afterwards seek to justify their actions by claiming they had wanted to turn that part of the monastery into a hospital. They never did so, of course, because the General's Quarter was too small (p. L. Saumery, Delices du Pays de Liège [1758], 2:50) and because, from the first, the hospital for the French soldiers was at the Abbey of Neufmoustier.

[194] The anonymous letter in the file on Dubois in the State Archives, Liège.

[195] Payment could be made in plate instead of cash "if it were first converted into ingots" (Grandmaison, Souvenirs de Huy, 36 and ff.).

other 50,000 pounds is to be shared out among the clergy, in proportion to their means, with the exception of the pastor of St. Mengold". [196] To meet this assessment of August 7, the Crosiers had to find 20,000 pounds.[197] Claiming that to do so required converting some of their timber into cash and borrowing against their grain-stores, they asked Lecourbe for an extension. He gave them five days.[198]

Thus began the more serious abuses. Within three days the Crosiers had sold a stand of grown trees for timber in order to acquire the funds which they claimed to need. Their success in raising comfortably more than the required 20,000 pounds made them bold, and they eagerly surrendered themselves to making money, even converting several of their pretiosa into cash.[199] Later that same year, one of them would admit that "he had pocketed cash just like all the rest".[200] Within a few weeks of the invasion, then, French prompting or the desire for personal gain had caused the Crosiers of Clairlieu to violate the principles of their religious life.

Such behavior is perhaps less surprising when one learns that the man quoted above was Jean Joseph Lacroix, the former prior of Virton and a convert to the Revolution's ideology from the first. After the pillage of Virton, Lacroix had sought refuge in Huy,[201] where his influence and actions must have set an evil example for the misdeeds of his confreres. But he

---

[196] He had abandoned his priesthood during the first hours of these tumultuous times.
[197] Archives, city of Huy, Register 403.
[198] Archives, city of Huy, French sources, file for year II.
[199] State Archives, Liège, letter of 17 Thermidor, year IV.
[200] State Archives, Liège, letter of 15 Fructidor, year IV.
[201] State Archives, Liège, letter of 15 Fructidor, year IV.

was not the only "stranger" to encourage their depredations. Some time before, Clairlieu had engaged a lawyer from Moha named Devaux to serve as its legal and business advisor, especially for the sale timber. He owed the Crosiers more than 3,000 francs from before the invasion,[202] but he was also a skillfully manipulative toady, always on the lookout for a profit or kick-back, and had so misled the giddy Crosiers that he managed to become the legal receiver of those in Liège. After September 1, 1794,[203] he played a major role in Clairlieu's financial administration and did not stop embezzling its funds until two years later, when he was caught with his hand in the till. Prior General Dubois took severe measures against his exploitations immediately after his return and would later declare that Devaux was chiefly responsible for the mischief at Clairlieu.

A third stranger was sowing weeds at Clairlieu, but his role requires some explanation. Under the new regime, military requisitions for forage, oats, bread, meat and other supplies were issued with dismaying frequency: six hundred and fourteen of them at Huy during the first eight months of the occupation.[204] At first the Crosiers thought to meet these exactions by selling more of their timber, but because their holdings had meanwhile been nationalized, they needed government permission to do so.

Devaux seems to have feared that he would compromise his position as the monastery's legal receiver if he became involved in this, so the delicate matter was entrusted to one of his henchmen, N. Donnay. A lawyer and staunch republican

---

[202] State Archives, Liège, letter of 17 Thermidor, year IV.
[203] State Archives, Liège, Crosier sources, the account-book of Subprior Noiville, 5.
[204] Dubois, Huy sous la Republique et l'Empire, 186.

well-known to the new administration, Donnay became the representative, publicity agent and self-styled champion of the Crosiers. Unlike Devaux, he was guided more by principle than self-interest and, as a Jacobin[205] extremist and sworn enemy of the ancien regime, regarded high-ranking ecclesiastics as tyrants and those under vows as victims whom he was duty-bound to rescue from the yoke of their superiors. Over time, the Crosiers became his dependents more than his clients, and in his claim to be their defender, he espoused and supported their causes with all the fervor of a Voltairean champion. Along with Lacroix and Devaux, this fanatical proponent of egalitarianism created a "climate" in the monastery and, when the Prior General returned, attempted to strip him of his authority over his community.

Donnay came to work for the Crosiers on October 25 or 26, 1794. His first task was to secure permission at Liège for them to sell their timber, which Fabry, the provisional president,[206] granted on October 27.[207] Such permission, however,

---

[205] A term commonly applied to those who supported the Revolution's more radical tendencies. It derives from a Breton group or caucus, the "Society of Friends of the Constitution," which met at the Dominican monastery of St. Jacques (Jacobus) in Paris. – Tr.

[206] The administration of the Department of the Ourthe was not finally established until November 24, 1795. (One result of the Revolution was the reorganization of France into eighty-three territorial and administrative subdivisions called departments. Each was further subdivided into a number of districts, or arrondissements, of roughly equal size and number in each department. Districts were subdivided into cantons, and the latter into communes or townships under the governance of a mayor and municipal council. Each district had a civil court, which encouraged settlement of cases by arbitration and mediation rather than by adversariallegal action,. and each department a criminal court. Jury trials took place only in the latter. – Tr.).

[207] State Archives, Liège, letter of 6 Brumaire, year III; see Annexe 9 (Fontaine, Jacques Dubois, 132).

required approval at a second level, by the Representatives of the People, which Donnay also sought and which this "citizen and dear friend" of the Crosiers handily obtained.[208]

Although France had officially absorbed Belgium on September 14, 1794, French despotism increasingly treated what had been the Princedom of Liège as if it were a conquered territory. A decree of January 6, 1795, required parishes to hand over "the bells, copper items and other furnishings found in the churches."[209] This time the Crosiers did not seek an extension, as they had the previous August, and even displayed a certain alacrity in complying with the new exaction, paying out a sum of 25,000 pounds. Perhaps they thought their generosity would move the conquerors to mitigate future demands, but it proved to be of no avail. They were no doubt somewhat disappointed when they realized, several days later, that their speedy compliance had hardly been noticed, either at Huy or in the former Princedom.[210]

The end of January 1795, brought the end of Lecourbe's military governorship at Huy, and on February 1, the National Agent[211] at Liège, Bouteville, assembled a municipal council. The younger L. Dewar became its president, but because the office had to change hands every ten days, we find Guerin, Ledrou, Wathour, Rouchet, Pfeffer and Piette succeeding each other at head of city government and each becoming more

---

[208] State Archives, Liège, undated letter.

[209] Daris, Histoire de Za Principaute, 3:33.

[210] Daris, Histoire de Za Principaute, 3:34.

[211] Beginning in December of 1793, the French government in Paris appointed national agents to the newly formed districts, or arrondissements. They soon became the principal officials of government in their areas, and their first duty was to purge municipal councils and local administrations of those whom they considered unreliable. – Tr.

despotic because of the problems caused by the obligatory use of paper currency, the assignats,[212] and the anger generated by the military's requisitions. From February 5, the day after the reconstitution of the city's government, Huy's city administrators were required, by order of Commissioners[213] Heetveld, Decuyper and Mainée, to make an inventory of all sorts of goods. Everyone was required to present at city hall a formal written declaration of the amounts of wheat, barley, rice, etc. and of the number of horses, cattle, sheep, etc. which he possessed, and to do so within twelve hours; everywhere, people's homes were ordered searched. What was involved, of course, was supplying the French forces bound for the Rhine and which marched through Huy without interruption.[214] A further decree, on February 22, requisitioned boots for the soldiers, of which Huy's clergy had to supply nine hundred and fifty pairs. The people of Huy suffered hunger and want in the wake of these ceaseless requisitions, and gathered each day at city hall to protest the military authority which took everything. There were even two riots.[215]

On February 12, Liège's Central Administration enacted its law governing the confiscation of the goods of those relig-

---

[212] Originally a large-denomination currency underwritten and guaranteed by the value of nationalized lands, it was intended to be retired after their sale; within a year, however, it had become a standard paper currency, in both large and small denominations, with a pronounced tendency to inflation. – Tr.

[213] The French constitution provided for the appointment of these officials whose primary tasks were to monitor departmental and municipal administrators, report on their compliance with the laws, and have them removed if it was deemed necessary. – Tr.

[214] For an idea of the number oftroops which passed through Huy in February of 1795 alone, see Grandmaison, Souvenirs de Huy, 42.

[215] Grandmaison, Souvenirs de Huy, 45.

ious communities which had absentee members. Lacroix, who periodically received some "help" from his confreres at Huy, seems to have been alarmed by this, for he returned to Clairlieu, where one of his first concerns was to betake himself to the city administration on February 24 and present to it a certificate of "unsullied good citizenship".[216] Did he think his gesture would better win him the clemency of the authorities in charge of the confiscation? He might have, but it made no difference. On March 12 (23 Ventôse) Commissioner Halein, two city officials and several religious were at Clairlieu to compile a catalogue of the furniture and various other objects in the monastery and the church. At the request of Subprior Noiville, who signed it, "the citizens religious were established as guardians of the said house and the objects listed there under their responsibility."[217] Six days later, Inspector of National Properties, Bourgoing, sent to the city of Huy the list of religious houses in its district whose goods were being confiscated on behalf of the Republic. There were eleven of them, and the local Crosiers headed the list. The next day Huy's municipal council affixed it *ad valvas* and forwarded a copy to all the townships in its jurisdiction, "in order that the tenants, bailiffs and debtors of the religious houses named might have to conform to the arrangements resulting there from."[218] In other words, the revenues owed to all the communities whose goods were being confiscated

---

[216] State Archives, Liège, letter of 15 Fructidor, year IV.

[217] The catalogue forms Annexe 10 (Fontaine, *Jacques Dubois*, 133-135) and reveals the pillaging which had taken place since August 1794. Among other things, paintings had already disappeared from the "David Room," so called because its chief decoration was a gallery of historical paintings illustrating the life of the biblical King David.

[218] Archives, city of Huy, Register 402, 92; see Annexe 11 (Fontaine, *Jacques Dubois*, 136).

would henceforth flow into the public treasury. That several of the communities so affected had no absentee members at all only made the measure even more unconscionable. On April 5, Representative Roberjot sought to keep the government "from taking possession of the religious communities which did not include several members accused of being émigrés."[219] But because three Crosiers were absent, Clairlieu's property remained confiscated, and Huy's municipal council immediately began to consider how they might exploit it. On April 8 (18 Germinal, year III), they summoned before them all those employed in the vineyards and hop-fields of Clairlieu. The council's purpose was to determine the nature and place of their work and to fix the conditions of their employment. The ten workers provided all the information requested of them, but declared that they would continue working only if they were paid twenty-five silver pennies a day and collected their salary every ten days.[220] The claims of the public treasury completely dislocated the administrative mechanism over which Devaux presided, and the Crosiers were desperately eager to have this disastrous decree annulled. On April 10, however, the Administration refused to allow them charge of their recently inventoried possessions "because three religious were absentees" and also ordered them to "promptly" make a contribution of 12,000 pounds to the government.[221] Ironically, Huy celebrated the planting of its Liberty Tree opposite city hall three days later (24 Germinal, year III) and the Crosiers and the members of the collegial chapter were required to par-

---

[219] Daris, Histoire de Za Principaute, 3:49.

[220] Additional details are in Annexe 12 (Fontaine, Jacques Dubois, 136-137).

[221] Daris, Histoire de Za Principaute, 3:47-49.

ticipate by pealing their bells.[222] Disappointed and embittered by their lot, the Crosiers again appealed to the Departmental Administration in Liège at the beginning of May in the hopes of recovering control of their property. The core of their appeal was "that they themselves had not emigrated, that they continued to occupy their monastery, and that it was therefore only just that they be allowed the necessary enjoyment of their substance, the more so because they had provided 20,000 pounds as a cash contribution". The Administration responded, on May 4, that the measures which had been applied to them because of their three absentee members remained in force but that, for the reasons given, "an exception was made regarding what was held under public lease, the kitchen-garden, two plots of vines and their arbors, with the express condition that their value be reckoned into the quotas which the assets and incomes of their house cost them."[223]

The confiscation of Crosier property soon came to be known among those on the lookout for easy profits. On May 10 (21 Floréal) Subprior Noiville protested to the city administration that "some miscreants had made free to graze their horses in the meadow located at Haut Chins and which belongs to the monastery under the lease recently obtained from the Republic." The city acceded to the complaint by threatening that "anyone who will be found with his animals at pasturage on any landed property whatsoever will be reckoned a brigand and punished according to the law."[224] It was a mere crumb of justice in the wake of the decision of May 4,

---

[222] Dubois, Huy sous la Republique et l'Empire, 24.
[223] State Archives, Liège, letter of 15 Floreal, year III; see Annexe 13 (Fontaine, Jacques Dubois, 137-138).
[224] Archives, city of Huy, Register 402, 185.

which in turn did little to mitigate the sanctions imposed on April 10.

The Crosiers were left greatly vexed, the more so because they were again informed that the source of their problems was their "absentee members". That was the ultimate source of their disaffection toward their Prior General, which a new decree of the Representatives of the People on May 25,1795 (6 Prairial, year III) must have furthered. The latter stated that "if more than two members of a community were absent, the Republic would receive their shares of the revenues and that the various rentals of their properties would be made before the Administration of the respective district."[225] The decree seemed to limit the effects of the confiscation to the émigrés alone, and the Crosiers at once appealed anew to the Central Administration in the hope of regaining their property.

This time their efforts got them somewhere, for they were able to avail themselves of "serious grounds". The historian, who was once Huy's city secretary, provides an insight into what precisely those were. "Citizens Lacroix and Tilman," Rene Dubois records, "canons regular of the Order of the Holy Cross, produced a declaration signed by ten religious of the Order in which they denounced Jacques Dubois, their Prior General, not only as an émigré but also as a thief, having carried off everything which the house owned, so that there no longer remained anything for them to live on."[226] Even granting the flowery style of the legal language of the period,[227] the Crosiers could not have found a more handy

---

[225] State Archives, Liège, letter of 25 Thermidor, year III.

[226] Dubois, Huy sous Za Republique et Z'Empire, 46.

[227] The language is not only worthy of Devaux, who would soon reap the reward of his great zeal, but pure Donnay as well. The narrative will show

argument, especially in a time when informers practiced what was deemed a civic virtue worthy of reward.[228]

As they must have known it would, the approach proved wholly successful. The Administration's president, Benoit Dumont, and its adjunct secretary, Bougman, arrived at Clairlieu on July 8, where they numbered and initialed the accounts of revenues in grain. (The other accounts would have to be refunded by the Inspector of National Properties.) At last, the Crosiers had regained control of their property.[229] Reassured by their success, Subprior Noiville paid Devaux four hundred florins that same day, i.e., all the fees they had incurred with him since the previous September 1, 1794.[230] Five days later, on July 13 (but dated July 8), there arrived at the Crosiers' door a decree stating that "from this moment they were authorized to govern and administer their property and, consequently, the objects belonging to them declared to be for rent as of the 26th and 28th of the current month would be removed from the list. Let a copy of the present decree be sent to the Inspector and Receiver of National Properties at Huy."[231] The most interesting aspect of this document is that it had been drafted and signed by Defrance, who was ardently anticlerical and, in it, reveals himself more obliging than had been the Representatives of the People on

---

that Donnay made the same accusation dozens of times without ever changing his hackneyed, word-for-word repetition of it.

[228] Dubois, Huy sous la Republique et l'Empire, 26.

[229] State Archives, Liège, letter of 29 Germinal, year IV; Indication no. 2.77. Repert. no. 822.

[230] State Archives, Liège, Crosier sources, the account-book of Subprior Noiville, 5.

[231] State Archives, Liège, letter of 20 Messidor, year III; Indication no. 3.992. Repert. no. 1.006; see also Annexe 14 (Fontaine, Jacques Dubois, 138).

May 25, for the document granted a simple and clear return of monastery's property without any reservation about its absent superior.

The Crosiers were still celebrating when Francken, the Director of National Properties, informed Belgium's Central Administration in Brussels that he did not agree with Liège's decision. Information provided by Rubin, the National Agent at Huy, indicated that three Crosiers were absentees and that the decision recorded in the decree of July 13 was therefore irregular. The Republic therefore ought to receive their shares of the incomes and proceed to rent their shares of the properties. The Administration at Brussels ought to revise the decision, he said, since it was contrary to the law.[232] Without considering that he might be helping those whom he opposed, Francken had entered into the register of decrees of Huy's municipal council, under the heading of the National Properties, directions that the property of the three absent Crosiers be put up for lease on July 16: to wit, of Warnotte and Demet, three vineyards comprising roughly six and three-quarters acres; of the Prior General, "a beautiful country house with a garden, comprising about four and a half acres, located at Lamalle."[233] The Crosiers resisted this parceling out of their property, hired two new lawyers, Raycken and Warzée, to bring suit at Liège and, in the first two weeks of August, sent their receiver Devaux to the Central Administration at least three times.[234] The two approaches proved

---

[232] State Archives, Liège, letter of 25 Thermidor, year III; see Annexe 16 (Fontaine, Jacques Dubois, 139-140).

[233] Archives, city of Huy, second Register of Decrees of the French Municipal Council, entry for 25 Messidor, year III (July 14, 1795); see also Annexe 15 (Fontaine, Jacques Dubois, 139.)

[234] State Archives, Liège, Crosier sources, the account-book of Subprior Noiville, 7 and 9.

somewhat successful. When Brussels notified Liège's Central Administration that, in light of Francken's protest, it disagreed with their decision, the Crosiers of Huy were told that the rights they had received would be continued, but only on the condition of their making known, within the next two weeks, the goods and incomes, both movable and real, belonging to the house. Only those of the absentees would be taken over by the Nation.[235] The sequestration of the absentees' property would thus affect them only upon their return to the country. Heartened by their success, the Crosiers eagerly had letters carried to a number of their debtors who had fallen into arrears because of these financial carryings-on. At the end of August, the monastery's usual auditor, Catoul, distributed forty-nine of these reminders himself, and in October Jacques Noël and his horse Bomba were engaged for the same task.[236]

Rather than easing the disaffection which they felt for their Prior General, however, their victory only increased it. It seems quite likely that heretofore their increasingly rebellious attitude had been checked by two of the community's elders, Vanderkam and Vanspauwen, both of whom had recently died.[237] Moreover, the imminent return of émigrés

---

[235] Daris, Histoire de Za Principaute, 3:52. We get some idea of what their declaration was to include from the excerpt of the May 25, 1795, decree issued by the Representatives of the People; see Annexe 17 (Fontaine, Dubois, 140-141).

[236] State Archives, Liège, Crosier sources, the account-book of Subprior Noiville, 9.

[237] They did not sign the "denunciation" of 1794. Because ten members of the house chapter did, two did not; that these were Vanspauwen and Vanderkam is supported by the establishment of "the Chapter" at Clairlieu around this time, which also consisted of ten members, whereas Father Henri Vanspauwen died on April 22 and Father Philippe Vanderkam on August 30 of 1795.

would have also increased their sense of agitation. These impassioned religious allowed themselves to be swept along by the new ideas articulated in Article 6 of the Republicans' Declaration: "The general will, expressed by the majority of the citizens, is the Law" and thus established themselves as the entity to which they soon gave the pompous name of "the Chapter". It became their ultimate, not merely temporary, embodiment of authority and to it they would attribute absolute power: they would give similar emphasis to that "Rule" which sprang from egalitarian theories.

A great calamity had taken place. When the Prior General returned home, he discovered that Clairlieu was on the verge of the most sorrowful hour of its history and he the most severe trial of his life. Even exhausted as he was by the trials and hardships of his journey, however, he was not a man to bend before the storm.

CHAPTER FIVE
PRIOR GENERAL DUBOIS RETURNS
TO HUY

Throughout Wallonia, the republicans and their supporters nurtured a vivid animosity against émigrés. In the spring of 1795, however, certain of them had been allowed to return to the country, viz., everyone who earned a living by manual labor, which was interpreted to include wholesalers, men of letters, and so forth.[238] One of the first citizens of Huy to take advantage of this privilege was Lambert Francotte, a lawyer and former burgomaster of the city. He was so involved in the events which followed that we must digress for a moment to provide some information about him.

Before the Revolution, Francotte had been Clairlieu's lawyer and legal advisor, a kind of successor to the medieval monastic chancellor; he had, in short, fulfilled all the roles which Devaux usurped.[239] He had emigrated to Germany with his

---

[238] Daris, Histoire de la Principaute, 3:49.

[239] Francotte drew up all the notarized documents in the Crosier files of the State Archives in Liège. He also represented several other religious communities in Huy (Archives, city of Huy, file for year V). R. Dubois says (H6tel de Ville de Huy, 21) that "Mr. Lambert Joseph Francotte, attorney at law, was chief magistrate of the city of Huy from July 1, 1792, until No-

family in 1794 and, while there, must have met Prior General Dubois on the latter's travels in exile, for Francotte had also been in Duisburg. More fortunate than Dubois in his return, however, he arrived in Huy on May 25, 1795. Ten days later, he succeeded in having himself issued a passport which allowed him to return to Duisburg with a cart and two horses to retrieve his wife and six children. His passport was worded in a way which also made it a request to officers of the French army that they not interfere in any way with the progress of his journey.[240] He was thus able to return to Huy ahead of the influx of the city's other émigrés.

In the meanwhile, Robespierre had been overthrown by the Thermidorean reaction,[241] whose effects were felt even in Belgium and created a more merciful attitude toward those who had emigrated. Indeed, the "patriots" were nearly the only ones who still wished to hinder the return of these "enemies". In spite of the opposition of such patriots, the Representatives of the People authorized a goodly number of the absentees to return. Thus, at the end of September 1795, more than fifty exiles from Huy hastened to return from abroad "where they had been exposed to all the deprivations

---

vember 29, when the French entered the city. On March 9, 1973, when the Austrians returned, he resumed his duties". Francotte passed to his eternal rest on July 20, 1842, at the age of ninety. He was the epitome of an honorable and Christian man (see the Rev. O. T. Halflants, o.P., Histoire de Notre-Dame de la Sarte lez Huy, second edition [Huy, 1871], 114-126).

[240] Archives, city of Huy, Register of Passports for 13 Prairial, year III (June 2, 1795); see Annexe 18 (Fontaine, *Jacques Dubois, 141*).

[241] So called because it was a reaction against the Reign of Terror (September 1793-July 1794) and led to the overthrow of Robespierre and his colleagues on 9 Thermidor (July 27). Although it began as an effort to moderate the violence of the Terror, the reaction itself descended into brutality as the clamor for retribution against those who had dominated the government under the Terror grew. – Tr.

of want."[242]

Prior General Dubois and Fathers Warnotte and Demet probably arrived in Liège around the middle of September. The city's Crosier monastery had suffered grievously from the fighting, and everything the Prior General would have learned there about the trials of the Belgian monasteries would have compounded the sad tale of the German monasteries. For the moment, however, he at least had the consolation of being able to inform himself of their fate.[243] Dubois stopped in Liège and had to stay there for two weeks, perhaps to recover his health. We can only wonder what the state of his health might have been: he was in his sixties, had just finished fourteen long months of travel, and was now faced with a whole new round of calamities.

We might also suppose that Francotte, whom he met in Du-

---

[242] Grandmaison, *Souvenirs de Huy*, 57.

[243] The sufferings which these monasteries had undergone can be summarized as pillage, molestation, forced quarterings of soldiers, contributions, requisitions, etc. Virton had been one of the first to have pay tribute to the victors of Fleurus: nothing remained of its movable property but debris (p. Roger, *Histoire de Virton* [1932], 394). Suxy, located in a clearing in the forest of Chimay which was crossed by the ancient Roman route from Reims to Cologne, had necessarily become a stop-over on the invaders' route. We can only suppose that the latter regularly preyed on the priory, which had a large agricultural establishment containing fifteen to twenty horses, fifty to sixty head of cattle and four to five hundred sheep (Rev. Rossignon, *Notice sur Suxy*, 1888). At Kolen, a French soldier had killed Brother Giles Claes in front of his stoves on March 2, 1795. That monastery had also been obliged to contribute cereal grains worth 7,000 francs, the cartage of which had cost it more than 1,200 pounds. Eight cows and fifty-one sheep were also requisitioned. (Daris, *Notices sur les eglises*, 1:413) At Dinant, Commissioner of War Muneret had directed that the cloister be used as storage bins for fodder. (E. Gerard, *Histoire de la Ville de Dinant* [1936], 131.) The monastery at Maaseik had been especially vulnerable, and had been subject to the incessant passage of both imperial and French troops.

isburg, had informed him of what was happening at Clairlieu. He thus seems to have deemed it prudent to take some time to fully inform himself about the inner workings of his monastery and the baneful influences which had so deeply affected it. Clairlieu had permitted enormous embezzlements, but who was principally responsible for them? It had dared denounce its Prior General and enthrone "the Chapter," but how and through whom had all this come about? On Thursday, September 20, Dubois instructed Demet to proceed to Huy.[244] His assignment, no doubt, was to personally investigate the nature and seriousness of the evil which someone had brought upon the monastery. After reporting back to his superior in Liège, probably on Saturday, September 29, he returned to Huy, this time carrying a letter from the Prior General to the municipal council:[245] the time which remained for Dubois to meet the requirements of the law governing repatriation was growing short. The law required that one had to present oneself before the municipal council of one's regular domicile within eight days and declare (the same form had to be used in all cases) that one "had become expatriate only because of the terrorism of Robespierre and that, having been informed of the changes which had occurred, was hastening to return to one's domicile, promising to conform oneself to its law."[246] But Dubois was unwilling to have to make such a declaration: it simply was not true in his case, and he was loathe to accept a formula which made him an émigré and implied that he had abdicated his duties as prior and prior general. Anyone accused of emigration was ipso facto deprived of any post in

---

[244] Grandmaison, Souvenirs de Huy, 57.
[245] Archives, city of Huy, Register of Decrees of the Municipal Council of Huy, years III and IV, 28.
[246] Ibid.

government, any administrative post and all rights of property. His letter to Huy's civil administration thus offered evidence to support his claim that his journey to Germany had been motivated by the obligations of his office and requested that he therefore not be charged with emigration.[247] At the meeting of Huy's municipal council on the day on which his request was received, however, the councilors rejected it, alleging "that formerly he very often delegated a definitor of the Order for the appointing of priors and that he had, moreover, taken abroad with him the most valuable possessions of his monastery."[248] Dubois learned of this decision on Sunday, September 30, and promptly determined that he would go to Huy himself and, since he had decided not to compromise on the issue, justify his absence. Given the delicacy of the matter, however, he resolved first to consult his lawyer, Francotte.[249]

On Monday, October I, Dubois rented a carriage and set out for Huy, accompanied by Warnotte. Reaching the city around noon, he went directly to the home of the former burgomaster, who invited him to dine.[250] We can easily 'imagine the subject of their conversation. Shortly after midday, the lawyer accompanied Dubois to city hall. Francotte was better qualified than anyone to attest that the Prior General had been away only and solely for the purpose of fulfilling his

---

[247] Archives, city of Huy, Register 403, 29.

[248] Ibid.

[249] This according to the contemporary source which we used above to describe how the French soldiers who entered Clairlieu were received (page 38, note 4). It also provides detailed information about Dubois' return to Huy; despite its anonymity and consequent partiality, we will continue to cite it whenever we can assure ourselves that its allegations are not contradicted by information which can be verified from other sources.

[250] Francotte lived at 248 St. Aldegonde street.

office, and Dubois himself rebutted the accusations, point by point, which had led to the denial of his petition:

> It was all the more necessary for me to go to Germany in person because, for the installation of a prior, I had to undertake a process concluded only on the fifth of August last. I further deny that, when I set out for Germany, I took with me the silver items, precious objects and archives of my monastery. The municipal council can verify this assertion by reference to the inventory which was made of the possessions of my monastery by the officers of the National Convention on the last day of 1792 and the first day of 1793. There they will discover that these objects had been removed a good deal earlier and that this had been done to avoid the unhappy consequences of the war. . . .. Know that I am very far from being opposed to any law or decree, insofar as it touches upon me personally.[251]

Despite his vigorous defense, the council maintained the decision "which regarded Jacques Dubois as an émigré."[252] Any

---

[251] Archives, city of Huy, Register 403, 31. In the margin of this account of Dubois' ap pearance before the council, an anonymous hand adds that the Master General "did not blush at describing his confreres as thieves and saying that they would pay for it." Beyond making us wonder what purpose such accusations could have had in helping him achieve the goal of this hearing, we may be quite sure that, had Dubois actually said such things, the council would have had them recorded in the minutes from which we have taken this quotation. We will see from what follows, twice in this same chapter, that whenever Dubois used some bold expression before Huy's municipal council, it was im mediately recorded verbatim, so eager was this hostile group to find fault with him. On the other hand, these minutes reveal nothing akin to the assertions in our anonymous letter. We should note, however, that that letter was written eight months after the General's return, Le., in the harrowing period when his enemies, of whom its author was one, were overwhelming him with their persecution. We will cite the letter extensively when the time comes to introduce it into our narrative.

[252] Archives, city of Huy, Register 403,31.

77

other result would have been astonishing, especially when one realizes that the council's president, Pfeffer,[253] had its vice-president, Arnold, replace him at this session: the latter was the defrocked pastor of St. Mengold and a confirmed republican.[254] Dubois left only after he had asked for and received a copy of the minutes.

From then on, the Prior General knew how fierce were the prejudices against him. Caught between the municipal council, which had in principle denied his authority, and "the Chapter," which disputed his exercise of it, Dubois sought a way out of the impasse. His most pressing need was to have the charge of emigration dropped. Thus, after leaving city hall and without going to Clairlieu,[255] he hastily made his way back to Liège, where he went to the home of a lawyer named Kiekens. The latter presented to the Central Administration a petition supported by seven attachments, including a copy of the minutes from Huy, in which he explained that Prior General Dubois had gone to Germany" only for just cause and in fulfillment of the duty attendant upon his state and condition of being Prior General of the Order" and therefore urged them "to grant his reinstatement in the enjoyment of his properties and revenues."[256] This last was cleverly worded, for it implied dropping any charge of emigration by reinstating Dubois in his office and prerogatives.

---

[253] He had presided at the meeting of the council on September 29 which had declared Jacques Dubois an emigre. (Archives, city of Huy, Register 403, no. 29.)

[254] Dubois, Huy jadis (Huy, n.d.), 2nd fascicle, 114.

[255] Our anonymous source here adds the spiteful comment, "it is true that he had been dispensed
from doing so."

[256] State Archives, Liège; see Annexe 19 (Fontaine, Jacques Dubois, 141-142).

The former followed from the latter: he who was reinstated in his property rights was simultaneously restored to his prerogatives. Dubois signed the letter with a somewhat shaky hand, which suggests his distress and his exhaustion by the events of the previous day.

When the Departmental Administration was informed of the matter, it seems to have hesitated. Some six or seven days later, it informed Huy of its intent to proceed with an investigation of insufficient grounds. The arrival of this message caused consternation among Huy's municipal council members, who had already shown themselves so hostile to Dubois' cause.[257] The whole council meeting on Thursday, October 8, seems to have been devoted to finding ways to block the defense which he had mounted. The members thus issued a decree that "anyone who removed or caused to be removed silverware, papers, records or any other precious objects before the entry of the Republic's troops into the country must return them to the place whence they had been taken, on penalty of being denounced as a plunderer of public property and, as such, liable to arrest."[258] Dubois was thus defeated before he had begun, and even made subject to an arrest warrant. Circumvented by this measure, which had also been contrived by Arnold,[259] the Departmental Administrators had to wait eight more days before opening their investigation.

---

[257] "Indeed, the city of Huy outstripped Liège in its pursuit of this grotesque persecution," is the opinion offered by Joseph Demarteau in his La Revolutionfranrais au Pays de Liège (complete 2nd series; Liège, 1889), 222.

[258] Archives, city of Huy, Register 403, 38; see Annexe 20 (Fontaine, Jacques Dubois, 142).

[259] Ibid.

The Prior General must have been informed that his case had been transferred to Huy, for he formally left Liège on October 8 to return to Clairlieu, where he would await the outcome of these new complications. Traveling by carriage and accompanied by Father Warnotte, he arrived at the approach to the monastery around 10:30 in the morning, and stopped to greet a man named Chapelle, a neighbor of the Crosiers, before going to the monastery gate. The first Crosier he met was Father Noiville, who seems to have found his prior and general superior stern of countenance and firm of voice. What disorder reigned in the General's Quarter, and what disorder of another, spiritual sort, had invaded Clairlieu! Our anonymous source[260] tells us that Noiville wished to "fraternize" but made it clear to the General that, in the setting of the new ideas, he was to recognize the primacy of "the Chapter." The Prior General rejected fraternity under such conditions: he reckoned that nothing authorized violating the essential precepts of the real Rule, which was not to be set aside. If the harsh trials of the present disrupted religious life, the challenge (and here his attitude betrayed him) was to advance religious life, not downgrade it.

Our source claims that Dubois "was resentful because no one had come to greet him with holy water and censer". Although one can argue that, informed about the situation before his arrival, he little expected to be received with pomp and circumstance, he might very well have taken umbrage at the omission, seeing in it a sign of the Crosiers' rejection of his office.

After this first contact with Clairlieu, Dubois went down "to the Chapelle home, at the gate of the monastery, to dine".

---

[260] As we shall hereafter refer to the letter cited on page 51, note 1.

That is a rather strange bit of information. On the other hand, it leaves one wondering whether the monastery might again have had "some officers residing at table," and whether the reason for our disapproving author's offended tone in recounting the General's action might not be that, in his eyes, Chapelle was a neighbor who knew too much and was too embarrassing an eyewitness.

.The next day the Crosiers "went in a body" to the General's Quarter and demanded that he have the valuables returned from across the Rhine. "Although he promised to give the request his attention," our source says, "he objected to it". That no doubt was the reason for a decree issued that evening by Huy's municipal council which declared these objects "public property" and which was promptly posted in all the usual places.[261]

Some days passed, which the Prior General must have used to put some order back into his residence. Although what had become of the investigation of insufficient grounds during this period is shrouded in mystery, Arnold had already arranged all the steps which the local administration would next take during the meeting of October 8, which had enacted the decree which we know about. The General's companions, Fathers Warnotte and Demet, were to be called first, the other members of the community the next day, and Dubois last of all. Subpoenas addressed to Warnotte and Demet arrived on October 12 or 13 and summoned them to appear on 23 Vendémiaire (October 15). Only two questions were posed to Warnotte: what objects had he transported into Germany and what had become of them? He replied that he had not been in charge of anything, except a chest containing

---

[261] Archives, city of Huy, Register 403, 38.143).

the monastery's possessions; that had been taken to Maastricht, by order of the Prior General, at the time of the first invasion of the country, and it was now at Duisburg.[262] Demet was interrogated on the same two points and gave the same answers as his confrere, but added that he had moved some of his personal effects and various others of the monastery's belongings.[263] The next day, all the Crosiers of Clairlieu, except Warnotte, Demet and the lay brothers, were subpoenaed for an appearance at city hall. All did so, except Fathers Deneumoulin and Tille. This time the interrogation was more detailed. Asked when the monastery's belongings had been taken away, the Crosiers confirmed that this had been done when the Republic's troops first entered the country. Asked to specify on whose order this had been done, they answered that they had not ever been consulted about it. Pressed to reveal if this had been done by order of the Prior General, they said they did not know. They were then asked whether additional objects had not been removed from the monastery at the time of the second invasion. They replied that they had indeed glimpsed a chest in the business office and had not seen it again after their procurator had left. Questioned at the last about where all these things were now, they dissembled, claiming "to have no knowledge of them; that probably only their superior and their two confreres who had emigrated could know where they were."[264]

The dignified and wary tone of these formal statements leave one with the sense that there was a certain regret about what

---

[262] Archives, city of Huy, Register 403, 39; see Annexe 21 (Fontaine, *Jacques Dubois*, 142-144).

[263] Archives, city of Huy, Register 403, 39-40; see Annexe 22 (Fontaine, *Jacques Dubois*, 143-144).

[264] Archives, city of Huy, Register 403, 40-41; see Annexe 23 (Fontaine, *Jacques Dubois*, 143-144).

had happened. There is real significance in how the answers become evasive each time a question tends to incriminate the General: perhaps a sign of a filial regrouping around him, like that which had so remarkably taken place at Liège sixteen years earlier?[265] During the General's long absence, however, too many subversive currents had risen against all legitimate authority, and there is every reason to fear that the strangers who had sparked the discord at Clairlieu continued to fan its flames. They had not ceased their activities, but had for the moment retreated into the background, fearful of the Prior General.

Huy's municipal council subpoenaed Dubois' appearance in their chamber for 25 Vendémiaire (October 17). On Saturday afternoon, October 17, he was brought into that large, low room adorned with republican emblems, from which the crucifix had been removed. The half-dozen well-known patriots, over whom Pfeffer presided this time,[266] sat enthroned on an improvised platform. We might imagine Dubois appearing before them with a sad but sincere countenance. Their questions fell like the blows of a hammer, as the transcript shows.

Q. Where are the archives, the silver items, the belongings, and so forth of your monastery?

A. At Duisburg, messieurs.

---

[265] I am convinced that, despite the whirlwind which had swept them up and was carrying them along, had these Crosiers been able to rid themselves of the scheming influences of Devaux and Donnay–the one of whom manipulated them for the sake of his loathsome greed and the other by his perverse ideology–a sense of respect for Dubois' worthiness and of concern for his misfortunes would have prevailed in his community.

[266] Recall that, in response to the General's petition on September 29, Pfeffer had classified him as an emigre.

Q. By whose order were these objects removed?

A. By my order, to remove them from the circumstances of the war.

Q. To whom are they entrusted?

A. To the monastery of the Crosiers of Duisburg. [Dubois seems to have next been asked who had packed up the missing objects and what had become of the monastery's money, for he went on:] It was Noiville, the subprior, who packed up the archives, and Jérosme, in his office of sacristan, the silver items; as for the coined money which might have been in the house, only the procurator could have knowledge of that. But all was done by my order.

Q. At what date was all that removed?

A. In the month of October, before the first entry of the French.

Q. The aforesaid objects having been removed at that time only to Maastricht, at what time after and on whose order were they taken to Duisburg?

A. That removal of the objects took place at the time of the siege of Namur, upon the second entry of the French, and that was again done at my order.

Q. Is it your intention to have them returned?

A. No, messieurs… for, I assure you, to share them among the community, should the case arise that it is suppressed, whereas they are now in safety.[267]

Q. Is it your intention to conform yourself to the decrees pertaining to émigrés and absentees, notably to that of 8 Brumaire [October 29, 1794]?

---

[267] Duisburg was not in the territories conquered by the French, but in Prussian territory on the east bank of the Rhine.

A. Certainly; however, I offer my declaration that I left this city on June 2 or 3 --I do not know the precise date—before the arrival of the French, to preside over the elections of priors of my Order and to make visitation of several of my monasteries, at the request of His Prussian Majesty and of the Palatine Elector. That has detained me until the first of this month, when I returned to this commune: the approach of the Re public's armies was in no way the cause of my absence.

[When asked to sign this transcript, he wrote:]

Fr. Jacques Dubois, General of the whole exempt Order of the Holy Cross[268]

Dubois thus once more showed himself unwilling to yield on matters of truth and justice.[269] Under the hostile gaze of these officials, he revealed himself a dauntless defender of Clairlieu's possessions, and into his" no" had entered all his soul as a solicitous and equitable father of his community. He had firmly taken full responsibility for the orders which he had given and for what he had done: his stand lacks neither greatness nor pathos, for he knew very well that an arrest warrant might follow. The despotic councilors, however, saw only too much candor. The reader will have noted that, if this hearing did not ignore its primary purpose, it was at the very least diverted from it. Supposedly held to deal with the charge of Dubois' emigration, it had focused entirely on those items which had been taken across the Rhine. Unable to convict him of emigration, the councilors had tied the majestic old man's fate up with his admissions about the "ob-

---

[268] Archives, city of Huy, Register 403, 45-46.
[269] Commenting on this episode, Grandmaison remarks, "One must say that it is a pleasure to see someone conduct himself like a man and make such a manly reply in the midst of the general abasement of character." (Grandmaison, *Souvenirs de Huy*, 60-61.)

jects removed". The "trap decree" of October 8 had made him subject to arrest, and if the councilors dared not do so immediately, their next action was hardly less odious: scarcely had Clairlieu's prior returned home than a gendarme was placed at his door to keep an eye on him.[270] Hereafter he would be a prisoner. It was the beginning of an unending and pitiless persecution.

On the morning of October 18, the day after this disheartening interview, the city government published, in the presence of the people assembled in the Great Square, the decree of the National Convention which annexed the Princedom of Liège to France. Inflammatory speeches followed, delivered by citizens Ista (a member and the representative of Liège's municipal council), Wathour, and Nansuy, the commander of the guard.[271] That evening, Huy's city hall was illumined in a gaudy display, which the Crosiers had to underwrite. [272]

Such impassioned demonstrations were not likely to neither mollify hearts nor incline the patriots to moderation. Three days later (October 21), the municipal council let it be known that it was less than satisfied with Prior General Dubois. Informed that he "continually received letters coming from various foreign places" and" considering that a monk such as he could not have such a large correspondence for the conduct of his affairs, fearing in consequence that this correspondence was contrary to the interests of the Republic," the councilors decided "to depute citizens Wathour, Piette and Rubin, as well as the commander of the guard, to call upon him for the purposes of verifying his letters, of as-

---

[270] State Archives, Liège, letter of 20 Brumaire, year IV.
[271] Archives, city of Huy, Register 403, 49-53.
[272] At a cost of nine florins; see State Archives, Liège, Crosier sources, the account-book of Subprior Noiville, 11.

suring themselves that they contained nothing which could prejudice the interests of the Republic; and, if anything of the sort was found, to take possession of them and to place the aforesaid General under arrest."[273] Although such measures were illegal,[274] the General was not overly upset by them. He showed his visitors the letters pertinent to his monasteries, declared that he did not have any others and added that, even if there were a secret correspondence, he did not reckon himself obliged to share it with the municipal council. That was bold language to use with those who, with Arnold, had engineered what we have called the "trap decree."[275] His four visitors promptly drafted a set of minutes which recorded the General's outspoken comments *word for word* and invited him to sign it, thus adding a bit more to his "indictment". Dubois did so without flinching.[276]

---

[273] Archives, city of Huy, Register 403, 57.

[274] Since January 13, 1795, the mails had been declared free of censorship and as of February 11 were no longer controlled by the Committees of Surveillance, which had also thereafter been abolished. (H. Pirenne, *Histoire de Belgique*, 4:65.) (These latter, also known as Vigilance or Revolutionary Committees, were local organizations patterned on one created in Paris which had given rise to "Committee of Public Safety" under the the Reign of Terror. Once established nationwide to insure "state security," they were to denounce any activities deemed contrary to the Revolution. – Tr.)

[275] Annexe 20 (Fontaine, *Jacques Dubois, 142*).

[276] Archives, city of Huy, Register 403,57; see Annexe 20 (Fontaine, *Jacques Dubois, 144*). It is unfortunate that these letters which Huy's municipal officials confiscated have all disappeared. Because the record of this interview says they came from the "superiors of the Order," they would have greatly illumined this crucial period in the General's life. Coming from Crosier superiors in the Netherlands and Germany, they must have reflected the fllial compassion which these men felt for Dubois, whom they knew to be exposed to the republicans' worst harassments and the disorders which had been enveloping Clairlieu.

Precisely in these days when its prior's cares weighed so heavily on his shoulders, Clairlieu gave a new sign of rebellion. Obedient to only God knows what demon of obstinacy (with Dubois under what amounted to house arrest, Donnay surely must have been snickering in the shadows), the Crosiers addressed letters to Huy's municipal council laying claim to the items taken across the Rhine. These, then, were the coveted prize, but how were they to be gotten hold of so long as the head of the monastery blocked any effort to do so? Two days after the unwarranted inspection of the General's correspondence, Huy's municipal council adopted a new stratagem. In a new inquiry to the Central Administration at Liège, they said: "The citizen Jacques Dubois obstinately refuses to have the valuables returned, and it is to be feared that he alone has possession of these valuables, which he has said he intends for all his religious in case of a suppression. This conduct is intolerable. Therefore we propose to send this man to you, so that you may confine him in a more secure place until the return of these items or, as it may be, until you determine the penalty which such a stubborn refusal merits."[277]

We may presume that none of the councilors really believed the General capable of making off with his monastery's possessions. They knew he was bound by his vows as well as his public commitment to share them among his confreres: it was a matter of "charging" an accused man against whom they themselves had taken excessive measures. They had put him under guard, but knew very well that their prisoner was quite capable of defending himself and even of confounding them. In their embarrassment, they sought to have him im-

---

[277] Archives, city of Huy, Register of Letters, 27, and Annexe 25 (Fontaine, *Jacques Dubois*, 144).

prisoned at Liège, at Fontainebleau instead of Savone.[278] To further assure themselves a successful hearing, they added to their letter copies of the minutes of the hearing at which the General had spoken his resounding" no" and of those compiled when his mail had been examined.[279]

The reply arrived the next day and was a prudent one: Liège doubted that the decree of 15 Vendémiaire (October 7)[280] applied to Monsignor Dubois. In view of the minutes it had received, however, the Central Administration was inclined to regard the General as "resistant to the law" and thus "believed the matter must be addressed directly to the government at Brussels, so that it might know what direction it should take regarding citizen Jacques Dubois." In the meanwhile, Huy was invited "to confine him with care," so that it might "be able to find him when he would be needed. It would soon be advised regarding the response of the Government Council."[281] Deeming the behavior of Huy's municipal council excessive and knowing the General's firmness, Liège deferred the decision to Brussels. Another delay followed. Fearing these delays could only work to Dubois' advantage (harassment had thus far not kept him from seeking his reinstatement), the municipal council and the Crosiers

---

[278] The reference is to the conflict between Napoleon and Pope Pius VII in 1808-1814. After being held prisoner in the Italian city of Savone from 1809 to 1812, the Pope was transferred to the Paris suburb of Fontainebleau because he still refused to accede to Napoleon's demands. He was released and allowed to return to Rome in 1814, having resisted the Emperor until the last. – Tr.

[279] Archives, city of Huy, Register of Letters, 27: letter of 2 Brumaire, year IV.

[280] That concerning superiors and members of communities who had caused valuables to be removed from their houses.

[281] Archives, city of Huy, Register of Letters, 32; and Annexe 26 {Fontaine, *Jacques Dubois*, 145).

lost all patience. Wanting to prevent his reinstatement in his rights, the latter brought suit against him before the civil court in Liège.[282] In a brief dated 4 Brumaire (October 26, 1795), they certified that they had recovered the right to administer their properties and wished to maintain themselves therein, to the extent which the law had not otherwise disposed of them.[283]

The municipal councilors first overdid Liège's instructions "to confine him with care" by doubling the guard on Dubois,[284] then risked another appeal to the same Central Administration. Declaring themselves astonished that they had received no response, they went on to state that "this individual was currently the object of an action before the civil court of Liège brought by the religious of his own monastery to make him give an account of himself, and fearing that a number of lawsuits would resolve him to escape them, they had judged it apropos, for the sake of security and in order to meet their responsibilities, to have him moved to a place within city hall, until Liège had prescribed the steps which were to be taken in regard to him. This they asked be done with briefest possible delay."[285]

Passion and animosity thus grew apace at Huy, but so did embarrassment and uncertainty. If the municipal councilors loaded new suspicions upon the General, they did so not merely to dishonor their victim further but also to justify to Liège the obvious bad faith revealed by their conduct, which was encroaching upon the authority of Brussels. Above all, they wanted to keep the Prior General away from Clairlieu

---

[282] Ibid.
[283] State Archives, Liège, letter of Rubin, 20 Brumaire, year IV.
[284] Ibid.
[285] Archives, city of Huy, Register of Letters, 69

and so exploit the disorders of which they themselves were a source.

In the meanwhile, Brussels delivered its decision. On October 30, the Administration informed Kiekens, the lawyer who had exerted himself so energetically on behalf of his client, that the Representatives of the People and national commissioners in Belgium, Perez and Portiez de l'Oise,[286] had granted the removal of the lien placed on the property of Jacques Dubois, General of the Crosiers, and directed the administrations to provisionally reinstate him in the aforesaid property.[287]

Out of spite, Huy's municipal councilors decided during that day's meeting to have the General appear before them the following morning at 10:00,[288] but then seem to have thought better of it, for the record of that meeting says nothing about his appearance. Besides, they took their revenge in another way, by consigning the decree which reinstated him in his property to an insignificant file labeled" inventories and other objects."[289] They could do nothing more to deride the order issued by the Representatives of the People even as they obeyed it.

The councilors seem to have decided, however, that they would do everything possible to keep the decree from taking effect. National Agent Rubin provides the first clue for such a decision by keeping gendarmes posted at the General's door. This so disgusted Francotte that he addressed a request to

---

[286] As is well known, these comissioners were for all practical purposes Belgium's rulers at the time.
[287] State Archives, Liège, letter of 8 Brumaire, year IV; and Annexe 27 (Fontaine, *Jacques Dubois*, 145).
[288] Archives, city of Huy, Register 403, 62.
[289] Archives, city of Huy, Register of Inventories and Other Objects, 62.

Liège asking that, in view of the reinstatement of the Prior General, these bothersome sentinels be withdrawn.[290] To Dubois' great disappointment, however, the Central Administration merely referred the matter to Huy by forwarding the petition to it.

This stung the insolent Rubin[291] to the quick. On November 11, with the support of the municipal council, he wrote a long letter to the Central Administration. Sneering at the petition of Francotte, he declared his opposition to the General's reinstatement and claimed that there were good reasons for the failure of Huy's municipal council to execute the decree. Admitting that serious reasons were obviously required to justify disregarding orders which came from higher authorities, he was not at all embarrassed to produce them. Mustering all the imagined complaints against Dubois, from Arnold's "trap decree" through the suit lodged by the Crosiers, he insidiously observed that Huy's municipal council was awaiting a response from Brussels: this, he continued, led him to conclude that someone had taken advantage of the Representatives of the People who had reinstated the Prior General.[292]

Opposition to Dubois thus was pitiless, and his enemies grew bolder as their numbers increased, all of whom sought to attack his prerogatives and to aggravate the rebellion at Clairlieu. Indeed, he seems literally to have obsessed them, and proof of that is not lacking. It was physically impossible

---

[290] State Archives, Liège, letter of 20 Brumaire, year IV.
[291] P. Verhaegen characterizes him as "a fanatic known since 1793 for extolling revolutionary opinions" in his *La Belgique sous la dominationfranraise* (1792-1814) (Brussels, 1935), 2:99.
[292] State Archives, Liège, letter of 20 Brumaire, year IV; and Annexe 28 (Fontaine, *Jacques Dubois*, 145-146).

for him to comply with a municipal decree issued on November 19 which stipulated that "within the period of a month, the General must have the valuables returned from across the Rhine":[293] issuing this new entrapment was nothing more than a further effort to put him at fault.

The prospect of a future which seemed to offer no conclusion to this dismal affair must have shaken the courage of one of Huy's conventuals, Father Henri L'Hoest. On November 20 he left the monastery to take advantage of the pension which the Representatives of the People had guaranteed to "those who left the cloisters,"[294] but he was the only one who gave in. In fact, despite the tension, which must have continued to worsen, and blinded as they were by the new ideologies, the Crosiers of Clairlieu in no way abandoned their priestly duties.[295] Soul thus seems to have played less role in their atti-

---

[293] Archives, city of Huy, Register 403, 75; and Annexe 29 (Fontaine, *Jacques Dubois*, 146-147).

[294] He continued to reside at Huy and received a pension of 900 pounds, payable in advance each quarter, but at no time were such payments made on the dates he wished. A review of the various documents pertaining to his case suffices to give one an idea of how little concerned, indeed, of how negligent the Republic was in meeting its obligations to its unfortunate victims. See Annexes 30 and 31 (Fontaine, *Jacques Dubois*, 147-152).

[295] As Subprior Noiville's account-book reveals in various interesting ways. Until the last, I.e., until that record ends in November 1796, the accounts of disbursements to meet the obligations of the Mass funds of Masters General Reynders (page 12), Fisen (page 16), Goffin (page 19) and d'Audace (page 25) at the proper times, to the "accounts for hosts paid to the Carmelite Sisters" (42 florins in all; pages 16 and 35), "the fashioning of wax candles" (136 pounds in all; pages 25, 30 and 33) and "the binding of 3 new missals and new canons" (page 25) clearly indicate that the sacred mysteries continued to be celebrated. In addition, "the church was washed" (pages 14 and 19), as were "the albs," the altar linens (page 20) and the surplices quite regularly, and "the sacristy linens mended" (page 23). All these entries clearly show that pious practice was continued

tudes than did mind.

December proved to be an eventful month. At Huy there was a nervous anticipation of the end of the first administration's term, and uneasiness and last-minute measures followed. Gendarmes Marmion and Degoiier were the first to be alarmed by the prospect, for they had not received a penny for "the surveillance rigorously maintained at the Quarter of their prisoner" and, fearing that compensation might be more difficult to come by under the new council, sent a petition to the Central Administration at Liège.[296]

Huy's municipal council, meanwhile, once more turned its attention to Dubois. At the meeting of 20 Frimaire, year IV (December 11, 1795), the councilors" decided to invite the commander of the guard to have the said General of the Crosiers transferred to a place in city hall... and to keep him under the constant surveillance of a sentry.[297] The risk of such a violent step did not, however, leave these Jacobins without some anxiety: that same day they deemed it prudent to advise Liège of their actions and justify them.[298] That their audacity masked a certain hesitation is further revealed by their request to the Administrators at Liège to respond "as soon as possible" and inform them about "what steps" they were "to take in regard to him".

They nevertheless achieved their goal. The "General, in full habit," says the liberal author of *Huy sous la République et l'Empire*, was jailed at city hall.[299] These tyrants, however, did

---

throughout 1795 and 1796, the two most chaotic years.

[296] State Archives, Liège, letter of 3 Nivose, year IV.

[297] Archives, city of Huy, Register 403, 94.

[298] State Archives, Liège, letter of 20 Frimaire, year IV; and Annexe 32 (Fontaine, *Jacques Dubois, 152-153*).

[299] Dubois, *Huy sous la République et l'Empire*, 46.

not foresee that news of his arrest would also gather a noisy crowd at the doors of city hall. The shouts and gestures of the people declared their indignation over the incarceration of the intrepid old man and, by December 13, the Prior General of the Crosiers had become such an object of veneration among the people that his imprisonment aroused wide-spread reproach.[300] Two men then emerged from the crowd and, braving the despotism of the local "patriots," entered city hall to plead for the General's release. They soon had the satisfaction of accompanying him down the building's steps. Although Rubin and his collaborators had had to give in to the people's protests, they managed to continue the General's supervised imprisonment in his own Quarter. His two bold liberators, G. Chapelle (his neighbor at Clairlieu) and F. E. Masson, were obliged to sign a statement entered into the record of council meetings that the General of the Crosiers would remain in his Quarter at Huy under their responsibility; that one of them, along with a military guard appointed by the municipal administration, would keep watch over him each night; and that they undertook "to produce him promptly upon demand."[301]

These two brave fellows seem to have dispensed themselves from bothering the General with their nightly presence. By an altogether singular coincidence, moreover, Masson was honored with an appointment as a city administrator only hours after Dubois' triumphant liberation. A dispatch arrived from Bouteville declaring the city's first administration dissolved; save for Piette and Rubin, all the men whom the Commissioner for the Department of the Ourthe the appointed to the municipal council were individuals who had

---

[300] Grandmaison, *Souvenirs de Huy*, 62.
[301] Archives, city of Huy, Register 403, 95.

held the magistracy before the Revolution. Former burgo-master Masson thus found himself seated next to Fran-cotte.[302]

Pressed for its advice about Dubois' incarceration, Liège's Central Administration meanwhile gladly took refuge in si-lence. It also declined to take up the petition which the two gendarmes had submitted at the beginning of December. It surely knew of the change in membership of Huy's munici-pal council, and no doubt reckoned that these new members would themselves put an end to this shabby local affair. But the new members had an abundance of other things to pre-occupy them, and faced merciless opposition. Annoyed that the gendarmes remained unpaid, Rubin supported their new appeal to Liège. Pointing out that "the Crosiers refused to accede to their request," he entreated the prominent citizens in Liège to "give a response, by the bearer's return, if possi-ble."[303] Only three days later, however, did a reply come from Liège, saying that it was for the monastery, not the General, to pay the two men.[304] Subprior Noiville did so on December 30, in the amount of "50 fl. 7 s. and 2 sols."[305]

At the turn of the year to 1796 two decrees indicating what fate awaited religious communities were passed. On January 6, the clergy were ordered to read out at Mass a declaration which pictured the people as the victims of high-ranking ec-

---

[302] Grandmaison, *Souvenirs de Huy*, 81.

[303] State Archives, Liège, letter of 3 Nivose, year IV; and Annexe 33 a, b, and c (Fontaine, *Jacques Dubois*, 153-154).

[304] State Archives, Liège, letter of 5 Nivose, year IV; and Annexe 33 c (Fon-taine, *Jacques Dubois*, 154).

[305] State Archives, Liège, Crosier sources, the account-book of Subprior Noiville, 15.

clesiastics.[306] Soon after came the decree ordering them to
inventory the silver plate and objects dedicated to cult in
their churches. Rubin moved quickly: the decree was dated
January 8, and on the 14th he was inside Clairlieu. He who
had been behind the whole persecution of the Prior General
was thus the one to poke into the cabinets in the monastery's
sacristy. He evidently bypassed Dubois completely: Jérosme
was the sacristan, and he sufficed. All was nosed into, in the
sacristy and in the church, and catalogued. The sacristan even
opened the tabernacle, "where was found a silver ciborium".
Everything was put "in custody," and Subprior Noiville and
sacristan Jérosme were made responsible "to produce them
promptly upon demand."[307]

The disagreeable memory of Rubin's descent upon Clairlieu
had not yet faded when resistance to Huy's new and radically
reorganized civil administration began. It had held office for
scarcely four weeks when it was blocked by the patriot ex-
tremists, who had compiled a new list of proposed members
and forwarded it to Bouteville.[308] Arriving in Huy on January
18, he dismissed the moderates with a stroke of the pen to
make room for Ledrou, the elder Lainé (a merchant), Piette
(a dyer), Jamolet (a shoemaker), Detelle (a merchant) and
Rouchet, who was chosen president. Former National Agent
Rubin became commissioner of police and was given the
task of compiling a catalogue of the silver plate and of cult
objects in Huy's churches. Liège' former deputy attorney general, Ista, about whom we will have much more to say, was

---

[306] H. Pirenne, *Histoire de Belgique*, 4:66.
[307] This detailed inventory of the Crosier church and sacristy in Huy is in
Annexe 35 (Fontaine, *Jacques Dubois*, 155).
[308] He had become Commissioner of the Department of the Ourthe on
December 13, 1795.

made Commissioner of the Executive Directory[309] for the commune of Huy.[310] The very select people who made up Huy's new municipal council would soon become famous for a series of measures which led to the suppression of religious orders in the city; they would also take it upon themselves to renew the struggle against General Dubois.

Thereafter the new council felt obliged to let not a month, not a week, pass without some new measure of persecution. On January 21, at the insistence of Commissioner Renard of Liège, it organized the taking of the anti-royalist oath in the market square at Huy.[311] From then on, the hateful oath was made obligatory for all priests, and the Directory enforced laws of revolutionary inspiration ever more strictly.[312] The next day, January 22, there appeared a decree obliging every inhabitant" of whatever status or sex" to wear the tricolor cockade: priests, too, who were forbidden to conceal it under the bands of their hats.[313] A law of December 10 had decreed a forced loan of 600,000,000 pounds, about which the pre-

---

[309] Under the French constitution of 1795, the five-man Directory, whose members were chosen by the legislature, formed the executive branch of government. – Tr.

[310] Grandmaison, *Souvenirs de Huy*, 84. Ista took up residence in Huy by moving his possessions into the Abbey of Neufmoustier. See Archives, city of Huy, Register 403, 136.

[311] The oath was taken by the city officials whom Bouteville had installed, by all whose office or work was somehow government-related, and "by a crowd of citizens and citizenesses of every age". The garrison fired a three-gun salute, and musicians played republican tunes–('a ira, La Carmagnole, and the like–"during which fraternal kisses were exchanged among all parties; when the ceremony was concluded, the municipal council provided two casks of beer for the refreshment of its brothers in arms." (Archives, city of Huy, Register 403, for that date).

[312] Grandmaison, *Souvenirs de Huy*, 64.

[313] Grandmaison, *Souvenirs de Huy*, 10.

vious municipal council had not much concerned itself. The new administration did, and on January 27, 1796, proclaimed in its usual despotic way "that within three days each person was to make a declaration at the office of the Commissioner of the Executive Directory of his goods and incomes. If the declaration was not made, the taxation would be applied automatically."[314] Huy was obliged to contribute 50,000 pounds but, as was typically the case, the bulk of it (28,900 pounds) was demanded of the clergy. In the list of the required sums, the Crosiers are set down for 6,000 pounds and the Prior General for 2,000.[315] The administration next drafted the stone-cutter Delhaise to efface and make invisible any religious armorial bearings or those which recalled the *ancien regime.* On February 11, it decreed that "those buildings, which at the end of an eight-day period, still bore these hateful emblems of the aristocracy will be confiscated," The Crosiers were set abuzz by this, for their church was surrounded by a gallery of such things. They summoned two plasterers who, over a three-day period, "obscured" all coats of arms ,[316] The escutcheon of Prior General Fisen on the pediment of the monastery's large carriage gate was not spared.[317] On February 30, the Crosiers were re-

---

[314] Grandmaison, *Souvenirs de Huy*, 50.

[315] Archives, city of Huy, Register 403. In this, too, the approach was typical. Whenever the rights of the Master General were involved, the municipal councilors declared that he had none, claiming that he had not been reinstated in his citizenship; whenever contributions were to be made, they counted him among those who had been reinstated and taxed him accordingly.

[316] State Archives, Liège, Crosier sources, the account-book of Subprior Noiville, 18.

[317] For its defacement, Delhaise received "2 flor. 2 s. 2 d". (the account-book of Subprior Noiville, 18).

quired to provide three sheep and a calf.[318] On 18 Ventôse (March 7), a regular requisition of *braz* was established, for which the Crosiers were taxed in the amount of 1,305 pounds.[319] On March 16, the city's religious houses were burdened with the requirement of providing vegetables to the troops of the garrison.

This avalanche of requisitions, added to so many previous exactions, must have eventually revived at Clairlieu a great interest in the valuables which had been taken across the Rhine. Had Donnay not availed himself of these claims to stir up the rebellion? Over the five months during which legal proceedings had gone on against the Prior General, he had burned with impatience to satisfy his hatred for this "high ecclesiastical dignitary". Since the character of the new municipal council made it certain that the illegal confinement of Prior General Dubois would continue, the moment could not have been more opportune for him to again approach the civil court in Liège about the urgency of settling the case involving the items which had been taken to Germany.[320] Liège thus informed the contesting parties of the date set for their court appearance. The unfortunate General, whose resistance up to this point no doubt reflected his confidence in appeals made to the courts, asked Liège for a continuance "in order to produce several documents bearing on his rights". In a decision handed down on March 19, how-

---

[318] Archives, city of Huy, file for year V.

[319] Archives, city of Huy, file for year V. *Braz* was a milled grain used in brewing; a hogshead of the stuff weighed two hundred pounds.

[320] Insistence on settling this matter was in all probability a collaborative effort between Donnay and Devaux: the latter made three trips to Liège during March, for which he was compensated by Sub prior Noiville. (State Archives, Liège, Crosier sources, the account-book of Subprior Noiville, 20.)

ever, the civil court decided that, in "shortening the continuance because of the urgency of the case,"[321] it awarded the defendant (Dubois) a period of five days in which to communicate to his opponents the pertinent titles and documents. Before 8:00 a.m. on the morning of March 23, the process-server Robert Catoul arrived to deliver the notice, countersigned by Donnay, to the Prior General. An equal period of five days was awarded the plaintiffs for their response and, at the end of it, the court would hear the case.[322]

Donnay used the intervening days to sharpen his weapons. Realizing how opportune the recent forced loan of 6,000 pounds assessed against them[323] had made this moment, he submitted, in the Crosiers' name, a petition requesting a twenty-day delay so that they might meet the requirements of this levy.[324] Over three-quarters of the petition, however, bore upon the Prior General, whose case he wished to prejudice. According to Donnay, Dubois had "emigrated," had carried "everything" off, had returned "nothing," was willing to render "no account," and had "given no account of him-

---

[321] So much had Donnay pestered Liège with his meddlesome "appeals". See Annexe 37 (Fontaine, *Jacques Dubois*, 156-157).

[322] State Archives, Liège; see Annexe 36 (Fontaine, *Jacques Dubois*, 155-156).

[323] To assure the successful collection of the six hundred million pounds, a system comprising sixteen different classes of property-owners had been created. According to the law, the sixteenth and highest class consisted of those whose wealth amounted to 500,000 pounds or more in capital, worth 1,790 pounds. [Father Fontaine's meaning is unclear. Father Brasseur suggests that he may have been comparing French pounds, which were constantly being devalued, with the local currency. – Tr.] The tax imposed on members of that class was set between 1,500 and a maximum of 6,000 pounds, depend ing on their gross worth. On directions from Huy, Liège had assigned the Crosiers to the sixteenth class and the General to the fourteenth. (Archives, city of Huy, Register 874, 136.)

[324] . State Archives, Liège; Annexe 37 (Fontaine, *Jacques Dubois*, 156-157).

self for five years."[325] Dechamp, president of the Central Administration at Liège, replied via Huy's municipal council that the Crosiers were granted their requested twenty-day delay.[326]

If these intimations of success gladdened Donnay's heart that morning of March 28, whatever satisfaction the Crosiers may have felt was overshadowed by the order of Commissioner Rose, issued the same day, that religious communities were to supply the meat demanded by the military, "their needy brothers in arms". The system developed to provide these supplies operated with the regularity of a clock. The Crosiers were to furnish all the meat needed for that day; the Celesti-

---

[325] Amid this heaping up of exaggerations, there are two points which might have caught the attention of the arbiters at Liège, viz., that the General had given no information about his affairs for five years nor had he done so since his return. But when one realizes, as Dubois would soon prove, that never in all his time at Clairlieu had he deviated from the community's rule about the administra tion of temporal goods being left in the hands of its procurator, and that the conditions created by war over the previous five years and more had hardly provided an opportune moment for the easy verifica tion of accounts, Donnay's allegations seem not only out of line but highly tendentious. If he was able to exploit the unfortunate circumstances which had obliged Dubois to absent himself from Huy since before the Revolution began at Liège in order to attend to spiritual matters in his Order's foreign monasteries, he knew very well that temporal matters had been attended to properly, as his "for five years" implies: the records kept since Dubois' arrival at Clairlieu in 1778 were clear and available. That Dubois may have indeed refused to render an account since his return is easily explained. In a time marked by an unnerving lack of understanding, he had to exercise a most prudent caution before enemies like Donnay and Devaux, who had no business and entirely too much interest in learning about things properly left to the discretion of Clairlieu's superior.

[326] Archives, city of Huy, file for year V, 8 Germinal; see Annexe 38 (Fontaine, *Jacques Dubois*, 157).

nes for the day after, 9 Germinal; the White Ladies[327] for the 10th; the Shelter of Aulne for the 11th; the Shelter of Val St. Lambert for the 12th; the Augustinians and Ursulines, half each, for the 13th; the convent of St. Aldegond and the Gray Sisters,[328] likewise half each, for the 14th; and if there was further need, the Crosiers would again meet it for the 15th, and so on.[329] The next day, March 29, four to six soldiers were sent to be lodged in each religious house, along with an invitation that they be supplied with a half-pound of meat each.[330] That did not keep Nansuy, the commandant of the garrison, from going to the Crosier monastery, confiscating an ox and having citizen Bihet slaughter it on the spot.[331] Soon afterwards, Commissioner Joubert of the Army of the Sambre and Meuse requisitioned 3,317 pounds of meat from Huy, under threat of execution by firing squad if the levy was not met. That exaction also fell upon the city's religious communities and its more well-to-do citizens. Clairlieu was

---

[327] As the calced Carmelites were known in Huy. – Tr.
[328] More commonly known as the Hospice Sisters, an order which claimed to have been the third order of sisters founded by St. Francis of Assisi. – Tr.
[329] Archives, city of Huy, Register 403, 180-181.
[330] Archives, city of Huy, Register 403, 185.
[331] Archives, city of Huy, Register 403, 186. Nansuy's action earned him a reproof from the city's administration, "considering that the commissioner of war, and his secretary the commandant of the garrison and the supply officer have committed an act most arbitrary, most tyrannical and most prejudicial to the security and preservation of the individual properties of the citizens by betaking them selves to the monastery of the Crosiers and there confiscating on their own authority an ox which they had slaughtered on the spot by Bihet, butcher of this commune, and that they had it carried off, as appears in the complaint which the Crosier monastery has just brought to us," as we read in the minutes of the council's meeting of 10 Germinal (March 30, 1796). The animal probably was needed for the monastery's spring work, for the Crosiers promptly bought another for 175 florins. (The account-book of Subprior Noiville, 19.)

exempted, "because an ox had just been confiscated from them," and only the Prior General was required to pay 200 pounds, in coin, to citizen Bertrand within twenty-four hours or face a firing-squad.[332]

The pressure was unyielding and pitiless. Monasteries like Clairlieu, which owned woodlands or engaged in sharecropping, also had to hire patrols and foresters to prevent the thefts which were on the increase, too.[333] The twenty-day extension which the Crosiers had been granted was therefore justified, but they used it with the same nonchalance they had shown in 1794. They sold cheap wines and measures of wheat, rye and spelt. All that was normal, but Devaux took it upon himself to convert into cash many of the monastery's possessions by making them over to the Mont de Piété at Huy.[334] Next, although their woodlands had been nationalized and cuttings there were strictly forbidden,[335] he dared suggest to the Crosiers the fiction of a sale for his personal acquisition of twenty oaks of considerable size. In concert with Father Jérosme, who did not at all bother to consult or inform his confrere Tilman, the community's agent for the sale of trees,[336] he marked twenty large trees and had a forester cut them down. So that he could claim that the sale had been concluded before the nationalization of the woods, and again with Jérosme's connivance, he predated the bill of sale

---

[332] Archives, city of Huy, Register 403, 192.
[333] State Archives, Liège, the account-book of Subprior Noiville, 20.
[334] State Archives, Liège, the account-book of Subprior Noiville, 2 and 3. (The Mont de Piete was a charitable lending institution from which one might draw loans by assigning movable properties to it as collateral. – Tr.)
[335] As Donnay had acknowledged in his request for the twenty-day extension.
[336] State Archives, Liège, letter of 17 Thermidor, year IV.

to read as if it had been concluded on August 17, 1794,[337] and so absorbed this sale of early April 1796, into the legal logging done in the summer of 1794, when the Crosiers had been obliged to pay 20,000 pounds in taxes. It was a purely gratuitous arrangement, from which Devaux made off with the lion's share by adroitly avoiding, to the detriment of the Crosiers, having to accept a higher public bid.

In all this drama born of the Revolution, the Crosiers of Clairlieu were both spiritually and materially the dupes and victims of meddlers from outside their community. As events unfolded, the atmosphere of the Revolution weighed more and more heavily upon them.

---

[337] . State Archives, Liège, letter of 17 Thermidor, year IV.

Illustration 1:
View of the sacristy in the Kolen Priory

Illustration 2:
Crosier Priory in Liége in the 18th Century

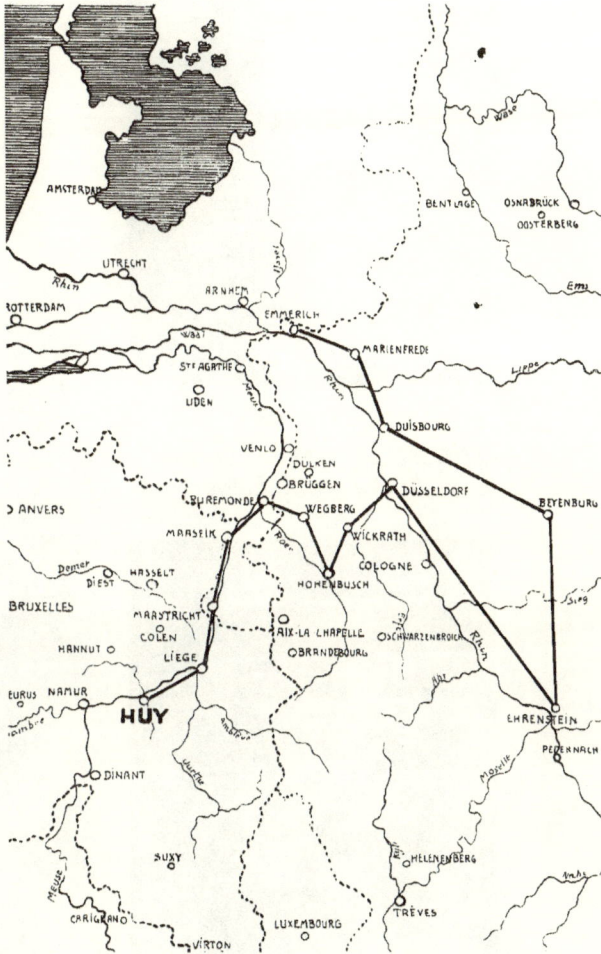

Illustration 3
Diagram of the last journey of Jacques Dubois, O.S.C.

Illustration 4
*Augustin Heuskin, O.S.C, former prior
in Paris and Liége*

Illustration 5:
*Lambert-Philippe Poswick, Commissioner for
the Executive Directory in Liège*

Illustration 6
Clairlieu in Huy in the 18ᵗʰ Century

Illustration 7
Château Lamalle, country home of the Prior General

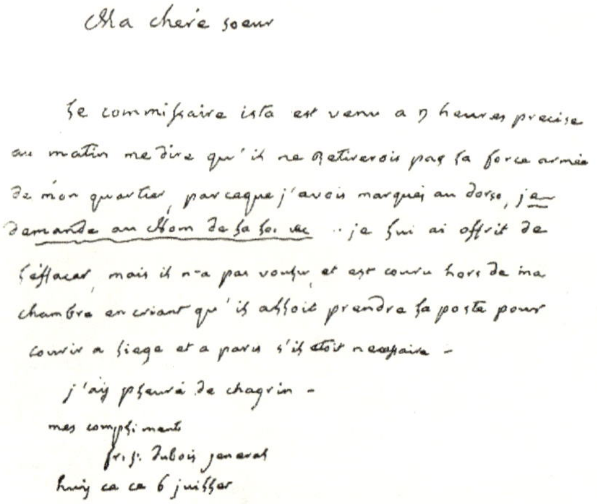

Ma chère soeur

Le commissaire ista est venu a 7 heures precise au matin me dire qu'il ne retireroit pas la force armée de mon quartier, parceque j'avois marqué au dorso, je demande au nom de la loi vec .. je lui ai offrit de l'effacer, mais il n'a pas voulu, et est couru hors de ma chambre en criant qu'il alloit prendre la poste pour courir a liege et a paris s'il etoit necessaire -

j'ay pleuré de chagrin -

mes complimens

fr. J. Dubois general

huy ce 6 juillet

Illustration 8

Facsimile of a letter of J. Dubois to his sister Madame Demany

Armoiries de Mgr Jacques DUBOIS

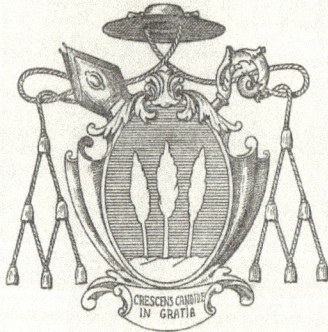

Illustration 9

Coat of Arms of Prior General Jacques Dubois

Prior General Jacques Dubois, O.S.C.

Illustration 10
Prior General Lambert Fisen, O.S.C.

Illustration 11
Former Crosier, Antoine Streel, in 1796

TABLEAU GENEALOGIQUE DE LA FAMILLE DU BOIS

Jacques du Bois et Eléonore Russon

Gérard	Gisbert	Jean-	Elisabeth	Jacques-	Marie-
28-5-1693	9-10-1694	François	9-11-1699	Nic.	Catherine
		né le		10-7-1702	30-7-1706
		20-1-1697			
		épouse le 6-5-1727			
		Jeanne Cologne (1)			
		née le 16-10-1701			

Eléonore	Catherine	Jacques	Jean	Jeanne	Jean	Catherine	Mathieu	Marie	Dieudonné
Josèphe	Jeanne	Gisbert	François	Josèphe	Ignace	Françoise	Nicolas	Agnès	François
5-3-1728	Josèphe	Joseph.	Joseph.	18-1-1735	Joseph	Josèphe	Joseph	21-10-1742	Joseph
	16-12-1729	19-12-1730	9-2-1733	épouse	1-2-1737	12-6-1738	9-6-1740		27-1-1744
				le					
				4-6-1770					
				Demany Servais-Jos.					

Jacques-Joseph.
1-6-1772

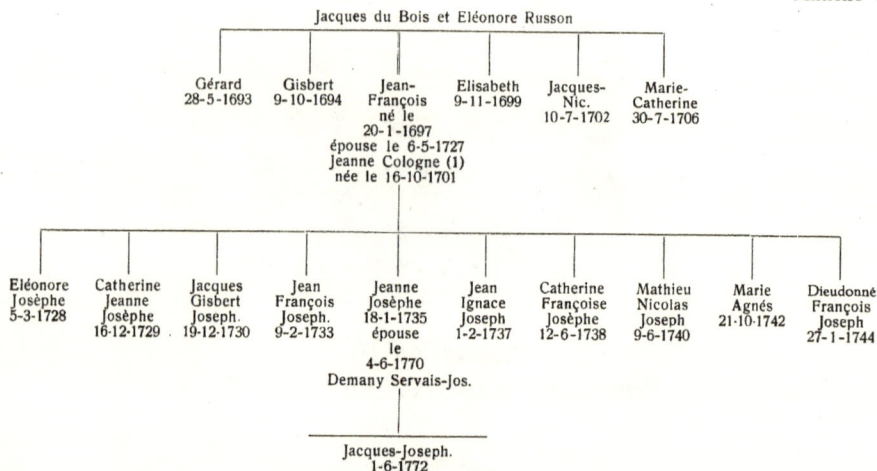

(1) Jeanne Cologne, fille de Gilles de Cologne et de Jeanne Bertho, fut baptisée à N.-D.-aux-Fonts, le 16-10-1701 et était la troisième des neuf enfants de cette famille : Marguerite, 12-4-1696 ; Gilles, 21-4-1697 ; Jeanne, 16-10-1701 ; Arnold-Jos., 2-2-1704 ; Jean, 22-2-1706 ; Marie-Gertrude, 8-4-1708 ; Mathieu-Nic., 13-2-1712 ; Marie-Thérèse, 28-10-1714 ; Jean, 25-2-1717.

Illustration 12
Genealogical Chart of the Dubois Family

Illustration 13
Clairlieu in Huy

Illustration 14
Prior General Jacques Dubois, O.S.C.

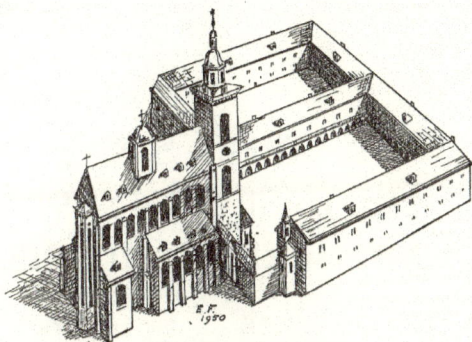

CHAPTER SIX
THE CASE AGAINST
PRIOR GENERAL DUBOIS

As Clairlieu endured dire calamity, the surveillance maintained over her Prior and Prior General kept him from coming to her aid. Sequestered from his confreres at Huy, Dubois was also isolated from the monasteries in the Netherlands and Germany. If letters kept him somewhat informed of their lot, the strict surveillance over him prevented his correspondence with them. Those circumstances must have weighed on him heavily in early April of 1796. On April 8, Father Demet set out for the border with a passport issued by the Central Administration at Liège, and probably charged by the General with a "secret mission":[338] it was, after all, important that the rest of the Order be properly informed about its General's detention and the status of his case.

On 22 Germinal, year VI (April 11), a government decree consigned the church bells to silence, and that same day Du-

---

[338] State Archives, Liège, letter of 21 Fructidor, year VI. He would have been unable to obtain this passport had he not been reinstated in his citizenship, as he and Father Warnotte were on 12 Brumaire, year V (November 4, 1795), by Representative of the People Lefevre de Nantes. See Annexe 39 (Fontaine, *Jacques Dubois, 157-158*).

bois received a summons to appear in civil court on April 13. Hoping to obtain some days of respite, he produced an affidavit from Doctor Bonhoulle which certified an alarming decline in his health.

At Donnay's insistence, however, Liège took no account of it and maintained the date scheduled for the hearing. That took place as scheduled, but the Crosiers were disappointed: their case was dismissed and Dubois was re-established "in the rights of governance vested in his office, in conformity with the customs of the community of which he is the Superior."[339] Wishing to restore harmony to his community, the Prior General had revealed Donnay's intrigues and offered to have the silver and other items brought back from across the Rhine.[340] To the "plaintiffs," however, this gesture of reconciliation was of no importance, and they lodged an appeal.[341] The real source of dissension thus seems to have been on the spiritual level.

The real loser on April 13, however, was Donnay. Six days later, on 29 Germinal, year IV, he sent a letter to the Administration at Liège demanding that management of Clairlieu be withdrawn from Dubois and returned to the majority of the canons.[342] In a second letter, he permitted himself an explosion of malicious glee: "Anarchy is at last complete in the fair monastery of the Crosiers of Huy." Thus he asked Liège "to charge the Executive Commissioner[343] to carry out the de-

---

[339] See Annexe 40 (Fontaine, *Jacques Dubois, 158-159*).
[340] Ibid.
[341] And greased the palms of the court with "21 flor. 7 I." to do so. (The account-book of Subprior Noiville, 22.)
[342] State Archives, Liège, letter of 29 Germinal, year IV; see Annexe 41 (Fontaine, *Jacques Dubois, 159-160*).
[343] That is, Ista. This may indicate that, by the end of April, Donnay had

crees of the Representatives against the General," by which he meant application of the laws against émigrés. That Brussels had restored the General's citizenship and the civil court in Liège thereafter reinstated him in office was of little consequence to him; he was very much counting on a "special decree" to overturn these decisions.

In response to Donnay, L. P. Poswick, Commissioner for the Executive Directory in Liège, declared that he "believed it incumbent upon himself to forbid that new proceedings prolong the disunity which reigned between the parties" and that his decision, therefore, was that the Prior General and "three deputies of the community of the Crosiers of Huy" appear at his Office of National Properties on the 15th of the month (May 4, 1796).[344]

Clairlieu was being more and more enwrapped in a web of outside influences and meddling. Dubois suffered greatly because of it, and his energies began to fail him: frequent bouts of dizziness so incapacitated him that he was unable to leave his Quarter to go to the church and even had to have

---

already won the support of the Commissioner of the Executive Directory. See Annexe 42 (Fontaine, *Jacques Dubois*, 160).

[344] State Archives, Liège; see Annexe 43 (Fontaine, *Jacques Dubois*, 160-161). The original offers several points worthy of note. The passages crossed out by Dechamp's censorship reveal that he did not share his colleague's noble sentiments about the government's duty to promote domestic as well as international tranquility and did not recognize the restoration of the General's citizenship and office. Equally noteworthy is Dechamp's removal of Poswick's proposal that the "three deputies of the community of the Crosiers" to appear before him be chosen from among its *oldest* members. Given the circumstances, this was particularly odious. As our narrative will show, it was the three youngest members of the community and the weak Noiville who were playing king: Dechamp must have known this as well as Poswick did.

help reciting the Hours.[345] As for the Crosiers, a sense of un-ease had hung over them since their setback, and the revela-tion of the misdeeds in which they had collaborated with Devaux, during the hearing on April 13, alarmed them even more. They were, to a great extent, putting their hope in the "special decree" which Donnay was seeking. We do not know whether they became impatient or, what seems more likely, whether Donnay brought their complaint before the Direc-tory's Commissioner, Ista,[346] but after having failed to have himself set up as arbiter, the latter improvised for himself the role of grand inquisitor. On the morning of April 24, he sent word that the Prior General was to appear at his private of-fice. Dubois declined the invitation, noting his poor health. Ista bristled, demanding a doctor's certification. Bonhoulle once more certified that "the health of citizen Dubois, Gen-eral of the Crosiers, had so declined that it was wholly im-possible for him to leave his house, considering the frequent bouts of dizziness and other difficulties with which he was afflicted."[347] Aware of Ista's impulsive nature, Dubois sent him the certificate that same morning. Angered, Ista immedi-ately arranged for one of the municipal councilors to accom-pany him to the General's Quarter and, the next morning, rapped on the door of the broken and sequestered septuage-narian. We do not know what transpired or what Ista said (he was known to be an abusive fellow), but one thing is cer-tain: although ailing, Dubois rallied his forces and resisted him. Our proof is Ista's report of the visit some days later to his friend Dechamp, president of the Central Administration. Although the account reflects his version of the meeting, it

---

[345] State Archives, Liège, letter of 12 Floreal, year IV.
[346] His second letter to Liège had, after all, suggested that the Central Ad-ministration refer taking further action against the General to Ista.
[347] State Archives, Liège, letter of 12 Floreal, year IV.

reveals that he was unable to intimidate the old man: "I saw a man in radiant health, who walked quite well…, a quarrelsome fellow, as stubborn as a mule, deaf to all possible reasonings."[348] His intention of forcing Dubois to surrender all claim to the civil court's favorable decision had run into a stone wall. From his own account of how a sick but strongwilled man had faced him down, we can conclude that, when confronted with this arrogant fellow, the Prior General had gathered his energies for a burst of courage and will. The information that Dubois was thereafter was afflicted with grave depression and frequent bouts of fainting supports our conclusion.[349]

During the most severe of these bouts, which reveal how shaky his health had become, Dubois received Poswick's directive of April 28 (9 Floréal, year VI) enjoining his appearance at Liège on May 4. At the limit of his strength, he informed Kiekens and, including with the letter a duplicate of Doctor Bonhoulle's certificate, begged his friend and advocate to see that his appearance be postponed to a later date. Kiekens immediately approached the Central Administration with an urgent request for postponement, arguing among other points that "the General of the Crosiers could not undertake the journey from Huy to Liège without running the risk of perishing en route."[350] The appeal was too manifestly sincere to be doubted, so Poswick issued a notification, countersigned by Dechamp, that the hearing at the Office of National Properties was definitely postponed until 10 Prairial (May 29). The Central Administration provided the

---

[348] State Archives, Liège, letter of 13 Floreal, year IV.
[349] State Archives, Liège, letter of 6 Prairial, year IV.
[350] State Archives, Liège; Annexe 44 (Fontaine, *Jacques Dubois, 161-162*).

same information to the opposing party.[351]

Even before they received notification of the postponement on May 2, the Crosiers at Huy, who increasingly danced to the tune of those behind the scenes, had submitted to Dubois a proposal for "reconciliation." The conditions were that "neither the General nor any other member of the community will be able to administer the community's property; all must be done by determination of the chapter through majority vote: in case of a tie, the General will cast the deciding vote.[352] Devaux must be retained at Clairlieu as the legal receiver. The General must ratify all the acts and business undertaken by his religious during his absence in Germany. He will render his accounts, will have the small collection of silver items returned, and must sign the receipt antedated by Devaux concerning the sale of the oaks." Thinking that mediation by Dubois' confessor, the Capuchin vicar general, would bring the matter to a successful conclusion, they requested "a response ... from the Most Reverend General by 4:00 p.m."[353] Were the Capuchin to fail, their plan was to have Rouchet, president of the municipal council, and one of his colleagues confront Dubois with the same conciliatory proposals.

The entire production around this "proposal" is typical of the lawyers contesting the General's authority, who now seem to have been doing nothing more than searching for ways to

---

[351] State Archives, Liège; Annexe 44 (Fontaine, *Jacques Dubois, 162*).

[352] Because the *majority* of "the Chapter" had succumbed to the current ideology, the right which it granted the General was illusory and meaningless. They had reserved to themselves the source and principle of power and were offering the General only its use and enjoyment. Although their formula sounds traditional, it is very much of the eighteenth century.

[353] State Archives, Liège; Annexe 46 (Fontaine, *Jacques Dubois, 162-163*).

increase the list of "witnesses for the prosecution" as the date of the hearing approached. Were he to accept the proposal without reservation, Dubois would effectively overturn the April 13 decision of the civil court which had reinstated him in his office and prerogatives as head of Clairlieu. Refuse it, and it would be his obstinacy to blame for the dissension in the community. In the wake of so many assaults delivered against his rank as General, this was surely the most unkind, for it was directed against his function. He was, however, unimpressed. "I will not sign this," he told the Capuchin priest, "because it is the handiwork of the lawyer Devaux, the receiver of my house."[354] Even as he firmly and indignantly rejected this proposal, which would have emptied the Order's constitutions of their substance, he nevertheless showed himself unwilling to burn the bridges between him and his community. As for the other embassy, from Huy's municipal council, events will show that their dismissal left them in no doubt that Dubois knew very well who was behind this new plot.

One member of the Crosier "Chapter" at Huy, however, did not sign the proposed compromise to which the rest had agreed as a body. Had Tilman then broken ranks with his confreres to at last be reconciled to his Prior General and to Warnotte and Demet? Indeed he had, but we must not get ahead of ourselves, and must first attend to the outcries which followed the refusal of the Prior General to sign.

Ista was the first to react. Immediately after 4:00 p.m. on May 2, he wrote two letters to Liège: one was to Dechamp, to offset Bonhoulle's medical certificate and so oblige Dubois to appear on May 4 (the General, he observed, "continues to

---

[354] State Archives, Liège; see Annexe 46 (Fontaine, *Jacques Dubois, 162-163*).

want to exalt himself above his religious");[355] the other, even more bitter in tone, went to Poswick,

whose moderation he wished to confound. In it he piled up one spiteful grievance after another against Dubois and to it attached the proposal for reconciliation, as if that were a court exhibit.[356] On May 3, Huy's municipal councilors in their turn dispatched a note

to the Central Administration, declaring that they put no confidence in the medical certificate which the General had sent and so thought he ought to appear on May 4.[357] But Liège remained unmoved, perhaps because of more accurate information relayed through Kiekens, and did not reverse itself; the hearing remained scheduled for 10 Prairial (May 29, 1796). Disappointed and annoyed, Donnay sent the administrators at Liège a virulent letter on May 4, claiming that "that priest toyed with them" and was an impostor who "was quite well," and as Ista had done two days earlier, when he had written "that [Dubois] may go to the devil if he is thinking of restoring the *ancien regime*,"[358] sought to raise the suspicion that his victim was an Austrian sympathizer. Donnay in his turn also enclosed a copy of the proposal of reconciliation,[359] and so verified for the historian that this effort was naught but a contrivance of that little coterie of Dubois' enemies. Thus the ground was prepared for the appearance

---

[355] For Ista, of course, the re-establishment of any authority at Clairlieu was the imposition of "tyranny." State Archives, Liège; see Annexe 47 (Fontaine, *Jacques Dubois*, 163-164).
[356] State Archives, Liège; Annexe 48 (Fontaine, *Jacques Dubois*, 164).
[357] State Archives, Liège; see Annexe 49 (Fontaine, *Jacques Dubois*, 165).
[358] State Archives, Liège; Annexe 48 (Fontaine, *Jacques Dubois*, 164).
[359] State Archives, Liège, letter of 15 Floreal, year IV; see Annexe 50 (Fontaine, *Jacques Dubois*, 165).

of the Prior General in Liège, now postponed until May 29. On May 7, however, Huy's municipal council, acting on its own authority, officially directed a local surgeon named Jacques to go to the residence of the Prior General and establish the true state of his health. They would, they thought, thus confound the overly complaisant Bonhoulle. But their expert found his patient in a very serious state. His note to the council observed that "the infirmities of the General of the Crosiers have become so serious that he has fallen even while in his Quarter and the briefest passage into the street places his life in imminent peril."[360]

Disappointed, the municipal council sought some other means of harassment. Knowing that the Departmental Administration was about to exact a new requisition of grain and meat from Huy, Rouchet and his colleagues were eager to designate those who would have to provide them. At the head of the list of the names of the twenty prominent citizens therefore appeared that of "the General of the Crosiers, who is obliged to pay 2,000 pounds." In eighteenth place were the Crosiers, charged only 200 pounds. The sums were to be paid within twenty-four hours, under pain of execution by firing-squad.[361] Faced with this new injustice to their General, Fathers Demet and Tilman openly rebelled. In these first days of May, they in fact showed such passion for his defense that they were arrested and jailed on Ista's order.[362] They in fact seem not only to have given public voice to their indignation but to have revealed something of the latter's less

---

[360] State Archives, Liège, letter of 6 Prairial, year IV; see Annexe 53 c (Fontaine, *Jacques Dubois*, 168).

[361] Archives, city of Huy, Register 403, 202.

[362] Archives, city of Huy, Register of Arrest Warrants, 15; see Annexe 51 (Fontaine, *Jacques Dubois*, 166).

than worthy conduct: in his descent upon the General's Quarter, Ista had "threatened him with being conducted to Liège by the gendarmes the very next day, repeatedly assuring him that he would be shot."[363] Ista was more than eager to report the audacity of these" monks" to Poswick and the conclusion of his letter, which his wrath seems to have rendered incoherent, did little to hide his intention of converting Poswick to the cause which so obsessed him. "Tell me," he wrote, "the day of your arrival... the friends which you have do not like to be caught napping..."[364] We do not know whether Poswick "had been fully informed about this affair," as Ista intended him to be, but it is certain that Demet had remained obedient and faithful to his General and that Tilman had followed his example.

Dubois seems to have been shocked by their arrest, for his condition again worsened. On May 21, Doctors Evrard and Bonhoulle went to his Quarter for an examination and consultation, after which they certified that it was absolutely impossible for the sick man to travel, so afflicted was he with dizziness.[365] Since there remained only eight days until his hearing and since the Directory had just scheduled the great "Festival of Victory" for that Sunday, the General asked a certain de Ponthière[366] to approach the Administration at Liège

[363] State Archives, Liège, letter of 25 Floreal, year IV, from Ista to Poswick.
[364] State Archives, Liège, letter of 25 Floreal, year IV, from Ista to Poswick; see Annexe 52 (Fontaine, *Jacques Dubois*, 167). He must have already known that Poswick would be in Huy for the coming "Festival of Victory" to celebrate Bonaparte's success in his Italian campaign.
[365] This according to a letter of 6 Prairial, year IV, from L. 1. de Ponthiere to the Central Administration at Liège.
[366] The request has been signed by "L. 1. de Ponthiere, pro...[illegible]." He must have been a colleague or confidant of Keikens, who perhaps was away. The letter and medical certificates are in Annexe 53 (Fontaine,

to see to the "rescheduling" of his hearing, with allowance made for his "serious and life-threatening" illness, confirmed by the three medical certificates attached to the letter.[367] On the 25th, it was done. In his request, de Ponthière informed the Central Administration that, if necessary, "the General authorized [it] to inquire about the state of his health among the impartial people of Huy, but he excepted from that group the members of Huy's municipal council, to whom he wholly objected, for they had not ceased, up to that very day, to oppress him in every way."[368] As a result, Liège provisionally took note of this, and one must wonder if their attitude of deliberation reflects the visit which three Crosiers from Huy, Jérosme, Hayweghen and Loncin, made there two days earlier, on May 23.[369]

On 8 Prairial (May 28, 1796), Huy's city administration deprived Dubois of all rights pertinent to the beguinages of which he held the conferral:[370] other, more serious, measures necessarily had to follow. That step and the celebration of the Festival of Victory on May 29 leads one to think that, when Poswick had come to Huy for the occasion, he had been received by the" friends" about whom Ista had written to him in such flattering terms.[371] Had the municipal councilors and their allies won him over? However that may have been, it was immediately after the Festival of Victory, the very

---

Jacques Dubois, 167-168).

[367] The third of these was a duplicate of that issued and signed by Doctor Jacques, whom Huy's municipal council had sent to "verify" Bonhoulle's claims.

[368] See Annexe 53 (Fontaine, *Jacques Dubois, 167-168*).

[369] State Archives, Liège, the account-book of Subprior Noiville, 24.

[370] Archives, city of Huy, Register 403, 206; see Annexe 54 (Fontaine, *Jacques Dubois, 168*).

[371] See Annexe 52 (Fontaine, *Jacques Dubois, 167*).

next day in fact (11 Prairial; May 30), that he issued a decree countersigned by Dechamp which deprived the Prior General of his prerogatives as chief administrator of Clairlieu and returned to "the Chapter" the administration of property "under the direction of the proper authorities and this Administration," i.e., under the management of Devaux. This time Poswick did Commissioner Ista the politeness of charging him with executing the decree.[372] He had thus made a complete about-face and had plunged Clairlieu back into the situation which had existed before the decision of the civil court.

This victory was altogether too unhoped-for and too complete for Donnay not to agree wholeheartedly. Had he not, after all, masterminded the whole scheme? Now it was the time for him to consolidate his victory, and he promptly applied himself to the task. Expert in the applicable law, he knew that, despite the eleventh-hour success of his "blocking" suit, it could not bring the issue to final settlement, so he would henceforth devote himself to obviating any attempted defense of the Prior General. Only a few days after Poswick's decree, therefore, he addressed an anonymous letter to the Central Administration in Liège.[373] This intermina-

---

[372] State Archives, Liège, decree of 11 Prairial, year IV; see Annexe 55 (Fontaine, *Jacques Dubois, 169-170*).

[373] While the heading suggests that the Crosiers of Huy wrote it, I have no doubt that it was Donnay's work. The text contains the same expressions and allusions and repeats the same points (usually word for word) which abound in previous letters to the Administration (compare especially those of March 25 and April 14). The use of the same style, studded with terms taken from revolutionary juris prudence, leaves no doubt about its paternity: it is pure Donnay. Were this letter indeed something they had written, we may be quite sure that the members of "the Chapter" would have signed it, just as they had been ready to sign the "proposal for reconciliation" which Devaux had composed twenty days earlier.

ble indictment rehearses matters from both during and after the General's absence, and reviews every criticism which had ever been voiced of him. In a further attempt to exploit the proposal for reconciliation, of which another copy was attached, Donnay then juggled the truth by making a case out of the "intentions" of the Prior General and a great to-do about his own clients' civic virtues and rights, and concluded with the statement that "the Crosiers affirm as irrevocable the decree of 11 Prairial."[374] Did Liège realize that Donnay had thus betrayed his specific purpose, and was obviously laboring to make Poswick's recent decree irrevocable? If Donnay defied the Prior General, he feared him just as much. It was not enough, then, to tilt the scales of justice against him; they had to be completely overbalanced.

Ten days after Dubois had seen his hopes collapse, Huy's municipal council presented him with a bill for 1,200 pounds and the Crosiers with one for 4,800 pounds: an additional tax over and above the previous forced loan.[375] A second decree was enacted on the same day, 19 Prairial (June 8), but by the Central Administration, and directed all heads of religious orders to have their valuables returned "within a period of forty days".[376] That same day Dubois sent Liège a memorandum which indicated his submission to the decree.[377]

What irony! Clairlieu had just been directed to have its carillon perform the revolutionary anthem, *Ça ira!*[378]

---

[374] State Archives, Liège; see Annexe 56 (Fontaine, *Jacques Dubois, 170-172*).

[375] Archives, city of Huy, Register of Letters, 197.

[376] State Archives, Liège, letter of 17 Thermidor, year IV.

[377] As a July 17 letter from Kiekens to Poswick notes.

[378] At the direction, no doubt, of Huy's municipal council. Subprior Noiville disbursed" 15 fl." for it. (State Archives, Liège, the account-book of

* * *

All recourse to Rome was forbidden. Any appeal to the definitors had been made impossible.[379] Thus constrained, the Prior General resumed his efforts to deal with the principal problem. Disregarding his doctors' advice, he informed the Central Administration that he wished to respond to its summons, despite the delay which the unfortunate state of his health had occasioned. To the bitter end, then, he would struggle to save his monastery from the clutches of its "enemies" and so ultimately determine his own destiny.

Oddly, whereas one might have expected Poswick to turn a deaf ear, as he had done not long before when the municipal council had suggested the General's imprisonment, he accepted. But this was a month after his devastating decision of 11 Prairial, which Ista had so hastily executed. Then, too, Kiekens had been Dubois' determined intermediary with Poswick and had become so passionate in his defense that, for the moment, the Commissioner would allow the Prior General provisional freedom and thus the withdrawal of the two gendarmes who were his constant nightmare.[380] Kiekens immediately informed Dubois of the twofold result of his efforts. That morning at 11:00, Dubois summoned to his Quarter the lawyer and bailiff L. Dispa, who prepared duplicate copies of the Central Administration's decree scheduling the appearance of the Prior General for 28 Messidor (July 16).[381] One copy was for Noiville and his confreres,[382] the

---

Subprior Noiville, 26.)

[379] Except for L. Meyers, they all lived outside French territory: W. Jacobs at Schwarzenbroich, J. Leurs at Maastricht, and F. W. Loverix at St. Agatha. Loverix, moreover, had died on October 24, 1793.

[380] State Archives, Liège, letter of 19 Messidor, year IV.

[381] State Archives, Liège, letter of 17 Thermidor, year IV.

other for Commissioner Ista. At the bottom of the second, the General added, "I demand, in the name of the law, that citizen Commissioner Ista consent forthwith and in conformity with the present decree remove the military force which he has had placed at my domicile and Quarter, that I might be able to enjoy my liberty and my tranquility, so disturbed by this guard to the prejudice of my health."[383]

Upon leaving the old man, Dispa went to knock at the monastery door and place the notification in Noiville's own hands. Finding Ista was not so easy. The bailiff went from one house to another where he might have expected to find him, but the Commissioner remained invisible.[384] In the meanwhile, the Prior General had asked Francotte to come to his Quarter, where they made provision for the most pressing matters required for the journey to Liège; Dubois' intention was to go there on July 11 so that he might have a preliminary conference with his lawyers Kiekens and Verdbois. Francotte sent Kiekens a note that same day, July 5, to inform him of what he and Dubois had planned. In it he also observed, "you will no longer see a Jacques Dubois; you will see a man who will leave you with no doubt about how heavily persecution has weighed him down," and underlined that last phrase with a heavy stroke. He further charged his col-

---

[382] On it the Master General noted, among other things, that he very much wanted to appear (thus responding to the summons recently issued, viz., the letter of 19 Messidor, year IV), and that he was offering to have the valuables brought back from across the Rhine.

[383] These sentries had watched and spied on Dubois for nine months. See the note dated 17 Thermidor, year IV, in Annexe 57 (Fontaine, *Jacques Dubois*, 172-173).

[384] One of our sources, however, informs us that he "had gone out secretly and would return only in the evening." (State Archives, Liège, letter from Prancotte to Keikens dated July 5.)

league to convey to the sister of the Prior General[385] an invitation to come visit her brother on July 11 and to share the "homely fare" which he would offer her.[386] At the lawyer's invitation, Dubois added a note to his sister at the bottom of the letter, in which he observed that "all is going very well." His hand shook so much that he was obviously unable to write more, but this tiny phrase suggests that, on Monday, July 5, the suffering man enjoyed a moment of hope.

Tuesday came, and the Prior General was impatiently waiting for someone to come and notify the two gendarmes that they had been ordered to leave. Ista had not returned the evening before, as he had been expected to, but he was about on Tuesday morning and had, in fact, just been seen in the streets of the city with Jérosme.[387] Around 9:00 came a brusque knock at Dubois' door. It was Ista himself, who entered like a blast of wind and began to shout that he had no intention at all of withdrawing the two gendarmes. He would, quite the contrary, order them to watch more closely than ever. That decree was groundless ... he would go to Liège and have it quashed. "Should I need to go to Paris to have it revoked, I will do so," he shouted.[388] This time the Prior General seems to have responded to his display of fury with nothing more than bewildered silence; but as soon as

---

[385] "Jeanne Josephe Dubois was born in 1735 and so five years younger than Monsignor Dubois had been baptized at St. John the Baptist (St. Thomas) on January 18 of that year. The marriage register of Notre Dame aux Fonts informs us that she married Servais Joseph Demany on June 4, 1770. They lived near the city hall of Liège. Demany was a bookbinder and his wife a seller of clothing. " (Th. Gobert, *Rues de Liège*, 3:631, 2.) See the Dubois family tree in Annexe 1 (Fontaine, *Jacques Dubois*, 125).

[386] State Archives, Liège; see Annexe 58 (Fontaine, *Jacques Dubois*, 173-174).

[387] State Archives, Liège, letter from Francotte to Keikens dated July 6.

[388] State Archives, Liège; see Annexe 59 (Fontaine, *Jacques Dubois*, 174).

his bewilderment passed, he had Francotte summoned.[389] Did they not have to act promptly, to keep Ista from succeeding in what he planned to do? Francotte immediately dispatched another letter to Kiekens in which he revealed how Ista had mocked the decree from the Central Administration and insisted on the urgent need to make every effort to see that the date of the hearing, July 16, was adhered to. The letter was placed in the hands of a friend and addressed to Mr. Kiekens in care of Madame Demany in Liège.[390] It arrived that same evening.[391]

His short conversation with Francotte must have poured a bit of balm on the troubled heart of the Prior General, but when he found himself alone in his room, which still re-echoed from Ista's wrath, the malign presence of the two gendarmes must have overwhelmed him, as the following scrap of a letter to his sister attests.

> My dear sister, Commissioner Ista arrived at precisely 9:00 this morning to tell me that he would not withdraw the armed guard from my Quarter, because I wrote on the back ""I demand, in the name of the law," etc. I offered to scratch it out, but he would have none of it and ran from my room shouting that he would make all haste to betake himself to Liège and to Paris, were it necessary. I wept with chagrin.

> My regards.

---

[389] The three Crosiers who remained unswervingly loyal to their Master General (Demet, Warnotte and Tilmen), and who must have helped him pray the Hours, presumably also performed errands of this sort.

[390] The sister of the Master General, with whose outstanding qualities Francotte was unacquainted, thus must have herself been able to reinforce, with ability and energy, the urgent watchfulness for which this letter called.

[391] As we learn from a notation on the back of it.

Prior General Jacques Dubois, O.S.C.

Fr. J. Dubois, General, Huy, this 6th day of July[392]

Upon receipt of this note, Madame Demany wrote to the members of the Central Administration at Liège, noting that "for nearly a year, the General of the Crosiers, her special brother, had been laboring under the burdens of oppression and calumny" and requesting that she be allowed "to bring him to Liège, in order to save him from certain death" and "so permit him to appear on the day set" by Commissioner Poswick. "The General" she went on "looks forward to that day as the end of his misfortunes and the triumph of his innocence."[393] Her hasty request must have borne fruit, since on July 16 there appeared before the Office of National Properties Prior General Dubois on the one side and, on the other, three delegates from the Crosiers at Huy, viz., Jérosme, Hayweghen and Loncin.[394] If we know little of what transpired in the course of that unpleasant hearing, we know enough to determine how the General appeared to his religious and his judges, as our account will show. For the moment, however, we note only that no final judgment was delivered on Saturday, July 16, and that the hearing ended with a postponement for deliberation *sine die*.

---

[392] State Archives, Liège. In both length and content, this is the smallest letter. The circumstances make it sadly poignant, and the doubled "this" of the date suggests eyes blinded by tears.

[393] State Archives, Liège; see Annexe 60 (Fontaine, *Jacques Dubois*, 174-175). The back of the letter carries the annotation, "the extremely urgent petition of the wife of Demany, of the Commune of Liège, on behalf of her brother, the General of the Crosiers," and to it were attached Dubois' short note and Francotte's two letters to Kiekens.

[394] As we may deduce from an entry in Subprior Noiville's account-book, which records the journey which these three made to Liège on July 16, 1796. Page 28 of that record also reveals that these three youngest members of the community went to Liège ten times during that one month.

One unhappy consequence of this delay was the paper chase of letters by which the two parties sought to sway the judges in Liège to their favor. In them, Donnay and his cronies maintained that Poswick's decree of 11 Prairial (May 30) was "irrevocable"; the Prior General wanted it overturned as contrary to the judgment handed down by the civil court on 23 Germinal (April 13), year IV.

Knowing only too well that Donnay's letters had supplied the grounds for Poswick's decision, Kiekens struck first. On July 17, he addressed a long brief to Poswick in which he reviewed all the wrongs done the Prior General by his own subjects and cordially invited the Central Administration at Liège to re-establish Dubois in his prerogatives as head of Clairlieu, to set the old man at liberty and to charge Commissioner Ista with the execution of this new decree. Aware of Poswick's reluctance to give in, and perhaps even more of his "flexibility," Kiekens sketched the outlines of a new decree.[395] To this lengthy brief he attached a copy of the judgment handed down by the civil court. (His vigorous efforts in this instance suggest that he wanted to make amends for his misplaced confidence before 11 Prairial.) His thorough reworking of Poswick's previous decree did not displease the latter but did leave him visibly embarrassed: the vertical strokes in the margins and across the text of Kiekens' brief give one an indication of the inner struggle between the "honorable" and the "flexible" Poswick. The evidence suggests that he regretted his previous casual and in fact ill-considered decree, but did not know how to go about changing it while the malevolent censor Dechamp, Ista's bothersome confidant and would-be twin, was looking over his shoulder.

---

[395] State Archives, Liège; see Annexe 61 (Fontaine, *Jacques Dubois, 175-177*).

Donnay seems to have quickly gotten wind of Kiekens' effort, for two days later, on July 19, he disgorged a four-page reply.[396] "There is an objection," he wrote, "which perhaps gives pause to one or another member of the Administration: these are allegedly the constitutions of the Order which must be followed, " but whoever might have scruples about the constitutions of an Order which are contrary to the Constitution [of the Republic] is indeed in the wrong place if he is set at the head of an Administration of the French Republic." And again, "it is going too far, citizens Administrators, when scruples about the constitutions of a religious Order can give an intelligent man pause." He concluded with, "You adopted the decree of 11 Prairial; stand by it, it is the right one.[397] For Donnay, then, the constitutions of the Order lacked any validity, and the whole matter was to be dealt with outside the barriers they imposed. But the overconfidence which allowed him to imply that Poswick was unworthy of his office if "scruples about the constitutions of a religious Order" gave him pause must have cooked Donnay's goose. The implication was galling, and must have cut Poswick to the quick. On July 28 Donnay dispatched to Liège a new request" on behalf of the Crosiers of Huy." It was a tactic that had proved successful on 11 Prairial, after he had deluged Liège with letters, while the file of the Prior General contained nothing but his doctors' certificates. Thinking once more to sway the balance in his favor, Donnay could have hardly imagined that Poswick no longer trusted him and had thrown his last letter into the wastebasket. Donnay came to suspect that such was the case, however; so much so that, every day until August 9, he went to the Administration's offices to learn what results

---

[396] The second-last paragraph of which is a nearly verbatim repetition of the last paragraph in the anonymous letter cited previously.
[397] State Archives, Liège; see Annexe 61 (Fontaine, *Jacques Dubois,* 177-179).

his petitions had.[398] His stay in Liège was, one suspects, occasioned by something more than curiosity.

Apparently wearied by these bothersome letters, the Administrators at Liège assigned Loneux to draft a new decree for July 29.[399] There is a hint of Poswick's influence on it in a first clause aimed at Donnay: "Whereas the Central Administration has, until the present time, been misled regarding the case brought before the civil court..." The draft then states "that the Administration revokes its previous decrees concerning the differences between the General of the Crosiers and the majority of his religious, and leaves the status of the parties in that established by the decision of the civil court on 23 Germinal [April 13]." There follows the statement "that the General should, without delay, send two of his religious to Duisburg to retrieve the silver objects and return them to the Crosier house of Huy." Finally, lithe majority of the Crosiers will have to justify within twenty days the cuttings made in their oak forest."

Supported by Loneux's recommendations, Poswick had effectively adopted Kiekens' proposal, save for one point: he did not dare charge Ista with its execution. It was, then, a victory over Donnay and nearly over Ista. At the bottom of the document, however, is a scrawled notation stating that, "this

---

[398] State Archives, Liège, a letter of Donnay dated 7 Fructidor, year IV. The account-book of Subprior Noiville (page 29) informs us that this stay in Liège cost 78 florins.

[399] An intellectual, Eugene Loneux had served as secretary of the provisional Central Administration in 1794. That same year he was assigned to inspect the city's prisons, and was the author of the report which led to the maintenance of "the Society of the Men of Charity for the Help of Impoverished Prisoners." He was one of seven professors named to the first faculty of the School of Engineering when the latter was established in April 1797. See Daris, Histoire de la Principaute, 3:26-117.

finding was read at the session on 11 Thermidor [July 29] and, when put to a vote, the draft was rejected by a majority of three to two,[400] which means that only Poswick[401] and

---

[400] State Archives, Liège; see Annexe 63 (Fontaine, *Jacques Dubois*, 179-180). It is interesting to observe how the censor's pen has carved up this document, too.

[401] Lambert Philippe Poswick was born at Limburg, in the province of Liège, and baptized there on June 22, 1747. His godparents were Madame de Reul (born de Tignee de Bonville) and, interesting ly, Lambert Englebert Fisen, Master General of the Order of the Holy Cross. On February 6, 1783, he married Marie Catherine de Lantremange (born and baptized at Liège on December 3, 1775; deceased November 29, 1834). Po swick attended the Jesuit secondary school in Maastricht and studied philosophy with the Laurencians [a branch of the Benedictine Order] in Cologne before beginning a three-year course in law at the University of Louvain. He received his licentiate on July 13, 1770, and the follow ing September was called to the bar before the High Court and the Superior Feudal Court of the Duchy of Limburg. Emperor Joseph II appointed him a member of the latter in 1776 and, on September 26, 1785, a judge of the High Court; on August 8, 1789, he became a counselor of the Superior Court of the Province. He held these offices until the time of the second French invasion of our country. On October 26, 1794 (5 Brumaire, year III), he was named president of the Central Administration in Limburg. In July 1796, he became the chief authority in the Department of the Ourthe when he was named Commissioner of the Executive Directory within the Central Administration at Liège. Poswick thereafter was frequently the target of jealousy and calumny; and the two Bassange brothers were espe cially zealous to see "that aristocrat" in the Central Administration removed from his post. On the oc casion of Poswick's election to a second term on April 11, 1797, L. Bassange attacked him in the *Courrier de I'Ourthe* of April 21 and subsequently charged him before the Minster of Police with hav ing engineered his removal from office. When the Minister demanded proof, Bassange replied, "I swear to you in confidence that it is nearly impossible to find a more blatant aristocrat than Poswick; he has spent his whole life in posts given him by the Emperor and the government of Brabant." Thanks to yet another of Bassange's efforts, Poswick was in fact removed from office on October 26, 1797. Although he was subsequently re-elected on April 17, 1798, the Executive Directory declared the elec tion null and void "because Poswick was not of its party." He was nevertheless named secre-

Loneux wished to re-establish Dubois in his prerogatives and that this act of justice had been blocked by the votes of Dechamp, Defrance and Digneffe.[402]

As one might expect, there were no few intrigues around this laborious draft, but new actors were about to appear on the stage. Two days later, Madame Demany, who would have been the last to lose hope, wrote to the administrators at Liège. "It is pressing that you deliver a decision on the conflict in question, so that you may put an end to the chaotic management exercised over the monastery by Devaux and

---

tary of the Central Administration that same year, and held that post until the prefectures were established on March 8, 1800. He then became provisional secretary general of the local prefecture until the organiza tion of the appellate court system on July 6 and August 26, 1800, after which he became clerk of the appellate court. On April 24, 1811, Napoleon appointed him chief clerk of court for the Imperial Court at Liège, a post which he held under both the French and Dutch regimes until his death on January 31 (or perhaps February 14), 1830. His home was on the Rue St. Etienne. See Daris, *Histoire de la Principaute,3:105-178.* Many of these biographical details we owe to the kindness of Mr. Guy Poswick, Justice of the Peace at Limburg. Thanks to him, too, we have been able to find a portrait of Commissioner L. P. Poswick [reproduced in Fontaine, *Jacques Dubois,* facing 112].

[402] Dechamp, the president of the Administration, "was one of the traitors who, along with Bas sange and Lesoinne, would plead with the Convention, over which Danton, Robespierre and Marat al ready ruled, for the annexation of the Princedom to France." (Jos. Demarteau, *La Revolution au Pays de Liège: conf. de la Societe d'Art et d'Histoire du diocese de Liège,* 2nd series (1889), 337-338.) "The cynic Defrance: his exploits surpass those of the iconoclasts. It was he who demolished the Cathedral of St. Lambert. He was removed from office by a decree of February 24, 1802, 'for hav ing carried out the demolition in his own self-interest. "' (Jules Helbig, *La Revolution a Liège et les beuax-artes,* 47, 85, 87 and 100.) Three years later, Digneffe would take his place on the Council of Five Hundred in Paris, to which he had been elected on the second ballot cast on April 14, 1799. (See Daris, *Histoire de la Prin cipaute, 3:279.)*

Jérosme and to return it to him on whom the constitutions of the Order have bestowed it, constitutions which have hitherto in no way been abrogated and by which the religious remain bound." She went on: "The Prior General appeared before you on July 16, confident that he would receive justice and armed only with his innocence. You then saw for yourselves how this fine old man, who could scarcely walk, successfully scattered, ... with a candor and frankness which those who have slandered him always fear, the false charges with which his cruel enemies have not been ashamed to blacken his name before you... The Prior General has readily and eagerly accepted that reconciliation with his religious which the Commissioner of the Directory has proposed... but they, relying upon Ista, have rejected it..."[403] "It is Devaux," she added by way of conclusion, "who has lit the fire of discord in the monastery of the Crosiers, probably with a view to benefiting from the divisions. . .; it is pressing that you have him render a clear and exact account of all the business which he has conducted these past two years in the monastery of the Crosiers."[404]

Unable to re-establish her brother in his rights, Madame Demany thus sought to wrench Clairlieu free of Devaux's tenacious grasp. He, however, had seen the threat coming. Judging himself dangerously compromised by the General's revelations,[405] he had managed to get himself a false deposi-

---

[403] Poswick thus seems to have gone to Clairlieu in the interim to make a private arrangement.

[404] State Archives, Liège; see Annexe 64 (Fontaine, *Jacques Dubois*, 180-181).

[405] Made through Kiekens when the latter proposed his draft of a new decree to Liège. Therein, for example, was the information that Dantinne, the Crosiers' forester, had testified under oath before the civil court that Devaux was clearly and truly the one who had despoiled the Crosiers' woodlands.

tion from the forester Dantinne with which to respond. At first afraid to use it, he waited for about ten days, but after Madame Demany's intervention, decided to forward it to the Administration at Liège on August 2.[406]

Did Devaux realize that he was finished? At the end of July he had asked Subprior Noiville to pay him his wages: 600 florins.[407]

* * *

Efforts like the deceitful letter concocted by Devaux and his fellow conspirator Jérosme[408] reveal the confusion reigning among Dubois' opponents, but the tide of ink had not yet exhausted itself.

The Crosiers of Huy opened the last act in the drama of Clairlieu by returning to the same ploy which had miscarried ten months earlier.[409] They engaged Huy's Justice of the Peace[410] "to speak with their General, under house arrest," on the pretext that forty days had passed and the silver objects had not been returned from across the Rhine.[411] But Madame Demany, who was henceforth listened to more frequently than her brother's other defenders, intervened to brand that action "merely a well-concealed ploy by all the suspicious

---

[406] Even though he knew he would himself be in Liège on August 9. See Annexe 65 (Fontaine, *Jacques Dubois, 182*).

[407] State Archives, Liège, the account-book of Subprior Noiville, 28

[408] That of 14 Thermidor, year IV, in Annexe 65 (Fontaine, *Jacques Dubois, 182*).

[409] The reader will recall that, on October 23, 1795, Huy's municipal council attempted to jail Dubois but had been blocked by Poswick's intervention

[410] In the French system, the judge or magistrate of the local court. – Tr.

[411] State Archives, Liège; the letter of 17 Thermidor, year IV; see Annexe 66 a (Fontaine, *Jacques Dubois, 183-184*).

characters at Huy," and went on to review all the proposals which her brother had made about these valuables and to again request that he be given his freedom. Her letter of 17 Thermidor (August 5) to the Central Administration also contained a forceful four-page indictment of Devaux,[412] boldly revealing the "underhanded deals" and "back-scratching" which he had engineered within the walls of Clairlieu.[413] The very next day, 18 Thermidor (August 6), she requested, on her brother's behalf, that passports be issued to Fathers Warnotte (the procurator) and Meyers, who had been assigned to retrieve the valuables left at Duisburg.[414] Poswick and Dechamp immediately signed the document accepting these proposals.[415] As for the man who was at the source of the exhausting controversy and who had been waiting since July 16, this was the right step.

With his courage reinforced by Madame Demany's interventions, Poswick personally took the matter in hand. That same day, August 6, he compiled a "report and draft decree" in which, after reviewing Loneux's rejected draft, the civil court's decision and the results of the meeting on July 16, he pro-

---

[412] State Archives, Liège; see Annexe 66 a and b (Fontaine, *Jacques Dubois*, 183-186).

[413] Her information also gave the lie to the risk which the Crosiers had taken (or rather, which Donnay had taken for them, since he is known to have been on the premises) when they placed a public statement in the *Gazette de Liège* about their sale of timber. See Annexe 67 (Fontaine, *Jacques Dubois*, 186).

[414] State Archives, Liège; see Annexe 68 (Fontaine, *Jacques Dubois*, 186-187). Seven years had passed since Meyers had become one of the twenty-three canons attached to the collegial church of *St.* Denis on October 30, 1789 (State Archives, Liège, French sources, list of former canons of St. Denis). He nevertheless remained one of the Order's sitting definitors, which may have been why Dubois entrusted him with this mission.

[415] State Archives, Liège; see Annexe 69 (Fontaine, *Jacques Dubois*, 187).

posed that the Central Administration revoke its decree of 11 Prairial and provisionally name citizen Bastin, a lawyer living at Huy, to be receiver of the monastery of Clairlieu, "in point of which, the religious who hold them will submit to him the pertinent records."[416] After prolonged labor, a decree very much in Dubois' favor was at last coming to birth. Not only did it effectively annul that of 11 Prairial, but finally got rid of Devaux and, more importantly, obliged him to appear before Justice of the Peace Couthuin "in order to render an account". If Clairlieu's temporal administration was once more to be entrusted to outside hands, the choice of Bastin was at least an acceptable one: he had been Dubois' advocate before the civil court.[417]

To the end of the document was attached a stipulation that copies be sent to the parties involved and to Commissioner Ista, to insure their compliance. The next day, August 7, the Director of the Second Office at Liège traveled to Huy to deliver copies to the Prior General, the Crosiers, Bastin and of course to Ista. When he went to the latter's home, however, he was accompanied, as Poswick had decided, by Huy's Justice of the Peace.[418] Hardly had the official from Liège departed when the shouts of protest began. The very next day, August 8, the Crosiers contacted the lawyer Brou and had him draft a "suit of appeal" to the Minister of the Executive Directory" for the nullification of any execution of the decree

---

[416] State Archives, Liège; see Annexe 70 a and b (Fontaine, *Jacques Dubois*, 188-190). To get an idea of the conflict between Poswick's sense of justice and Dechamp's part, one must examine all the passages in the draft which were censored (Annexe 70 a). Poswick used these abridgements, however, to give the final version a directness which better focused its purpose.

[417] State Archives, Liège, letter of 24 Thermidor, year IV.

[418] State Archives, Liège; see the decree of 18 Thermidor, year IV.

of August 6."[419] They waited somewhat, however, before lodging it. Donnay seems to have first threatened Liège with it, were Bastin's substitution for Devaux enforced, for when he learned that Liège was standing fast on the matter, he declared on 24 Thermidor (August 11) that "the religious deem that no departmental authority may assign them a receiver contrary to the will of the CHAPTER ..., otherwise, the latter will have no choice but to make appeal."[420]

While this desperate assault on the success of the Prior General was under way, he busied himself with having those things left at Duisburg returned to the country. On August 14 he asked a member of the Administration named Ouwerx[421] to request, at that day's meeting, the issuance of passports.[422]

If Poswick ignored Donnay's pettifogging arrogance in denying the government's authority to name Bastin Clairlieu's receiver, his fellow Administrators Dechamp and Digneffe found it annoying and chose to extricate themselves from the matter by referring it to Paris. On 27 Thermidor (August 15),

---

[419] State Archives, Liège; see Annexe 71 (Fontaine, *Jacques Dubois, 190*).

[420] State Archives, Liège; see Annexe 72 (Fontaine, *Jacques Dubois, 190-191*).

[421] Since he was the treasurer or finance officer attached to the Central Administration at Liège, he was the logical choice for this task.

[422] State Archives, Liège; see Annexe 73 (Fontaine, *Jacques Dubois, 191*). The concern of the Master General for prompt action about the return of these items must reflect the threatening atmosphere of August 1796, when rumors about the "suppression ofreligious houses" were growing. Had he not told Huy's municipal council on October 17, 1795, that he intended "to share them among the community, should the case arise that it is suppressed"? He thus intended to keep his word, even if it had led to his imprisonment for eleven months. That such indeed was his purpose finds support in the Central Administration's failure to issue the requested passports to Meyers and Warnotte before September 9 and 10, respectively. Was Liège suspicious? (State Archives, Liège, 1st Register of Passports, fol. 13 and 15.)

they drafted a statement which would have sent a copy of their decision on August 6 to the Ministry of the Interior "tomorrow and by the first courier".[423] Poswick took care to "have added a letter which would develop the reasons which had led the Central Administration to take this step".[424] How would Paris reply, and in whose favor would it decide?

Around the same time, there took place another incident of some interest. Huy's municipal council again accused Dubois of failing to pay the additional tax imposed on him as head of his Order the previous June. He thereupon promptly deposited the required 1,200 pounds with Ouwerx, the treasurer at Liège, who informed Huy of it, and added some pointed remarks: "But I think it helpful for you to note, citizens, that you must have been misled about the resources attributed to the General. I know to what extent his revenues have been reduced. I also know that, for quite some time, he has not received them and that, because of your belief in his presumed wealth, he has been taxed beyond his means in forced loans and contributions, and much more so than the community which collects the revenues. I am equally aware that, ere long, justice will be done him."[425]

Neither Paris nor Huy were giving any sign of life, and almost two weeks had passed since Ista was to have informed Liège that the decree of August 6 had been carried out. Poswick became impatient and asked Huy's city administration to inform him, without delay, whether this had been done and if Bastin was in possession of Clairlieu's account

---

[423] State Archives, Liège; see Annexe 74 (Fontaine, *Jacques Dubois, 191-192*).
[424] State Archives, Liège; see Annexe 74 (Fontaine, *Jacques Dubois*, 191-192).
[425] Archives, city of Huy, Register of Letters, 134; see Annexe 74 (Fontaine, *Jacques Dubois*, 192).

books. Huy could only say no: Ista had done nothing. Angered, Poswick again issued formal directions to Ista, on 6 Fructidor (August 23), to carry out the decree "in all its parts, by having all the documents and records used by Devaux and the Crosiers delivered to Bastin, or face a charge of insubordination." Things had become serious, and Dechamp was obliged to countersign this menacing dispatch.[426] Ista could not dream of dodging the issue again and, the next day, August 24, did as he had been instructed, but in his own way: he merely informed the Crosiers of what the Departmental Administration had required him to do! We do not know if Noiville had any reaction to this, but Jérosme did yet not consider himself defeated. That same day he sent Ista a note[427] and a copy of that statement of opposition which we have already seen. The moment to introduce at Liège this suit which had been readied seventeen days earlier seemed to have finally arrived. On 11 Fructidor (August 28), Donnay took it upon himself to play this last card, but his accompanying protestation lacked the arrogance of those which had preceded it.[428] Liège did nothing more than file the two documents, and for good reason: the same day it received a

---

[426] State Archives, Liège; see Annexe 76 (Fontaine, *Jacques Dubois*, 192-193).

[427] State Archives, Liège; see Annexe 77 (Fontaine, *Jacques Dubois*, 193) Three days later, on August 27, 1796, the Directory of the Council of Five Hundred introduced and adopted the measure which suppressed Belgium's religious houses and confiscated their possessions. That was enough for Ista to order, at twilight that same day, a furious ringing of all the church bells in Huy, as he recounts in his letter of 11 Fructidor, year IV. (Under the French constitution of 1795, the Council of Five Hundred was the lower house of the legislature, which was able to introduce and discuss laws; to enact them, however, required the approval of the legislature's upper house, the Council of 250 or of Elders. – Tr.

[428] State Archives, Liège; see Annexe 78 (Fontaine, *Jacques Dubois*, 193-194).

succinct reply from Paris saying that "the latter decree seems to me a wise modification of the former, and I believe the dispositions ought be approved."[429] Poswick's defense of the Prior General had been successful, and that day Dubois must surely have savored his victory.

But the Paris Directory's approval, on August 27, of the law which suppressed religious houses inspired Ista to crow triumphantly in his turn, as we can see from his letter of the next day to Dechamp: "The decree of suppression enacted by the Council of Five Hundred has given me revenge for the efforts of Poswick and the aristocratic scheming of the partisans of the General of the Crosiers. That salutary decree has been received here with joy. The ringing of the bells first announced it to the monks and fanatics in which this city abounds. We laughed greatly."[430]

Ista probably found Poswick's injunction less laughable. On 13 Fructidor (August 30) he tried a diversionary tactic, viz., an effort to dissuade Bastin from taking his appointment at Clairlieu. Bastin returned the note with a response which in effect said, "Commissioner, mind your own business".[431] It was not quite the coup de grace, but Poswick was about to deliver that. "As of this date, our express wish is that citizen Ista, Commissioner for the Executive Directory in the city of Huy, upon reception of these presents, execute the decree of

---

[429] State Archives, Liège; see Annexe 79 (Fontaine, *Jacques Dubois, 194*).

[430] The letter ends with a quatrain. "And that means: Against you, may the blind believer / squeal his passionate prejudice. / May the red-clover tyrant over mortals, / fanaticism, tremble at this decree!" (State Archives, Liège; see Annexe 80 [Fontaine, *Jacques Dubois, 194*]). (During the revolutionary era, the derogatory terms "fanatic" and "fanaticism" were commonly used in reference to Catholics and their faith. – Tr.)

[431] State Archives, Liège; see Annexe 81 a and b (Fontaine, *Jacques Dubois, 195*).

18 Thermidor [August 6], under pain of being removed from office for insubordination in failing to execute the decisions of higher authority."[432] But Ista did nothing, neither upon receipt of Poswick's orders nor the day after. Since the latter was September 1, the day on which the Directory enacted the law suppressing religious houses in the departments newly annexed to France,[433] Ista very well may have again taken some time to laugh. He did nothing at all until September 5, and then did exactly the opposite of what he had been directed to do. Simultaneously portraying himself as both totally uncomprehending and utterly irreproachable, he suggested to his superior in Liège that he "date his letters" and "write more intelligibly" and pleaded with the Administration there to "provide definite instructions about what he should do in case of a refusal of the decree." To this note he attached copies of the pro forma notification sent to the Crosiers, of Jérosme's protest, and of the appeal filed by Brou.[434] At nearly the same moment, Liège received a letter from

---

[432] State Archives, Liège; see Annexe 82 (Fontaine, *Jacques Dubois, 195-196*).
[433] This seems to have frightened off Clairlieu 's domestic staff. On September 7, Martin Fastre, the cook, and Matagne, the porter, asked for the wages due them since July 20 and 24, and the Subprior paid them 160 and 100 florins respectively. During these same days, even citizen Donnay seems to have remembered that he was owed some money and received 97 florins "for the sum payment of his fees." (State Archives, Liège, the account-book of Subprior Noiville, 31.) The day after the law of suppression took effect, Lacroix, who was a conventual of Huy but also prior of Virton, wrote a long letter to the Central Administration asking it "to enjoin the Crosiers of Huy" to grant him a share in the objects from across the Rhine, and "to ratify" the power of attorney which he had given to Commissioner Ista to obtain that share. By an ironic twist of fate, Lacroix was pushed aside in this final act of Clairlieu's drama when Liège again concluded that" it was not its place to decide" his request. See Annexe 83 (Fontaine, *Jacques Dubois, 196*).
[434] State Archives, Liège; see Annexe 84 (Fontaine, *Jacques Dubois, 197*).

Bastin stating that nothing had yet been handed over to him and that, as a result of the failure to execute the decree, new embezzlements were taking place at Clairlieu.[435] The arrival of these two letters on Poswick's desk must have decided him to make a clean sweep of the affair. In a long formal notification dated 24 Fructidor (September 11), he directed Ista to do his duty within twenty-four hours or be removed from office.[436] So blinded by rage that he was unable to conquer his partisan impulses, even in his own interest, Ista resigned, thus sacrificing his career to his intransigent hatred. [437]

With the defeat of Ista came that of all the rest: Donnay, Devaux, the municipal council and the Crosiers. At 8:30 the next morning, however, the Crosiers gathered "in the chapter room" and with Brou's help prepared a statement in which, "fully intending to stand upon their rights," they declared that "the Chapter again protests the arbitrary actions of the Administrators of Liège... who, in defiance of the Constitution itself, have dared to attack the rights of man and the people..."[438] Receipt of this declaration was recorded at Liège the same day, September 14, and Donnay forwarded a copy to the Departmental Administration.[439]

As one might expect, Liège's response was an estoppel. The

---

[435] State Archives, Liège, decree of 24 Fructidor, year IV
[436] State Archives, Liège, decree of 24 Fructidor, year IV; see Annexe 85 (Fontaine, *Jacques Dubois, 197-198*).
[437] He subsequently lost the suit which he brought before the civil court. His provisional replacement was the municipal administrator, Ledrou, and on December 16, 1796, Bouteville named Barbaix as Commissioner for the Executive Directory in the canton of Huy. (Archives, city of Huy, Register 403, 282.
[438] State Archives, Liège; see Annexe 86 (Fontaine, *Jacques Dubois, 198*).
[439] Brou must have drawn up two official copies. (State Archives, Liège, the account-book of Subprior Noiville, 32.)

only effect which this" declaration of grief" by the Crosiers had was to become the last item in the file sadly labeled "the case brought against the General of the Crosiers of Huy."

CHAPTER SEVEN
DEATH OF PRIOR GENERAL DUBOIS

On October 30, 1795, Prior General Dubois had been cleared of the charge of emigration; on April 13, 1796, he had been reinstated in his rights as Prior of Clairlieu; and on August 6 of that year, he had been fully restored to his office of Prior General. These successive reconciliations of truth with justice owed more to the evidence of the facts than to the judicial system.

Even though he had finally escaped the legal chicaneries, he was not yet free of the hostility which surrounded him. If he was no longer a prisoner,[440] he had been proscribed. That, despite Bastin and his mandate, was the work of Devaux,[441]

---

[440] On September 21, 1796, and on orders from the chief of police, Subprior Noiville paid the last money due the two gendarmes whom Ista had posted at the General's Quarter: "29 flor., 16 sols, 1 liard." (State Archives, Liège, the account-book of Subprior Noiville, 32.) Ista thus seems to have kept them at their post right up until the day he was removed from office.

[441] He continued to be the "man of business" for the Crosiers ofHuy even after his removal: proof of which is his payment on December 12, 1796, of the annual income owed by the monastery to the pastor of Bas aha (State Archives, Liège, Register of Incomes to the Pastor of Bas aha, 1742-1781, 81) and his assignment by these Crosiers to be their legal representative in the acquisition of the farmstead of Envoz on 13 Pluviose, year V (State

and indeed of the whole world of the time. Thus was Clairlieu blown along before the winds of its misfortune.

Increasingly the monastery's atmosphere of quiet was disrupted by the hubbub around the grain wagons supplying its bake house, where bread was prepared for the whole parish of St. Remy,[442] and thus were the last traces of its discipline of silence and the last vestiges of its solitude utterly obliterated.

Clairlieu would henceforth live under the imminent threat of inventories, official sealings and plunderings. The Crosiers would soon have no alternative but to sign the act of suppression and agree to the seizure of their property: but never would the hand of Jacques Dubois, on which gleamed the ancient ring of the Order's priors general, ratify that forfeiture.

On September 22, the fourth anniversary of the establishment of the Republic, the municipal council publicly enjoined the religious communities and parishes to "ring all their bells at 6:00 p.m. on the eve of the festival and on the day itself at 6:00 a.m., midday and 3:00 p.m."[443] Dying Clairlieu was thus obliged to participate in these eccentricities, which would bring the final ringing of its bells. Nor should we forget that in its cloister, now profaned and in the final throes of its history, there flared the covetousness of those who awaited the return of Fathers Warnotte and Meyers with the valuables taken across the Rhine.

Archives, Liège, French regime, National Properties: aff. 7, no. 8.)

[442] Archives, city of Huy, Register "Committee of Police," 13; and Register 403, 306. Preparation of any bread other than a specific form of loaf which had to be called "the bread of equality" was forbidden.

[443] Archives, city of Huy, Register 403, 245.

In token of reproach and in abandonment of the atmosphere which would thereafter weigh so heavily on his soul, the Prior General withdrew from and closed his Quarter. He might have sought shelter from his misfortunes and the ease of his mind in his lovely country house on the other bank of the Meuse, but five miles may have been too far from his monastery. Instead, he went only a hundred paces down the hill and stopped in the Rue des Sœurs Grises, opposite Clairlieu's bell-tower; there he became a humble recluse in the house of a poor old man named Martin.[444] This retreat would sanctify his agony, its silence make his holocaust fruitful. He was alone, at the summit of his own Calvary.

But not quite. Huy's municipal councilors continued to pursue him in his sad isolation. One last time they raised the business of those silver items because of which he had already endured so many hardships, but seem to have been unwilling themselves to face the doughty old champion who had beaten them all. They ordered Father Demet to appear before them, then summoned Francotte in his turn. The interrogation was brief: they merely wanted to ascertain whether those who had been entrusted with the retrieval of the valuables had returned.[445] These last probings seem to have been not unrelated to the act of suppression, which was promulgated at Huy three days later, on September 29.[446]

These spiteful officials next remembered that Dubois held the conferring of the beguinage of Catherine Tille de Liège and, on October 14, officially deprived him of it, so that they

---

[444] This information was provided by Mr. E. Dantinne, Huy's city archivist; see Annexe 87 (Fontaine, *Jacques Dubois*, 199).

[445] Archives, city of Huy; see Annexe 88 (Fontaine, *Jacques Dubois*, 199-200).

[446] Archives, city of Huy, Register 403, 284.

might make a gift of it to "citizeness Marie Françoise Ista, resident at Huy."[447]

Huy's municipal council thus took a malign pleasure in persecuting their victim to the very end. Ten days later, Commissioner Harzé and his staff came to Clairlieu to compile the inventory which had to be completed before its possessions could be confiscated. These official government plunderers from Liège needed twenty-nine days in the monastery to finish their work. How could the dismal news of it not have reached the haven of the isolated Prior General?

At this point, the chest of valuables was brought back from across the Rhine.[448]

These sorrows and afflictions, joined to the anguishing vision of the imminent collapse of Clairlieu and indeed of the whole Order, were like a prayer to Heaven to set a time of final rest for the Prior General, bleeding upon his cross. The agony of his heart entailed the final agony of his body.

Dubois remained in seclusion in the Rue des Sœurs Grises until these last matters were finished, but he did not die in Huy.[449] His passing came at the Crosier monastery of Liège,[450] on Wednesday, December 21, around 9:00 in the

---

[447] Archives, city of Huy, Register 403,243; see Annexe 89 (Fontaine, *Jacques Dubois,* 200). They had been unable to do so earlier because the foundress was still alive: she died sometime in the first days of October.

[448] More information about this inventory and the return of these valuables from Germany will be provided in a forthcoming article entitled "The End of Clairlieu." (added as Chapter Eight of this English translation. – Trans.)

[449] Grandmaison was mistaken on this point: see L. Grandmaison, *Conference de Za Societe d'Art et d'Histoire,* 4th series (Liège, 1891), 176 and ff.

[450] Hermans *(AnnaZes,* 3:589) says "in domo nativa," which usually means "in the house of his profession" and in Dubois' case would mean Liège.

morning, and was comforted with the Church's last sacraments. He died precisely one month after the seizure of his
monastery at Clairlieu.[451]

Thus did God set his valiant witness free and so spare him
the ultimate insult, viz., the "retirement benefit" offered by
the lords of the time: his "benefit" was his holy death and his
"retirement" heaven. A similar thought concludes the magnificent eulogy which a confrere who was a contemporary of

---

The question is whether or not the Liège Crosiers were still in their monastery. The act of suppression had been promulgated in that city on September 14 and its Crosiers had received their "benefits" on November 25. That
should have meant they had to evacuate the premises within twenty days,
and so would have been gone by December 15, six days before Master
General Dubois died. But that was not the case. The law allowed suppressed religious first to lease then try to repurchase their house. Such
leases were available at Liège on December 12, three days before the Crosiers would have had to move out, and a priest named Richard, the under-
secretary of the synod, rented the monastery for them and let them have
use of it for the time being. (Daris, *Histoire de Za Principaute*, 3:85.)
Moreover, Commissioner Thonart completed the official list of the members of the monastery and the inventory of its possessions only on 9
Nivose, year V, i.e., December 29, 1796. (See Annexe 91 [Fontaine, *Jacques
Dubois*, 201-202.]) The Crosiers may, in fact, very well have still been there
at the beginning of March 1797, since Duckers and Thomson finished the
final appraisal of their property, at 55,665 francs, only on 2 Pluviose, year
V (January 21, 1797). Sale of it was put off, and in the meantime the Crosiers repurchased one of their farmsteads at Emburg, near the town of
Chenee in the canton of Fleron, on 21 Ventose, year V (March 6, 1797),
for 70,085 pounds, 10 sols. This had the advantage of assuring them a
place of retreat after the beginning of March but also seems to have had
the unfortunate result of leaving them with sufficient funds to repurchase
their monastery. On 27 Germinal, year V (April 16, 1797), a former Crosier named Streel offered the asking price of 55,665, but the sale was not
approved and the monastery remained in the government's hands.
(Gobert, *Rues de Liège*, 1:358; and *Bulletin Archeologique liegeois*, 16 (1881)
508.)

[451] That harsh and spiteful act was concluded on November 21, 1796.

the drama of Clairlieu prepared in his memory.[452]

Unconquered in spirit, Dubois must have decided to die in the monastery where he had professed his vows and which he had barely saved from extinction. He was unwilling to entrust his remains to the holy hillside of Clairlieu, over which dismay and sacrilege now loomed, and thus firmly set his preference upon the monastery in Liège, which had experienced no defections during these years of torment.[453] Then, too, we would not be rash to assume that Madame Demany, who had expressed her desire" to bring her brother to Liège" the previous July, was aware of his last wishes. Perhaps after a brief stay in her home, he made known his wish to be taken to the Crosiers. Near death, he would have found among them the last upwellings of religious dignity and faithfulness which allowed him to slip his final ties to life.

No tolling of the death-knell marked his passing,[454] no obsequies, no cortege followed,[455] and if some ceremony did take place, it was carried out in secret behind closed doors, for no priest could perform any liturgical ministry unless he had sworn obedience to the laws of the Republic.[456] Prior General Dubois must have been buried beneath the flagstones of the choir, where stood the burial vault of the famous family of Lamarck; it was also the final resting place of Prior General

---

[452] Hermans, *Annales*, 3:589-590; see Annexe 90 (Fontaine, *Jacques Dubois, 200-201*).

[453] See Annexe 92 (Fontaine, *Jacques Dubois*, 202-203). That contemporary source declares that "no religious of this community of Liège has left the cloister." (State Archives, Liège).

[454] Church bells had been silenced by a law of April 11, 1796 (22 Germinal, year IV). Verhagen, *La Belgique sous la dominationfranrais*, 2:290.

[455] If one may judge by what was done in the department of the Deux Nethes. See Verhagen, *La Belgique sous la dominationfranrais*, 2:288.

[456] Grandmaison, *Conference de la Societe d'Art et d'Histoire*, 63.

George of Briiggen, whose memory was likewise surrounded by a halo of great suffering endured in the course of a strong and gentle guidance of the Order.[457]

Prior General Dubois' was a death unnoticed and without epitaph, for the times which followed also set upon his tomb: the Crosier church in Liège was demolished in 1817.[458] He thus lies buried beneath the ruins of the Revolution. The last Prior General at Clairlieu, he showed himself worthy of its illustrious founder, Blessed Theodore de Celles. Indeed, if he who founds a religious order reveals his soul, he who perishes in saving it reveals no less. His tomb has disappeared, the example of his dedication to his community lives on.

If the name of Prior General Dubois has heretofore recalled the downfall of Clairlieu, it will hereafter be at the service of the high-mindedness of generations to come. Dignified in the face of injustice, great in the midst of ruin, he remains a vital example of what a religious animated by the flame of faith and of love of the Cross can achieve.

When we look back on the dark days of the Revolution, we can have no doubt that the example and the memory of Prior General Dubois were the source of the unity and strength which insured that the Order was not extinguished without renewal.[459] Through the inspiration of this great standard-

---

[457] George of Briiggen was the Order's twenty-first Master General. Hermans *(Annales,* 1(2):115) says that "in the reformation of monasteries, especially those at London and Toulouse, he exposed himself to many labors and hardships."

[458] Moulin, "Recueil de particularites," *Bulletin de l'Institut Archeologique liegeois* 2 (1855) 162.

[459] After the suppression of the Crosiers in Belgium, French law extended its effects to Germany, where the Order's surviving monasteries were closed

bearer of the cross, the institution once more found living enthusiasm in the way of life and the peace of the Cross.

---

by Napoleon. Only two of them in North Brabant and Holland, St. Agatha and Uden, and only four religious, were eventually all of the Order's vast structure which survived into the reign of William I, and they were forbidden to admit novices. In them the four old men who had resisted Napoleon resolutely awaited the accession of William II in 1840. Thus was the continuity of the Order of the Holy Cross preserved without disruption.

CHAPTER EIGHT
END OF CLAIRLIEU

From the first days of 1796, the Belgium of the *ancien regime* no longer existed.[460] The Republic's military successes had forestalled both any Austrian counteroffensive and any counterrevolution. In this new situation, Bouteville hastened, on orders from the Directory in Paris, to reorganize the country under the French system of departments, districts and cantons. Because whatever might be irritating or confusing in the new legislation was enforced by a military government, most people quickly adjusted themselves to the new system. Individuals might of course continue to feel upset about the oc-

---

[460] Father Fontaine annotated the title of this chapter/article, published as "La Fin de Clairlieu" in Clairlieu 9 (1951) 6-42, with the comment that it was intended to complement his biography of Master General Dubois and that its preparation had been "prompted primarily by the lack of any previous publication on the topic. Although Mr. Leon Wilmotte touches on this history in his 'Notice historiqe sur le Couvent des Croisiers de Huy' (Annales du Cercle Hutois des Sciences et Beaux-Arts 20 [1927-1929] vol. 3), he wholly disregards the principal archival source of information of which he might have made profitable use, viz., the numerous documents constituting the bulky collection labeled"no. 485, Sources: French Prefecture, files pertinent to the religious houses of Huy" in the depository of the State Archives at Liège. Thus, while there are some excellent qualities in Mr. Wilmotte's work, it also has some notable gaps and the occasional obvious error."

cupation and exploitation of their country, but for those not of the privileged classes, the conquest was a fact of life: the Revolution was over.

For religion, however, it had only begun. A violent persecution of the Church, notably of its religious and priests, and of the latter before the higher clergy, would soon follow: in every instance, all means would be allowed and all injustice be legal.

That such was to be the fate of the regular clergy was made clear at Huy on August 27, 1796: the day the Directory of the Council of Five Hundred decided to dissolve Belgium's religious orders. Even as the blow of that fearful news fell, the Executive Directory's Commissioner at Huy, Ista, took the occasion to provoke laughter and jeers among the citizenry by ordering that evening a pealing of all the city's bells.[461]

This flagrant display of prejudice was the prelude in the city which had been the home of Peter the Hermit to the assault on religious institutions which followed. The local authorities stood ready to support the powers of the time in their confiscation and destruction of monasteries and convents.

Thus delivered into the Revolution's hands, what fate would Clairlieu suffer?

There could be little doubt that its final hour had struck. On 15 Fructidor, year V (September 1, 1796), the French government suppressed all religious congregations in its newly-acquired territories, and on the 26th of the month the city of Huy decreed the annexation of all their goods and incomes to the Republic. The process went forward without hesitation or delay.

---

[461] See page 91.

As a result of the French decree, an Office of National Properties was soon established. On 24 Vendémiaire (October 15),
city officials entered Clairlieu at the orders of Legressier, who
supervised the registration of such properties, to "examine
the seals affixed to the library and remove them."[462] This
seemingly innocuous act presaged the seizure of the monastery's goods. Eight days later, on 2 Brumaire, year V, a delegation arrived from Liège. Led by Commissioner Harzé and N.
Billotey, president of the municipal council, they said their
task was to examine the monastery's accounts to determine
in detail its real property, titles and incomes. Harzé then pro-
ceeded to catalogue the monastery's furnishings: a long and
detailed inventory whose compilation required him and his
colleagues to spend twenty-nine days at Clairlieu. Only on 1
Frimaire, year V (November 21) did this high-ranking plunderer finish his list and have it countersigned by the Crosiers
who remained: J. P. Noiville, L. A. Hansotte, L. Tille, C.
Deneumoulin, L. Hayweghen, P. Loncin, J. F. Jérosme and
Walthère Heusquet, a lay brother. Those who by their absence refused to sign this act of confiscation were Prior General Dubois, who had already moved to the Rue des Sœurs
Grises at Huy, and H. Demet and J. Tilman.[463] Father
Warnotte's signature is also missing, for he had not yet completed his mission of retrieving the valuables taken to Duisburg in 1794.[464] The absence of their signatures also marks
their final eclipse in the affairs of Clairlieu.

When another of the last months of the monastery's agony
had passed, Prior General Dubois died on December 21, fal-
ling prey at the last to the misfortunes and affronts which

---

[462] Archives, city of Huy, French regime, Register 403, 254.
[463] The text is in Annexe 1 (Fontaine, "La Fin de Clairlieu," 33-36).
[464] See pages 88-89.

had burdened him during these disastrous times. Until his last breath, he had struggled with all his might against the Revolution's enterprises; his death spared him having to witness the unhappy spectacle which followed.

The death of their prior and general superior also brought an end to the incredible presumption which these Crosiers had shown from the first. They now enjoyed a new freedom to act and did not hesitate to make full use of it. Save for those who had not chosen to participate by signing the inventory of Harzé, they immediately assumed collective responsibility for their fate in the exceptionally critical circumstances in which they now found themselves.

For somewhat less than four months, they had known that they were living under a suspended sentence of banishment. What were they to do? They first claimed the provisional right to manage the monastery's property, as the law of suppression allowed, and then, on 9 Nivôse, year V (December 29, 1796), eight days after the death of the Prior General, they formally and collectively petitioned the local administration for that right, taking advantage of the sixth article in the law of 15 Fructidor. Huy's municipal council acceded to their request, "on condition that the ex-Crosiers conform themselves to the said sixth article, stipulating that the petitioners would be responsible for the objects placed in their care."[465] That was no small favor, for it was the equivalent of an economic rehabilitation. Bastin, the lawyer who had been imposed on them as Clairlieu's temporal administrator in the wake of the disheartening legal battle of the preceding months,[466] was thus stripped of his mandate: after barely five months, the Crosiers had succeeded in freeing themselves

---

[465] Archives, city of Huy, French regime, Register 403, 284.
[466] See page 88.

from what they deemed his burdensome supervision.

If they reckoned this change something of a break in the clouds which overshadowed these days, it would not last long, for that gloom had also concealed preparations for their final expulsion. Aware of the cruelty entailed by the law's application, Huy's municipal council first sought to fuel the bold secularism which was the order of the day. On the morning of January 21, there was a great to-do in the city square; "amid airs and songs, and the sound of bells and of the carillon, there occurred the first takings of *the anti royalist oath.*"[467] Five days later, the deed was done, and the Crosiers were the first victims.[468] On 7 Pluviôse (January 26) "retirement benefits" were issued. Most of the religious in the Department of the Ourthe deemed it legal to accept them,[469] and the Crosiers, including one lay brother, did so; only Fathers Tilman, Tille and Demet refused. All of them, however, were required to lay aside their religious habits and to leave their monastery within twenty days.

Faced with that requirement, they first tried to lease and then to "repurchase" their monastery. It was in vain. Huy's municipal council, which had hitherto been so ready to hasten the plunder of religious properties, now deliberately delayed the sale of what had been nationalized. Caught in a double bind, the Crosiers tried a different approach, relying, as before, on the law which would henceforth govern them. According to that, those who could not repurchase their monastery but could acquire lease of it at public auction were thereby authorized to remain in it with the title of "exempt

---

[467] Archives, city of Huy, French regime, minutes of the meeting of 2 Pluviose, year V.

[468] The Augustinians would be the last, on February 15, 1797.

[469] Daris, *Histoire de la Principaute,* 3:82.

caretakers." Aware that acquiring such a right could allow them to stay on for several years, and with a confidence bolstered by their futile but honest efforts to legally rent, the Crosiers asked to be assigned as "caretakers" of Clairlieu. This at first met with no more success than previous efforts. Now only five days remained until they would have to leave Clairlieu and scatter. Again they submitted their request, emphasizing how, before this, they had always acted in accord with the law and made their requests well in advance.

While they were left to squirm in their eleventh-hour fears, the government considered their urgent plea. Then, on 21 Pluviôse, year V (February 10, 1797), the municipal council and the Manager of National Properties "agreed" to it. The decree which allowed them to stay on noted that they were "deservedly" assigned to be caretakers of the monastery, but also stipulated that "this appointment is granted only provisionally, and that the petitioners will be held responsible for every damage which might occur to the national property of which they have care."[470]

They were thus left in a precarious security while their responsibilities were increased. What dominated this necessary step to ransom their situation, however, was that it made them caretakers of their monastery without outside interference, and so left them in a better position to consider the course of events before seeking to determine their future.

They had held their new post for a less than a month when two gentlemen named Duckers and Thomson came from Liège and, escorted by Commissioner Barbaix of Huy, presented themselves at the monastery's gate. Their task was to make a full assessment of the property which formed the

---

[470] Archives, city of Huy, French regime, Register 403, 307-308.

monastic enclosure. Although Duckers was only a small con-
tractor and Thomson a mere carpenter, the Central Administration had decided that these were the men to make this"
appraisal" of what had once been described as the fairest and
richest monastery in the city of Huy.[471] Their vague and tor-
tuous report, dated 28 Ventôse, year V (March 16, 1797), reveals their blatant incompetence. Its only value is that it gives
a quite different description of the monastery's buildings
from what one sees in illustration of Saumery. Our inclusion
of the text, with its orthography, thus seems to have some
merit:

> Summary of the appraisal on 28 Ventôse Year V
>
> Appraisers: Duckers and Thomson, visiting the property
> accompanied by citizen Barbaix:
>
> Know that the monastery of the Crosiers located upon
> parcel no. 390 of the city of Huy is composed of a consid-
> erable number of buildings which may be divided into
> the old and new monastery; first upon entering into the
> second courtyard, one finds to the right a group of build-
> ings, of which part comes forth from the coach-houses
> and stables, of a length of about 220 feet, then 30 to 36
> feet in depth; opposite that is a considerable building part
> of two stories, making of it the one of the old monastery
> of 340 feet in length and 25 to 30 feet in depth, 3 wings
> attach to this building and form between the two court-
> yards, of which one with cloister walks attach to the
> church, they are together 340 feet in periphery and several
> widths from 26 to 35. These parts are very old, are decay-

---

[471] See Saumery, *Delices du Pays de Liège* (Liège, 1740), 2:60, and Boussin-
gault, O.S.C., *La guide universelle de tous les Pals-Bas ou des 17 Provinces*
(paris, 1668), 72-73.

ing, are likewise very damaged by the considerable quartering of troops and have been designated for demolition. The new part of the monastery, newly built, is a group of double buildings, about 158 feet in length and 36 in depth, of two stages, the one built in bricks and dressed stone and communicates with the church by a corridor. The church is very large and very high; it is at least two hundred feet in length and 100 at its greatest width. All these buildings are contained in an enclosure where are many terraces and gardens and contains about two boniers, four large verges, three small. In which the buildings alone occupy a surface of 54,000 feet or 10 large verges, a dozen and a half small. The property is found located beyond the gate of the Crosiers and all opposite, between the street of the Hauts-Chênes on one side and that of Larrons on the other.[472]

Two days later, on March 18, came a new cause for alarm. Huy's municipal council declared, by means of placards, that "no one shall any longer fulfill the ministry of any cult in any place whatsoever if he does not first make the civic declaration before the local Administration."[473] A hint of how lit-

---

[472] State Archives, Liège, French regime; Nationalized Lands. It should be noted in passing that this lends credence to our suggestion on page 54, for it is consistent with the assumption that some detachments of soldiers were garrisoned in the "wings" of the monastery when the Master General returned to Clairlieu. Moreover, how else might one account for them being so damaged that they were to be demolished, unless such damage is a hint that "the considerable quarterings of troops" had not yet ended when the General decided to withdraw to the Rue des Soeurs Grises (see page 95)?

[473] Archives, city of Huy, French regime, Register 403, entry for this date. (The "civic declaration" was an oath binding one to the terms of France's Civil Constitution of the Clergy, which effectively put clerics on the government's payroll and subjected them to its regulation. – Tr.)

tle sympathy Huy's municipal councilors felt for their victims can be gleaned from the fact that, during the "Festival of the Sovereignty of the People" celebrated that same day, those chosen to speak found no better topic than "to declare their indignation against the Roman Curia and their admiration for the virtuous Romans who had just thrown off the yoke of their tyrannical pontiff."[474]

Perhaps we ought also see behind that noisy demonstration a fevered preparation for the municipal elections scheduled for March 22. As a result of them, however, several of those who had been noisy patriots only a few days earlier were turned out of office, including Wathour, the president of the municipal council, who received only ten of the six hundred and sixty-nine votes cast.[475] Among the voters of record were Crosiers Deneumoulin, Hansotte, Hayweghen, Heusquet, Jérosme and Noiville. Clairlieu's church served as the polling-place for the ward of Hoyoux.[476]

With the new administration would come the organization of the sale of nationalized lands, and the Crosiers at Clairlieu knew it. On 13 Pluviôse, year V (February 2, 1797), they had a document prepared by the lawyer Chapelle of Huy which granted Antoine Devaux[477] power of attorney" to act as their special proxy to tender for and acquire the nationalized lands

---

[474] Archives, city of Huy, French regime, Register 403, entry for this date. (The reference seems to be to the ceding of certain papal domains to France by the Treaty of Tolentino on February 2, 1797: a result of Napoleon's first Italian campaign, conducted while he was still a prominent and successful general in the service of the French government. – Tr.)

[475] Archives, city of Huy, French regime, file for year V.

[476] Grandmaison, *Souvenirs de Huy*, 86.

[477] The same ardent republican who had been their receiver until the Central Administration dismissed him on August 6, 1796; see page 88.

which corresponded to their possessions. "[478] A first piece of Clairlieu's holdings, some meadowlands consisting of six bonniers and called Haut Mat,[479] was auctioned off on 22 Floréal, year V (April 11, 1797) and purchased by General Songis of Brussels, acting as proxy for a former Carmelite, at a price of 15,000 francs. We do not know if Devaux tried to recover that bit of land, which was contiguous with the monastic enclosure, but the next month, on 2 Floréal, year V (April 21), he repurchased for his employers the farmstead of Envoz lez Couthuin for 200,000 pounds. Consisting of one hundred and fifteen bonniers and seven large verges of land and of seven bonniers and fourteen large verges of meadows and gardens, it once again became Crosier property, or rather the property of six Crosiers: Jérosme, Deneumoulin, Noiville, Hayweghen, Hansotte and Loncin.[480] We can only speculate as to whether the absence of the names of the other Crosiers indicates some difference of opinion over this purchase.

Amid the excitement engendered by the first steps taken to eradicate religion, some efforts were also made at Huy to reach an accommodation with the law governing the free exercise of worship. On 23 Floréal, year V (May 12, 1797), for example, a dozen priests made the civic declaration at city hall, among them Fathers Jérosme, Loncin and Hansotte.[481]

The business of plundering was now in full swing and, while

---

[478] State Archives, Liège, French regime, National Properties, aff. 7 no. 8; the text is in Annexe 2 (Fontaine, "La Fin de Clairlieu," 36).
[479] P. Clerx, "Liste generale des Eglises et Couvents de la province actuelle de Liège, vendus comme proprietes nationales du ler vent6se an V (22-2-1797) au ler juillet 1808," *Bulletin de l'Institut Archeologique liegois* 16 (Liège, 1881) 508.
[480] See Annexe 3 (Fontaine, "La Fin de Clairlieu," 37).
[481] Archives, city of Huy, French regime, Register of Declarations, 3 and 4vo.

it went forward from the spring of 1797 until well into the fall,[482] there were also efforts to remove bells and crosses. In the first days of July, employees of the Lannoy Company, who were the auctioneers of the city's bells, came to Clairlieu to lower the nine bells from the church tower and the carillon. In doing so, they damaged "the clock and the ironwork attaching to it." The Crosiers angrily registered a protest with the Central Administration, claiming that "in no way can this object be considered as having a use pertaining to worship." Poswick forwarded their protest to the Manager of National Properties for the canton of Huy, who decided that there was good reason to accede to it.[483]

For six months, then, the Crosiers fulfilled their double charge of caring for and managing their property for the best. In August, however, there occurred something which would compromise their already insecure hold on Clairlieu. The facts recorded in the court records follow.

During the night of 12 Fructidor, year V (August 29, 1797), Huy's chief of police, Séguin, was making a patrol of the city accompanied by his clerk and his assistant, Carré and Graffar, and three soldiers. Hearing a noise, they surprised two men named Sacré and Crousse near the Crosiers' entryway. The two carried a small church candle set in the bottom of a basket to light their way and were making off with the bell from the monastery parlor in a second basket. Arrested and

---

[482] On 12 Thermidor, year V (August 30, 1797), there was an appraisal of the country house of the Master General at Lamalle in the township of Bas Oha lez Huy. The text, which briefly describes the buildings and their setting, is in Annexe 4 (Fontaine, "La Fin de Clairlieu," 37). The Pommier Company purchased the property in 1798; in 1830 it was sold to the Melotte family, who later sold it to the Laminne family.

[483] State Archives, Liège, no. 485, French Prefecture.

questioned, the miscreants admitted to having made off with several other of the monastery's possessions and taking them to the part of the city called Saint Mort, to a garden owned by a man named Rouchet, who lived near the city square. To his record of the interrogation Séguin added, "I will make a report of this to citizen Lemarié, Receiver of National Properties, to show him how the ex-Crosiers, who have been assigned to care for the Republic's property, are given to pillaging it."[484] This denunciation of the Crosiers, caught in the act of burglarizing their monastery's property, had soon to have its consequences. On 18 Fructidor, year V (September 5, 1797), the Departmental Administration permanently revoked the Crosiers' appointment as caretakers and, six days later, made it over to "citizen Wathour":[485] a sop of consolation tossed to the zealous Jacobin whom the voters had recently turned out of office. What made this especially galling was that the man who had had such a hand in all the nets woven about Prior General Dubois would now preside over Clairlieu's death throes.

The Crosiers were given a week to pack up and move out. When it had passed, their last ties to their monastery were finally severed. In these critical hours, the unhappy exiles seem to have been guided by a specific, threefold decision. They first of all established their place of refuge in the neighborhood of the monastery, viz., in the part of the city called le Sarte Next they divested themselves of the farm at Envoi, which was a way of converting some resources into capital and, more notably, of freeing themselves of certain incomes which had become overly burdensome to them. This they did the next month, on 3 Brumaire, year VI (October 24,

---

[484] Ibid.
[485] Ibid.

1797).[486] Finally, be cause they were determined to continue celebrating Mass each day, as they had been able to do behind closed doors since January 1,[487] they freed themselves from the restrictions on the practice of cult. On September 11, 1797, the very day on which they had to be out of their monastery, Subprior Noiville, who hitherto had not done so, and Father Hayweghen went to city hall and there together made the civic declaration.[488] Once more, however, fortune failed them. Five days later, on September 16, a new law, which had been enacted on 19 Fructidor, year V (September 6), was promulgated at Huy. This rescinded the obligation to make the declaration, but required all priests to take the "oath of hatred for royalty and anarchy" under pain of imprisonment or exile.[489] What were the Crosiers to do now, in the face of this new and redoubled pressure? That same day, Jérosme and Noiville and seven other priests of the city took the requisite oath, the one before Detelle, the other before President Rouchet.[490] Twelve days later, on September 28, Noiville felt obliged to rectify his failure of nerve somewhat. Returning to city hall, he had it recorded that he chose to exercise his priesthood at the church of St. Mengold.[491] After September 16, however, no other priest took the despised oath. Determined to break all resistance, the city administration then enacted threats against" nonjuring clergy." Two more Crosiers, Loncin and Hansotte, consequently gave in on 19 Vendémiaire, year VI (October 10, 1797), and took the

---

[486] The text is in Annexe 5 (Fontaine, "La Fin de Clairlieu," 38).
[487] Since then, all churches served by priests who had not made the civic declaration had been closed; see Grandmaison, *Souvenirs de Huy, 64.*
[488] Archives, city of Huy, French regime, Register of Declarations, 4vo.
[489] Archives, city of Huy, Register 404, 68-69.
[490] Archives, city of Huy, Register of Declarations, 8 and 8vo.
[491] Archives, city of Huy, Register 404, 76.

168

oath be fore Rouchet.[492] In all fairness, however, we must note in their defense that they were the first of the twenty priests that took the oath before them who, like Noiville, chose to add a condition to it by requesting that a note be made on the record that they chose to exercise their priesthood at St. Mengold and St. Denis respectively.[493] In spite of everything, however, including the pronouncements of Vicar General de Rougrave,[494] nonjuring clergy remained numerous. On 22 Vendémiaire, year VI (October 13), Spiroux, who was chairman of the grand jury charged with matters pertaining to the clergy, ordered that all such priests were to appear before the municipal council between 9:00 a.m. and noon and between 2:00 and 5:00 p.m. that day. Three did so, including L. Hayweghen, who claimed St. Mengold, as his three confreres had done before him.[495] The next day, twenty more priests did the same, aware that the municipal council had decided to round up those who would not. At the end of October, in fact, the local police, accompanied by armed men, set out at 2:00 a.m. to hunt down at home those who had not taken the oath. At the instigation of Bassenge, the fanaticism of this brazen pursuit grew in intensity and would

---

[492] Archives, city of Huy, Register of Declarations, 11.

[493] Once expelled from their monasteries, religious priests usually chose to function in the church nearest their new homes. Hansotte, who was a native of Huy, returned to his family home in the Rue St. Domitien and so chose St. Denis. Noiville, Loncin and Jerosme, who were living in Ie Sart, the part of the city next to Clairlieu, preferred St. Mengold, which was located behind city hall.

[494] He not only failed to condemn taking this oath but, in a letter of December 14,1797, approved doing so and, less than two months later, on February 1, directed the clergy to submit to it. The Bishop of Roermond, on the other hand, condemned taking the oath, and when Pope Pius VI was consulted in December 1797, he declared that doing so was illicit.

[495] Archives, city of Huy, Register of Declarations, ll[vo].

last until May.[496]

* * *

With this business of the oath, the Crosiers concluded two months in exile and Wathour a similar period as "caretaker" of their former home. We must now trace the course of his "reign" over his prize in order to witness the ancient monastery's death.

Hardly had two months passed when Wathour sought to renew his appointment as "assigned caretaker" on 26 Brumaire, year VI (November 17, 1797).[497] Hoping to hasten its renewal by the Central Administration, he urged "that consideration be given to his recent misfortunes and his difficult situation."[498] Not only did the government at Liège pay no attention to his doleful plaints but even declined to take action on his plea.

Had it perhaps gotten wind of something? Whatever the case, even as Wathour sought to renew his appointment, the monastery of the former Crosiers had become the scene of grave mismanagement. The version of events which follows is that recorded in various contemporary minutes and transcripts.

Knowing that Huy's local government would proceed to the public auction of furnishings belonging to religious communities during December, Crosiers Jérosme and Loncin had conceived a plan for making a clean sweep of their sup-

---

[496] Archives, city of Huy, Register 404, 162-187; and Grandmaison, *Souvenirs de Huy*, 62. (Of the two thousand French priests arrested for refusing to subscribe to this oath, five hundred were from the Belgian departments. – Tr.)

[497] Such appointments were usually made for only two months under the Republic.

[498] State Archives, Liège, no. 485, French Prefecture.

pressed monastery and had soon lured Wathour into being their accomplice by offering him a share in the plunder. On the appointed day, Clairlieu's "caretaker" set off for Liège, thereby giving himself an alibi should things go wrong. On November 14, meanwhile, Jérosme and Loncin had met with H. Crousse (a carpenter living at St. Mort), his uncle, N. Crousse (the man whom Séguin had recently interrogated), J. Berlot, and a fellow named Sacré, who had been the Crosiers' organist. The plan called for them to strip the Quarters of the Prior General of everything that could be carried away. In view of the risk, the four had at first hesitated, but Jérosme had calmed their fears by telling them "that they could do the job with confidence because everything would be done in broad daylight, and if ownership of the items was disputed," he told them, "he would return them."[499] Thus instructed and reassured, they set out with him for Clairlieu. Revealing nothing of his intentions, Father Jérosme asked Mrs. Kinaple[500] to open the door to the General's residence. Hardly had she turned her back when the pillage began. For two hours, sometimes under the watchful eyes of Wathour's son, cartloads of items were dispatched to Mottet, one of the Crosiers' pieces of property, for storage. At some point Mrs. Kinaple challenged the younger Wathour's failure to intervene, but he dodged by saying "that he was going to write to his father, who was in Liège, to see if the Quarter of the former General was being stripped of its furnishings in this way with his approval."[501] The plundering continued the next day, but on that when Crousse and Sacré were preparing to

---

[499] State Archives, Liège, no. 485, French Prefecture.
[500] J. P. Kinaple, a native of Liège and the Crosiers' brewer, had occupied the outbuildings to the right of the monastery since 1781.
[501] State Archives, Liège, no. 485, French Prefecture, deposition of Mrs. Kinaple given on 15 Frimaire, year VI.

make their" final assault," the elder Wathour unexpectedly arrived on the scene, purporting to be on his way home from his daily walk. Deceitfully assuming an attitude of mixed surprise and displeasure, he accompanied the movers to Mottet.[502]

This plundering, which had been carried out in broad daylight over several days, seems to have been noticed by too many people to keep tongues from wagging and investigations from being started. L. Lemarié, the Receiver of National Properties, was the first official to be involved. Accompanied by President Delloye of the municipal council, he descended upon the Crosiers on the morning of December 1 and was wholly taken aback by what he saw: furnishings, doors, paneling, heaters, even the locks, had all been removed from the General's Quarter, and the shutters had even been wrenched from the windows. "It is surprising that the walls were left..." he commented in his report of findings. He also got Mrs. Kinaple to talk, and she gave voice to the rumors: "there were two perpetrators of the crime, and everything was done either by the order or with the knowledge of the caretaker, Wathour." That same day, Lemarié sent an indignant note to Barbaix, the Commissioner of the Executive Directory, in which he noted Wathour's probable connivance in the episode and so settled the latter's hash for him: "it seems to me that assignment as caretaker of the Monastery of the ex - Crosiers ought to be withdrawn from him immediately."[503] His wrath provoked Barbaix. Upon receipt of the letter of Lemarié, the Commissioner went to see for himself. Shocked beyond belief, Barbaix the next day, 12 Frimaire (December

---

[502] Ibid.
[503] State Archives, Liège, no. 485, French Prefecture, letter of 11 Frimaire, year VI.

2), sent a laconic note to Wathour, saying that he no longer had any confidence in him and, consequently, required him to return the keys to the "primary Monastery of the ex-Crosiers," along with everything which he had taken from it. "The rest," the Commissioner added, "is up to the courts."[504] The parties involved were thus led to expect a formal investigation by the court of inquiry.

Two days later (14 Frimaire or December 4), Mrs. Kinaple received a summons to appear on December 5. Before Huy's Justice of the Peace, A. Pfeffer, she gave a detailed account of everything which had happened and, although she did not refuse to give his name, observed that "an ex-Crosier canon" was at the head of the band of movers.[505] The next day everything which had been removed and stored at Mottet was returned to Clairlieu. Séguin oversaw the operation, which cost him 19 pounds, 10 sols, and for which Lemarié reimbursed him on January 8.[506] Eleven days after his expedition to Mottet, on 27 Frimaire, year VI, Séguin replaced Wathour as caretaker of Clairlieu, but that did not keep the investigation from proceeding.

On 5 Nivôse (December 24), Séguin and his clerk, L. Carré, questioned Crousse and Berlot, who said they "had been un-

---

[504] State Archives, Liège, no. 485, French Prefecture, letter of 12 Frimaire, year VI.

[505] State Archives, Liège, no. 485, French Prefecture, deposition of Mrs. Kinaple given on 15 Frimaire, year VI.

[506] State Archives, Liège, no. 485, French Prefecture. What eventually became of these items remains a mystery: all the more so because on the same day Mrs. Kinaple gave her deposition before the court of inquiry (December 5, 1797), Huy's municipal council informed the Central Administration in Liège that "the sale of extant furnishings in the suppressed religious Houses had ended," a claim manifestly contradicted by what follows. (See Daris, *Histoire de la Principaute*, 3:233.)

173

der the directions of Jérosme and Loncin, both of them ex-Crosiers."[507] Next came Wathour's turn. The municipal council invited him to appear before it on 7 Nivôse, year VI (December 26) and read to him the letter and decree of the Central Administration, which directed that he "be queried regarding the facts." His judges, good patriots all, were so moved to pity for the lot of their former president that, at the end of the meeting, they addressed a letter to Liège stating that "in their opinion, his dismissal by Barbaix had been precipitous and neither justified nor authorized by any of the constituted authorities... it was an arbitrary action taken against citizen Wathour."[508] When the Central Administration received this bit of cheerleading for the defendant and an appeal on his behalf, it forwarded a copy to Barbaix and invited him to comment on the facts in it.[509] Infuriated, Barbaix rose in wrath against this attempt to justify Clairlieu's former caretaker and, in four long pages (accompanied by an equal number containing three items of corroboration), demanded that the Administration uphold his dismissal of such an obviously guilty fellow.[510] Wathour, meanwhile, was writing letter after letter to Liège in an effort to exculpate himself and to neutralize Barbaix's restatement of the case against him. Oddly, Barbaix's letter to the Administration seems to have been misplaced, for they sent him a reminder,

---

[507] State Archives, Liège, no. 485, French Prefecture, transcript of the interrogation of 5 Ni vose, year VI.

[508] State Archives, Liège, no. 485, French Prefecture, letter of 8 Nivose, year VI.

[509] State Archives, Liège, no. 485, French Prefecture, letter of 18 Nivose, year VI.

[510] State Archives, Liège, no. 485, French Prefecture, letter of 25 Nivose, year VI.

again asking for more information.[511] Annoyed, Barbaix merely referred to his (apparently misplaced) letter and its reasons for his cashiering of Wathour, adding that "this shows you, citizens, how much trust you ought to place in the letter from our municipal councilors."[512]

Did the latter now realize that their inept handling of the Commissioner might compromise Wathour's success? Be that as it may, the individuals who made up the "Constitutional Circle of Defenders of the Country" now took umbrage with Barbaix, and on 10 Ventôse, year VI (February 28, 1798), sent Liège a letter of complaint about him over twenty-two signatures.[513]

No more support could be contrived for Wathour, clutching at his "rank" of caretaker of Clairlieu and suffering from the harm to his "honor": all his hopes now rested on the understanding and indulgence of the departmental authorities. Four days later, on 14 Ventôse (March 2, 1798), the decision which he so fearfully awaited finally arrived. The decree merely said, "The Central Administration, the Executive Commissioner being in agreement, confirm the dismissal of citizen Wathour from his office as caretaker of the Monastery of the ex-Crosiers of Huy: both the city administration and the Commissioner are, respectively, charged with the execution of this decree."[514]

---

[511] State Archives, Liège, no. 485, French Prefecture, letter of 28 Pluviose, year VI.
[512] State Archives, Liège, no. 485, French Prefecture, letter of 5 Ventose, year VI.
[513] State Archives, Liège, no. 485, French Prefecture, letter of 10 Ventose, year VI.
[514] State Archives, Liège, no. 485, French Prefecture, letter of 14 Ventose, year VI.

Séguin, meanwhile, had for all practical purposes surrendered his responsibility to care for Clairlieu by handing it over to G. Mataigne, formerly one of the monastery's domestic servants. The latter, however, seems to have been discouraged by the risks connected with such a responsibility and had increasingly dissociated himself from it. These new irregularities were reported to Liège by one Servais Dony, who took the opportunity to also seek the post for himself, since he reckoned it was vacant. On 4 Floréal, year VI (April 23, 1798), the Central Administration forwarded his request to Huy for decision.[515] Although he had no business doing so, Wathour thereupon requested a hearing during the meeting of 14 Floréal (May 3). Again he laid claim to his "right" to be appointed caretaker of the Crosiers' monastery and sketched the "injustices in which he had been steeped." The municipal council was inclined not to consider Dony, until Barbaix remarked that the whole exercise was pointless, since "before long, all these properties were going to be sold." In the end, the decision was put off to another day,[516] and because Barbaix was not at the council's next session, S. Dony had to be appointed" caretaker of the Monastery and contiguous properties of the ex-Crosiers." He was entrusted with the various keys and told "to see to it that no damage was done that national property."[517] For the battered and bloodied Wathour, this was the last straw. On 14 Prairial, year VI (June 3) he sent to the Central Administration a letter occupying thirty inches of stamped paper, in which he sought to prove that he

---

[515] State Archives, Liège, no. 485, French Prefecture, letter of 4 Floreal, year VI.

[516] State Archives, Liège, French regime, year VI, Register of Meetings, 10 and 11.

[517] State Archives, Liège, French regime, year VI, minutes of the meeting of 17 Floreal, year VI (May 6, 1798).

had been the victim of hostile machinations "while the authors of the pilferage," whom he had incriminated, "went unpursued." This letter gushed such misery, however, that the Administration must have found its contents a bit much. "Citizens Administrators," he moaned, "it makes my heart bleed once more to see the ratification which the Central Administration has made of my provisional dismissal by Barbaix," and the like. Toward the end, he wrote, "I invite you, citizens, to assist me again to make your Administration understand: that it might be willing to re-examine my documents and render me justice. .. consider them clearly once more, and my character and my misfortunes, then better informed, it will graciously receive my long and toilsome requests." When Huy's municipal council forwarded this last card to be played in the appeal of Clairlieu's former caretaker, they added to its first page a warm note of commendation on behalf of a man whom they claimed "to be an honorable and unfortunate republican.[518] What result did this final play of the game's last hand have? It is in a scrawled comment on the back of the letter's fourth page: "in view of the sale of the property of the ex-Crosiers of which the petitioner solicits being made caretaker, there were no grounds for discussing it." Such was Wathour's final removal: he was never paid for his services, either.[519]

---

[518] State Archives, Liège, no. 485, French Prefecture, letter of 14 Prairial, year VI.

[519] Even after Clairlieu lay buried beneath its ruins, all who had served as its caretakers gained no profit from the post, except Seguin. The first to seek recompense was Mataigne, who entered a claim for four months as caretaker. The Central Administration dodged the issue by referring him to Seguin for settlement of the account. S. Dony put forward a similar claim soon after, "for two months as caretaker of the Crosiers' furnishings." When it was ignored, he reapplied. He was then informed that there were

We have recounted this last episode and its tangled proceedings at some length, above all because it reveals so clearly the atmosphere which pervaded Clairlieu after the unhappy exodus of its inhabitants. Beyond that, one cannot help noting how Wathour, who so tormented Clairlieu's last Prior General, was himself soon chastened, and with good reason. There is indeed some satisfaction to be found in noting that the former president of Huy's municipal council was himself toppled from his pedestal and so joined Devaux, Donnay and Ista in their fall:[520] all once rising stars of the new regime, now in sad disgrace.

* * *

The Central Administration had been right about the impending" sale of the property of the ex-Crosiers" when, in early June of 1798, it had rejected Wathour's request to be named caretaker of Clairlieu. Public Notice No. 60, announcing the sale of "the conventual House of the ex-Crosiers, which consists of several groups of buildings, church, courtyards, terraced gardens, forming an enclosure of two bon-

---

no grounds for his claim, since the Crosiers' furnishings "no longer existed during the period in question." Finally, a quarrel broke out between Mataigne and Seguin, for the latter pocketed everything and paid his successor nothing. Wathour also made one last claim, again in a request carrying the recommendation of Huy's municipal council, for what was owed him for his two and a half months as caretaker. He was informed that, "he must first find evidence of the decree which had as signed him to be caretaker: that there then must be an investigation of whether he had properly fulfilled his duties and whether, through his negligence, he had not allowed the monastery of the ex-Crosiers to be damaged." A decree passed on 25 Thermidor, year VII (August 13, 1799), ordered that the former president of Huy's municipal council receive a check for seventy-eight francs, "payment in full for his term as caretaker." (State Archives, Liège, no. 485, French Prefecture.)
[520] See chapter six.

niers, four large verges, thirteen small, located in the commune and canton of Huy" had already appeared in the usual public places, especially in Huy, on May 3 of that year (14 Floréal, year VI). In pursuance thereof, the Administrators of the Department of the Ourthe gathered at 9 :00 on the morning of 7 Prairial (May 26, 1798) in the auction-room at Liège to set the date of and opening bid for the initial auction. The opening bid to be accepted on 17 Prairial (June 6) was fixed at 380,250 francs: three-fourths of the value determined by the appraisal of March 16, 1797. On the date set, the same Administrators (the younger Huberty, Lafaulx, Piette and secretary-general Soleure) assembled in the court room. The auction was to proceed "at the pace of the bidding," which began at the sum set during their previous meeting. Five higher bids followed, with the highest from" citizen J. P. Henkart," a lawyer from Liège; a sixth was made, but not a seventh. Article six of the law which regulated this procedure required that the auction not be concluded until ten days later, viz., not before 27 Prairial (June 16). The bidding was reopened that morning at 9:00 with the first session's last bid of 410,000 francs serving as the opening bid. Three higher bids followed, until the offer stood at 504,000 francs, again from J. P. Henkart, acting on behalf of several buyers. No higher bid was made. Thus, at 5:00 that same afternoon, Henkart and his associates appeared in the offices of the Department of the Ourthe to make their declaration of proxy.[521] That reveals who had really purchased the monastery of Clairlieu: Libert Devillers, a man of independent means from Liège, claimed two of the nine shares; Antoine Thomson,[522]

---

[521] Required by French law from one who had made a purchase at auction on behalf of a third party. – Tr.
[522] The same fellow who, with Duckers, had appraised the property on March 16, 1797.

carpenter, resident at Liège, two shares; Leonard Defrance, artist and painter, resident at Liège, two shares; Dieudonné Five, resident at Liège, one share; P. E. Rouma, resident at Liège, one share; and C. N. J. M. Barbaix,[523] former captain in the service of Holland, one share. Henkart and his associates promptly arranged payment: a tenth in cash, the rest on contract. Four days later, on 2 Messidor, year VI (June 20, 1798), upon payment of the 504-franc registration fee, they took receipt of the official copy of the record of auction,[524] which made them owners of everything within the monastic enclosure.

Clairlieu was thus sold without any involvement of its original owners, who had several times tried to ransom it. Might they have been victims of some behind the scene manipulation? We do not know. It is quite unlikely, however, that they could have made another attempt to save their former home when the sale actually took place. Devaux had made clumsy use of their resources to recover the property at Envoz and, as we have already noted, when the Departmental Administration finally sent them packing, they had had to sell that farmstead and its goods lest their lack of ready funds leave them impoverished.

---

[523] His wrath at Wathour's pillaging of the Crosiers' furnishings was not, therefore, entirely disinterested.

[524] The same document from which we have drawn this information. The thirty-ninth item of another document, which is dated 26 Pluviose, year VII (January 25, 1799), and records the transfer of nationalized lands for the previous year, informs us that the four houses and the mill which the Crosiers owned in Huy were disposed of as follows: the house at Haut Mat went to Brialmont of Liège; that on la Sarte to Antoine Peree, resident on la Sarte; that in the district of Ie Sart to Herman Herla, a tanner; that at 324 Rue de Mottet to the same H. Herta; and the monastery's mill in the Rue St. Domitien was sold to L. Bihet, a tanner, and Basile Lebrun on November 2, 1798, for 15,000 francs. (Archives, city of Huy, file for year V.)

The subsequent course of events reveals that the predatory Defrance had also had an eye on Clairlieu. Indeed, it would be surprising had he not, for we know that he visited the place not long before the auction.[525] From the moment the auction of .Clairlieu began, however, it could not have fallen into hands more skilled in demolition. Defrance and Devillers had been two of the three men who had organized and carried out the demolition of the Cathedral of St. Lambert in 1796. He and his associate Thomson had also recently acquired (in April 1797) and wholly demolished the church and monastery of Liège's Franciscan Minims.[526] This revolutionary trio, presided over by the unholy P. J. Henkart,[527] thus would oversee the vandalism perpetrated on the home of "the ex-Crosiers of Huy" beginning in that same summer of 1798.

The monastery, the church and the cloisters all fell before the pickax: everything was leveled. The only thing which slowed the methodical sack of the place was its library and numerous books, which some time earlier had been earmarked for the central school in Liège.[528] In August, Huy informed the Central Administration that it must take steps to halt the depredations to which the Crosiers' library was being ex-

---

[525] On 24 Pluviose, year VI (February 12, 1797), he had been assigned to visit churches and designate those objects worthy of being shipped to Paris. (Archives of the Central Administration, Register 49, 544.)

[526] Gobert, *Les Rues de Liège*, 2: 490.

[527] After extensive participation in the revolutionary movement, Henkart married a former nun from the Abbey of Herkenrode. He died in 1815. (Archives of the Prefecture, file 93/3).

[528] Wilmotte, "Notice historique," 40. R. Dubois is of the opinion that the books from the Crosiers' library were kept in Huy for so long, and thus exposed to pillage, because the central school originally planned for Huy, to be erected on the site previously occupied by the Augustinians, was not established. (See R. Dubois, *Les Rues de Huy* (Huy, 1910), 37.)

posed, and on the 19th of that month, Liège directed Pirnéa to move the library to its own central school. That transfer (by boat!) took place only in late September, however, for it was on September 30, 1798, that Pirnéa wrote to the Prefect that "the library of the ex-Crosiers of Huy was yesterday deposited in the central school at Liège."[529]

If we can and ought not go into the details of Clairlieu's destruction, which went on for several years, we should at least include Gorissen's eyewitness account of the demolition of its church. "In the case of the vast church of the Crosiers," he writes, "they removed the ironwork, the lead, the woodwork and the marbles; then the columns were undermined and left supported only by wooden stanchions; a fire was set and the edifice collapsed with a crash."[530] The "entrepreneurs" responsible were driven by the urgency of making money from the debris, and by their thirst soon to realize other sources of income, too.[531]

Thomson, who particularly seems to have been out to make a killing, again returned to the scene of Clairlieu's desolation in February 1811, to pay before the notary, Chapelle, local fees on four and a half of the nine shares of the ruined monastic enclosure. The ancient monastery, which only a few years before had stood so majestically on the heights of la Sarte, had by then been reduced to It a small building, mate-

---

[529] Daris, *Notices sur les eglises*, 1:317-318, and Th. Gobert, *Bulletin de l'Institut Archeologique* 37 (Liège, 1907) 15,52,55 and 57. Gobert adds that Pirnea was scandalized by the numerous acts of negligence, tactlessness and plunder which he witnessed.
[530] Gorissen, *Histoire de la ville de Huy*, 485.
[531] The sack of Clairlieu had not ended when Thomson turned to the demolition of the remaining large tower of St. Lambert's in 1803; he undertook the destruction of a similar tower belonging to the church of St. Adabert in 1809. (Gobert, *Les Rues de Liège*, 1:609 and 190.)

rial left over from demolition, stones, limestone, lots, gardens, courtyard, open space and the tower."[532]

By early 1811, then, only the large, tall, square tower of the monastery church had survived the work of the master demolitionist Defrance.[533] In 1818, however, this also had to come down, by an order from the Dutch government issued shortly after King William's visit to Huy in June 1817. The stones were to be used for the construction of Huy's present fortress.[534] Had things been otherwise, that monumental piece of stonework might well have remained standing among the ruins for long years afterward: a gigantic tombstone over the grave of the Order's cradle.

Some scattered bits and pieces escaped the legalized pillaging of the ancient monastery and the impiety of those responsible for its heinous destruction. Among those worth noting are statues of St. Theobald, St. Helen and the Blessed Virgin, also a bust of St. Odilia which is now preserved in the collegial church of Notre Dame at Huy;[535] "the magnificent censer and beautiful monstrance" which have figured in several expositions of art from the Meuse region and which now belong to the church of St. Remy in Huy;[536] the organ, which

---

[532] According to the notarized contract between Thomson and J. Sikivie, a carpenter and a resident of Huy.

[533] This gloomy fellow died on February 25, 1805, and was buried at Huy in the garden of his friend Henkart after a secular ceremony. (Gobert, *Les Rues de Liège*, 1:381.)

[534] R. Dubois, *Notices sur la ville de Huy*, 37.

[535] H. Demaret, *La Collegiale N.D. il Huy*, 3rd part, 51-53.

[536] These were preserved, Grandmaison informs us, by the piety of certain citizens of Huy who, during the night of September 3 or 4, 1795, removed what they could from the condemned churches. (Grandmaison, *Souvenirs de Huy*, 64.) Something similar happened at Clairlieu on September 30 of that same year, when one gilt and four silver chalices were removed from

was first installed in the collegial church in 1807[537] but afterwards given to that of Forges at Condroz, and is now a ramshackle instrument of poor tone; the great and richly framed painting of Christ on the cross which was removed by Father Jérosme and is now the property of Mr. van den Berg of Liège; the precious reliquary made in 1292 (the oldest surviving example of Liège's tradition of painting)[538] to hold the relics of the Order's patroness, St. Odilia, which was saved through the efforts of L. Hayweghen, one of the Crosiers of Huy, who moved it to Looz and, in 1828, gave it to the church at Kerniel; numerous manuscripts and incunabula which were first taken to Liège's central school and, around 1815, shared out between the Grand Séminaire and the University;[539] and various objects discovered when the embank-

---

the church during the night. Subsequent investigation failed to reveal who had been responsible for the theft. (Archives, city of Huy, French regime, Register 403.)

[537] *Annales du Cercle Hutois des Sciences et des Beaux Arts, 5:245.*

[538] For a description, see J. Helbig, *Le Beffroi,* 2:31; H. van Lieshout, O.S.C., *Rond het Reliekschrijn van Sint Odilia* (Hasselt, 1935),91 and following; and Daris, *Notices sur les eglises,* 1:391-392.

[539] The two collections reveal that (1) the art of calligraphy was cultivated early and enthusiastically at Clairlieu; (2) there are unmistakable traces, for more than a century (1424-1541), of a constant study of astronomy and mathematics and of an interest in keeping abreast of scientific progress (see C. Le Paige, "Notes pour servir a l'histoire des mathematiques dans l'ancien pays de Liège," *Bulletin de l'Institut Archeologique liegois* 21 (Liège, 1888) 470-472); (3) there was also an appreciable involvement in the great humanistic revival at the end of the fifteenth and beginning of the sixteenth centuries; (4) part of the importance of these collections is that they suffice to establish the existence of a climate of asceticism at Clairlieu across the ages; and (5), when printing began, the Crosiers of Huy so specialized in bookbinding that their artful work soon surpassed masters of the craft and brought their work shop a notable popularity (see J. Brassinne [professor and head librarian at the University of Liège], *La Reliure Mosane,* 2 vols., Liège, 1912 and 1932). Among the other libraries which

ment and convent of the Poor Clares of St. Colette were built on the site of Clairlieu's church, viz., a finely carved wooden crucifix, two heavy oak pedestals a meter in length, a small oak altar in the style of Louis XV which has a large Crosier cross carved on it but lacks a reredos,[540] and the statues of St. Lambert and St. John Népomucène which probably once adorned the church's portico and today enrich the entryway to the church at Bas-Oha.

Aside from these precious relics, now scattered to the four winds, nothing remains of Clairlieu's robust beauty. The site of the monastery has been so cleared that, save for some ashlar blocks lying here and there about the foot of the hill, all vestiges of it have been deeply buried under successive levelings and constructions. All that has survived destruction is a set of buildings on the site of the old monastery brewery (which now serve as a residence for the church-wardens of St. Remy), the retaining wall along the Rue des Hauts-Chênes, and the great carriage gate at the corner of the latter and the Rue des Larrons.[541]

That monumental gate is an appropriate and moving memorial: the last heritage in stone of a splendor which no longer

---

possess manuscripts or books stamped with the ex-libris of Clairlieu are Belgium's Biblioth~que Royal, the Biblioth~que du Petit Seminaire of St. Trond, the Library of the British Museum, the Bibliothèque Mazarine in Paris and many more.

[540] These objects were generously returned to the Order in 1923 in exchange for copies of them fashioned of lindenwood.

[541] Known as *Tra de Creuhis* [At the Site of the Crosiers], the gate consists of two pilasters supporting an architrave, which is surmounted by a heavy, curved fronton adorned with a coat of arms. The arms were probably those of Master General Fisen; despite their defacement during the revolutionary period, what seems to be the date" 1742" is still more or less visible. The gateway is fitted with a double door.

exists, a granite gateway which resisted the storm and has stood there ever since, sublimely adamant in its defiance of time and oblivion, covered with memories, as if standing guard over the godliness and the loss once associated with this blessed place, so ravaged by the unholy fury of the revolutionaries.

It remains, then, to sketch something of the subsequent history of the hillside of Clairlieu, the cradle of the Order of the Holy Cross. We will be brief.

By 1811 the property had been parceled out into lots of some fifteen bonniers to two bonniers, four large verges and thirteen small and was acquired that year by Thomson of Liège and Sikivie of Huy in joint venture. In 1821 the whole of it passed to N. Delhaise, professor of music at Huy, who sold a joint half to his son, A. J. Delhaise, an agriculturalist, in 1823; the younger Delhaise became sole proprietor in 1828. Barely two years later, he had to sell it to P. J. Daxhelet, a local brewer, and the year after that, a claim was made for a joint half, through an act of subrogation, in support of the construction of the new cathedral in Liège. In 1834, the property was purchased by P. J. F. Wilmotte, a man of independent means from Flémalle, who also assumed the burdensome clauses on behalf of the cathedral of Liège. Four months later, he sold the whole property to Caroline and Adele Hansotte, the directors of a private boarding school.[542]

---

[542] In 1875, Miss Virginie Nottret became superintendent of this school. She was an outstanding educator, as well as a very talented writer and a member of the panel of judges for the literary competitions organized by the Commission of the "Cercle Hutois des Sciences et des Beaux Arts" (see the latter's *Annales*, 5:205). After her death, Miss Brichot, whose reputation as a teacher was marked by a similarly fine tradition of education, assumed direction of the school built on the land which had once belonged to the Crosiers (see *Journal de Huy*, 97 annee, 98 [December, 1947] 17). A chapel

After their deaths, Mrs. Pauline Hansotte-Thirifays inherited the land in 1893. Not long after, the courtyard and buildings belonging to the school, which occupied a little more than a third of an acre, were sold to the workers' society of *St. Joseph.* A second parcel, slightly less than a third of an acre, was sold to the Collettine Sisters in 1908. The next year, at the request of Mrs. Hansotte-Thirifays' residuary legatees, what was left of the property which had once belonged to the Crosiers, about three and one-eighth acres, was put up for public sale: the asking price was 26,500 francs.[543] The land was purchased by Mr. Smets, a lawyer, who had to divest himself of it in his turn in 1945.

The legal documents which allow us to reach back to the time of the Revolution in sketching our little account of the changing ownership of what was once Clairlieu obviously contain many other details about the multiple transfers summarized above, but it would be wearying to dwell at length on the particulars of their history. The inescapable reflection engendered by the story of this diminution of the Church's possessions, however, is that since its profanation at the end of the eighteenth century, the property has brought little good fortune to its successive owners. Indeed, at nearly every stage of the various transfers of that holy enclosure, one encounters hints of a shameful awareness of the ecclesiastical censures which fell upon its first purchasers,

---

has been arranged in the basement, a wing of which is built up from and still rests upon the foundations of part of the old monastery buildings.

[543] At the bottom of the 1909 handbill announcing this sale of "the lovely Property of the Crosiers" is an advertisement in bold print claiming that, "By its location, which is somewhat isolated but still within the city limits, this property is admirably suited for someone who desires quiet, *for a religious community,*" etc. What an ironic reversal, after precisely one hundred years!

and hints also of a kind of immanent misfortune which affirms the reality of a past which remains always present: the suppression of the Crosiers, the plundering of their home, and their scattering.

* * *

That scattering of the last Crosiers of Huy is all which remains for us to consider, and so still the final echoes resounding from "the end of Clairlieu."

After two years of rigorous oppression, the religious who lived in the conquered territories had yet to endure five years of terror. In the closing years of the eighteenth century, however, what dominated events and fascinated the masses was not the hardships which continued to befall victims of the suppression but the great to-do surrounding Napoleon's victories. As a result, nearly all these outlawed religious are without a history. The stories of their lives, like the few traces of them, inevitably pass silently away into the pain of isolation, hardship and oblivion. What follows are mere gleanings from the small and scattered historical sources, gathered for the most part alongside the paths of misfortune which mark the routes into exile taken by the Crosiers of Clairlieu so long ago.

Henri DEMET returned to Liège, where he had been born on November 7, 1753, and took up residence at 821 Rue Féronstrée.[544] On 27 Germinal, year V (March 17, 1797), he accepted the retirement benefit which he had refused the previous January 26 and which enabled him, on 17 Messidor, year VI (July 5, 1798), to repurchase from a former Capuchin named Daenen the farmstead known as la Menagerie, which was located at Embourg and had once been the property of

---

[544] *Bulletin de la Societe d'Art et d'Histoire* 24 (1932) 183.

the Crosiers of Liège.[545] On May 12, and again on June 20, Huy's municipal council informed Liège that, because H. Demet was "predisposed to emigration," he "ought to be put on the list of those sentenced to be deported." The Central Administration refused to do this and, on 21 Fructidor, year VI (September 8, 1798), replied that "these were deplorable presumptions against this citizen."[546] In the summer of 1802 Demet was still living in Liège, for on July 1 of that same year, the city's mayor made a formal declaration that he was a resident and on 16 Messidor (July 5) provided him with a certificate attesting that he had made the promise of fidelity to the Constitution,[547] one of the conditions necessary "for being added to the roll of ecclesiastical pensioners."[548] Demet subsequently left Liège and moved to Bettincourt (or Bettenhoven), where he enjoyed a pension of 267 francs paid three times annually,[549] and must have lived there in retirement, in the home of a family member or friend, while awaiting an opening in a parish, for in the spring of 1816 (on March 9), he became pastor of Darion and also served Ligney, Omal and Manil. He seems to have been able to meet these heavy responsibilities only until the summer of 1819, since the last baptism which he recorded was on July 5, 1819, whereas the record of a marriage, on the following September 5, bears the signature of his successor, Father

---

[545] See E. Fontaine, O.S.C., "Les Croisiers de Liège en face de la suppression", II *Clairlieu* 7 (1949) 39.

[546] State Archives, Liège; see Annexe 7 (Fontaine, "La Fin de Clairlieu," 39).

[547] Among other provisions, the Concordat signed by Napoleon and the Pope in 1801 did away with the revolutionary oaths demanded of the clergy and allowed them to declare their support of the French government. – Tr.

[548] State Archives, Liège, French regime, files pertinent to ecclesiastical pensions, no. 2227.

[549] Archives of the Chamber of Records, Brussels, no. 411.

Pasque. We may conclude that, by the fall of 1819, this former Crosier's health was failing and that he must have died around the age of sixty-six.

Our last trace of the presence of Christophe Deneumoulin[550] in Huy coincides with the sale of the farmstead at Envoz, from which he was entitled to one-sixteenth of the payment. By then (October 24, 1797), however, he had already left the city. He seems to have separated himself from confreres in exile when he saw them accommodate themselves to the civic declaration, and to have taken refuge in his native city of Tongeren.[551] There, in September of that same year, he categorically refused to the oath of hatred and thus was put on the "fatal list" of the Lower Meuse, canton of Tongeren, and sentenced to be deported.[552] He certainly must have sought to escape, but we do not know if he was arrested. Since there is no death-record for him in Tongeren, he probably did not die there; no modern record in that city bears his family's surname.

---

[550] He was the son of Servais Deneumoulin and Marie Hermans, and had been born at Tongeren on August 20,1753. One of his several brothers, Hubert Antoine (born November 18,1766), had joined the Franciscans and became pastor of Meth after the suppression of Belgium's religious houses; he died at Tongeren on January 30, 1832.

[551] There he must have encountered other Crosiers who had, like him, been expelled from their homes and taken refuge in the same city. Three had belonged to the monastery at Kolen and the fourth to that at Maaseik: Jacques Nicolas Cornely, also one of the nonjuring clergy, who died at Tongeren on March 11, 1829, at the age of eighty-four; Henri van Langenacker, who died at Tongeren on July 6, 1856, at the age of eighty-seven; Bernard Domen, also one of the nonjuring clergy, who died on November 1, 1797, at the age of fifty-five; and Jean Guillaume Lemmens, a member of the nonjuring clergy and sentenced to be deported, who died at Tongeren on May 25, 1814.

[552] Daris, *Histoire de la Principaute*, 4:159.

Prior General Jacques Dubois, O.S.C.

Born at Grandville on March 24, 1752, Martin Germeau had been prior of the monastery at Suxy while remaining a conventual of Huy. He took refuge at Noiseux, in the province of Namur, and was still living there in 1803, when he made numerous efforts to claim a pension under the terms of the Concordat. Because he had not accepted the retirement benefit and therefore did not appear on the list of the Crosiers of Huy compiled at the time of their suppression, he was refused any claim to a pension.[553] He thus became the victim of a galling negligence, and we have no idea of whether he was later more successful in asserting his claim. We also know nothing about when or where he died.

Louis Antoine Hansotte was born at Huy on March 5, 1731, the son of Jean François Hansotte and Dieudonné Feuille. Because he was tonsured at Liège on June 3, 1746, by the suffragan bishop P. L. Jacquet, the young man was very probably a seminary student at the time. He entered the Crosier monastery in his native city only in 1750, and made his profession there on April 19, 1751. He was ordained a subdeacon on September 23, 1752, a deacon on June 16, 1753, and a priest on March 15, 1755. Installed as prior of Carignan on July 14, 1780, he enjoyed neither a long nor happy term of office. From 1787 onwards he was in conflict with members of the French clergy hungry for prebends and was denied his right to confer benefices on the grounds that he was not a French national. The only result of this conflict was his being placed under a restraining order.[554] Ousted, Hansotte returned to Huy and resumed his place at Clairlieu, but not for

---

[553] State Archives, Liège, French regime, files pertinent to ecclesiastical pensions, no. 2230.

[554] National Archives, Paris, file on the Crosiers of Huy, G. 9 136, formerly 0 636. An account of this incident appears in our article, "Mgr. Jacques Dubois et la fin du Prieure de Carignan," *Clairlieu* 8 (1950) 46-66.

long, since Belgium's religious houses were suppressed on September 1, 1796. Of advanced age and twice banished, he did not survive to suffer. He retired to his family's home in Huy, where he died on September 2, 1798, at the age of sixty-seven, only two years after the suppression of his monastery. Until recently, the Hansotte family kept up and decorated the small shrine to St. Domitian in Huy. The custom, says R. Dubois,[555] most certainly traces its roots back to this former Crosier.

We have seen that, so long as the Crosiers of Huy remained caretakers of their monastery, they resided in that part of the city known as le Sarte, Lambert HAYWEGHEN, who had been born in Looz on July 31, 1753, must have lived there with them for about four years, and necessarily so. He had hidden the reliquary of St. Odilia and, so long as rigorous measures were taken against the clergy, he could not move it elsewhere: all religious were obliged to record any change of residence, and harsh reprisals were taken against those who had removed things from their suppressed houses. We must assume that Hayweghen could have risked the bold step of moving the reliquary only after the signing of the Concordat, so it must have been around 1801 that he took it to Looz, in Limburg, where he guarded it for most of the next thirty years. When he realized that he had not too many more years to live (he was seventy-five), he entrusted his precious prize to the church at Kerniel. He died at Looz six years later, on July 20, 1835. Daris, the historian of the diocese of Liège, knew him, and was so edified by the example of this elderly priest that he considered himself honored to have sometimes helped him recite his breviary.[556]

[555] *Les Rues de Huy,* 186.
[556] G. Monchamp, "Le chanoine Daris, " *Revue ecclesiastique de Liège* (Liège,

Jean François Jerosme[557] also took up residence in the district of le Sarte and likewise must have left Huy only some years later. What especially kept him on seems to have been certain civic duties. On 1 Prairial, year VII (May 20, 1799), the Central Administration appointed him a "trial juror for the canton of Huy,"[558] and to a second such three-month term on 1 Ventôse, year VIII (February 20, 1800).[559] He was thus the only Crosier of Huy who assumed public functions, and in his second term was reunited with Ista, who had in the meanwhile become president of the court of petty sessions. On February 20, 1800, in company with Noiville, he took the oath of loyalty to the Constitution of the Clergy.[560] On August 11, 1802, he requested and obtained a passport, number 133, which was valid for one year and allowed him to travel in the various adjacent departments of Belgium.[561] His travels in early August 1802, must have been occasioned by the steps he had to take to receive the pension provided for by the Concordat and to finally establish a permanent residence for himself. Jérosme also had in his possession some items removed from Clairlieu and was no doubt very anxious to move them. He finally came to rest in Braives, somewhat under two miles from the village where he had been born. He must have been welcomed there by his parents and his brother, Jean Pierre Jérosme, a former Franciscan

---

1905) 186.

[557] The son of Gregoire Jerosme and Marie Annes Colmet, he had been born at Avennes on January 13, 1753.

[558] Archives, city of Huy, Register 406, 126. There were five such jurors, selected for a term of only three months but eligible for another after each.

[559] Ibid., 217.

[560] Ibid., 219.

[561] Archives, city of Huy, Register of Passports, no. 11, for the date specified.

who had already taken up residence in the same area. The Crosier Jérosme died on June 11, 1828, at the age of seventy-six.[562] The vault of the Jérosme of Avennes still stands in the cemetery of Robermont, and we are left to suppose that the remains of this former Crosier of Huy now rest under its aristocratic marble.

Jean Joseph LaCroix, who had been prior of the monastery at Virton while remaining a conventual of Huy, was appointed caretaker of his suppressed and confiscated monastery. The auction of Virton took place on 21 Pluviose, year V (February 9, 1797), and Lacroix repurchased the place for himself at the price of 14,700 francs, which he paid from his retirement benefit. A legal document prepared by Michel de Virton informs us that, two years later, on 21 Germinal, year VII (April 10, 1799), he sold to Mr. Jean Louis Magnette all the properties which he had acquired on February 9, 1797, in consideration of an annual return and lifetime annuity of 420 florins or 900 pounds tournois. On February 3, 1800, Lacroix "resigned his citizenship" to the municipal council and left Virton. In 1824, he was still alive and residing at Longuion; we do not know when he died.[563]

We know nothing of what became of Pierre Philippe Joseph Bernard Loncin[564] after the suppression of Clairlieu. Until September 1797, he lived at number 318 in the district of le Sarte with his confrere Jérosme. In the quieter days which

---

[562] C. Thimister, *Necrologe du clerge liegeois, 336.*

[563] P. Roger, *Notices historiques sur la Ville de Virton* (Virton, 1932), 395-396. This valuable work contains so much information about the Crosiers of Virton that there is no further need for someone to write the history of their monastery. The sources of which the author has made special use are in the Crosier files of the State Archives at Arlon.

[564] The son of Pierre de Loncin and Marie Isabelle Hoyoux, he had been born on January 17, 1757. (parish archives of Villers le Temple).

followed the signing of the Concordat, he most probably would have reported his residence as Villers le Temple, where he was born, but we cannot be sure. Loncin had two brothers and two sisters, and the lack of any subsequent trace of the Loncin at Villers suggests that they moved elsewhere and that their Crosier brother retired in one or the other of their homes. The archives of Villers le Temple are wholly silent about what became of this former Crosier and our search there for the date of his death proved vain.

After the Crosiers had been dismissed as Clairlieu's caretakers, their former subprior, Jean Paul Joseph de Noiville,[565] lived by himself at number 93 in the district of le Sarte On February 20, 1800, he made the promise of fidelity to the Constitution and, during 1801, was issued passport number 458, but left no record of his proposed destination. In the wake of the Concordat, he provided several attestations on behalf of his former confreres at Huy. Two such are recorded for September 13, 1802 and 1803: one on behalf of Theodore Tille, who was living at Tihange, and the other on behalf of Martin Germeau, the former prior of Suxy.[566] Documents of this sort attested that the interested parties had been Crosiers of the monastery at Huy and declared whether or not they had received the national retirement benefit, i.e., the two former religious were seeking to regulate their standing under the law governing ecclesiastical pensions. We may assume that, because of his office at Clairlieu, Noiville would have provided similar information about others of his former confreres, too. Although he had been born in Namur

---

[565] The son of Jean Paul de Noiville and Marie Catherine Lambert, he had been born at Namur on July 23, 1733, in the parish of St. Michel.
[566] State Archives, Liège, French regime, files pertinent to ecclesiastical pensions, no. 2230.

and, assuming they were still alive, had two brothers and a sister there, Noiville seems never to have left Huy, for he died there on 20 Ventôse, year XIII (March 9, 1805).[567]

Although born in Liège on December 10, 1746, Lambert Theodore Tille chose to seek a place of refuge in Tihange, near Huy. Unless there was another individual with the same names and also a religious, Lambert Theodore Tille refused to take the oath of hatred. To avoid pursuit, he withdrew for some time to Liers, near Liège. Apprehended all the same, he was imprisoned for three long months and freed only by a decree of July 11, 1799.[568] On September 11, 1802, he took the oath of allegiance to the Concordat by declaring himself in communion with the bishops nominated by Napoleon.[569] If he died at Tihange while still residing at number 609, the parish records furnish no information about it.

Jacques Joseph Tilman at first refused to accept the retirement benefit of 15,000 francs when his monastery was suppressed in January of 1797. After Rome decided, on February 4 of that same year, that it was licit to use such benefits to repurchase the possessions of one's monastery,[570] however, Tilman requested and received his (no. 3980 in the records), but it was later annulled.[571] He managed to avoid both making the civil declaration and taking the oath of hatred, but did make the promise of fidelity to the Constitution at

---

[567] Archives, city of Huy, Civil Records.

[568] Daris, *Histoire dela Principaute*, 3:290; see also the appendix to the same volume, xlv.

[569] State Archives, Liège, French regime, files pertinent to ecclesiastical pensions.

[570] Daris, *Histoire de la Principaute*, 3:86.

[571] On 25 Vendemiaire, year X (October 17, 1801), according to the State Archives, Liège, French regime, files pertinent to ecclesiastical pensions, no. 2224.

Huy.[572] In the fall of 1803 he was still living in that city, for on September 13 of that year he accompanied his former confrere, Father Germeau (then sixty-one years old), to city hall to help him get a certificate of residence.[573] We do not know where or when Tilman died.

From the suppression of Clairlieu until the signing of the Concordat, there is no trace of Pierre Lambert Warnotte[574] in Belgium. On 29 Germinal, year VI (April 18, 1798), when the hunt was on for non-swearing clergy, the city of Huy informed Liège that "former Crosier Warnotte was a fugitive."[575] Had he perhaps joined those in Germany? He was declared an exile, and only in 1802, with Napoleon's suppression of religious houses in the Rhineland and the availability of the pension in Belgium, did he give some sign of life. Instructions came to his mother, Mrs. E. Brassine, the widow of J. Warnotte and owner of a farmstead at Remicourt, "to go to request for him an attested affidavit from the City of Huy." With the help of the lawyer Francotte, his mother succeeded in having the document issued on 16 Pluviôse, year X (February 6, 1802.) Emboldened by this first success, Warnotte returned to Belgium and got himself a certificate of residence near Maire de Remicourt. Four months later, on 19 Prairial, year X (Tuesday, June 9, 1802), he appeared before the Prefect, seated in consular rank, to make the promise of fidelity[576] and fulfill all the legal formalities required for re-

---

[572] Archives, city of Huy, French regime, Register of Meetings, 15 Fructidor, fol. 9, 59 verso.

[573] Archives, city of Huy, French regime, Register of Passports, no. 2; see Annexe 8 (Fontaine, "La Fin de Clairlieu," 40).

[574] The son of Jean Warnotte and Elisabeth Brassine, he had been born at Remicourt on June 22, 1751.

[575] Grandmaison, *Souvenirs de Huy,* 73.

[576] State Archives, Liège, files pertinent to ecclesiastical pensions, no. 2240.

ceipt of a pension. He must never again have left his native city, for he died there on 14 Fructidor, year XII (September 4, 1804) "at three o'clock in the afternoon."[577] He was only fifty-three.

Something essential would be missing from this note about Father Warnotte if we did not refer to his connection with the fate of the valuables and archives taken from Clairlieu to Germany during the early stages of the Revolution, which he and L. Meyers were sent in search of at Duisburg.[578] But is this not a disputed point? Can we be sure the two Crosiers ever completed their mission? The answer is no longer a problem. That the two men set out for Duisburg is proven by the passports which the Central Administration issued them at the time: Meyers' on 22 Fructidor, year IV (September 9, 1796) and Warnotte's the next day. The records also clearly stipulate that the purpose of their journey was "to retrieve the silver objects, the records and effects of the Monastery of the Crosiers of Huy.[579] What remains to be determined is whether they did so and when. Precise answers to these questions are provided by Warnotte t s mother herself. In the sworn affidavit cited above she says that, when her son was" sent to the conquered territory of Germany with the commission of his confreres to go there to recover the objects and, because of the war, move them to a monastery of their Order, he remained there until about the month of Frimaire, year V."[580] Because Frimaire of year V corresponds to November 21 through December 20, 1796, we can be sure that

---

[577] Remicourt, Civil Records, year XII; document of 14 Fructidor, year XII.

[578] See pages 88-89 and 96.

[579] Archives, city of Huy, French regime, no. 346: 1st Register of Passports, fol. 13 and 15; see Annexe 9 (Fontaine, "La Fin de Clairlieu," 41).

[580] Archives, city of Huy, French regime, Register of Passports, no. 2; see Annexe 10 (Fontaine, "La Fin de Clairlieu," 41).

the items in question were returned to Huy before the death of Prior General Dubois on December 21. Further confirmation of their return can be found in the fact that the record *Pro luminario albo*, which the Crosiers of Huy several times declared, during 1795 and 1796, was in Duisburg, today rests among the few odds and ends which comprise the "Sources: Crosiers of Huy" in the State Archives at Liège.[581] Herewith, then, is the solution of a problem which we have encountered at each step of our investigation, i.e., the mystery of Clairlieu's "vanished" archives.

Such, in sum, was the end of Clairlieu: assailed by the Revolution, swept up in its whirlwind, delivered over to its judgment, devastated by its pillage and, at the last, laid low by pickax and crowbar. The mother house which once embodied the hope of the Order's stability and perpetuity was so hatefully leveled, so literally swept from the earth, that today not a single ray of hope shines over its ruins. Never had the Order undergone a misfortune more dire or more cruel, never had its vitality received a blow more grievous or more catastrophic. But ruin was not annihilation. With its six centuries of life at an end, Clairlieu stands forever in the memory of the Order of which it was the cradle: an imperishable memory which has survived the fragile buildings which the cataclysm turned to dust. However much threatened with extinction, the Order of the Holy Cross retained sufficient sources of vitality to survive those tumultuous times and to lay the foundations of its rebirth.

---

[581] See also Annexe 1, notably the comments which follow no. 28 (Fontaine, "La Fin de Clairlieu," 34).

CHAPTER NINE
DEFINITORIUM, 1796-1803

Few religious orders have found themselves in so precarious a situation as did that of the Holy Cross at the time of the French Revolution.[582]

With origins in the early thirteenth century, the Order had encompassed more than eighty monasteries scattered about the European continent at the height of its splendor. In less than three centuries, however, it had grown considerably smaller. Henry VIII had suppressed the English monasteries. In the next century, the Protestant Reformation had made the first inroads against those in Germany, notably in the Netherlands.[583] Joseph II had subsequently leveled three more in the Austrian Netherlands. Finally, the Revolution of 1789 had dissolved the fourteen in France. These successive mutilations had left the Order some thirty houses spread across Belgium, the Netherlands and Germany when Jourdan's victory at Fleurus on June 25, 1794, delivered Belgium into French hands. That day the Order might have sensed that it

---

[582] This article appeared in Clairlieu 10 (1952) 28-36 as "Le Definitoire (1796-1803)." – Tr.

[583] Parts of the modern Netherlands were then part of the old Hapsburg or Austro-German Empire. – Tr.

would experience anew the misfortunes of the previous centuries, for it was soon wholly within the net of the invaders' secularization.

The drama began on September 1, 1796, when all religious congregations in Belgium were suppressed and their possessions confiscated by the state. This proscription thus struck at the Crosier monasteries of Virton, Suxy, Dinant, Huy, Liège, Kolen, Maastricht, Maaseik, of Venlo and Aachen, too, and eight others on the left bank of the Rhine. For the latter, however, the effects of the act of suppression would be felt only later; after that, the seven other of the Order's monasteries on the right bank of the river would be harassed and sacrificed in their turn. The first victims, however, would be the Belgian monasteries, beginning with the most important of them: Clairlieu at Huy, the mother house of the whole Order. In 1797, its members were expelled, and their monastery sold, then totally demolished.[584]

Only two monasteries in the Dutch republic, those of St. Agatha and Uden, both in south Brabant,[585] had some chance of escaping the catastrophe. That does not mean, however, they were able to avoid the depredations of the French. Quite the contrary; St. Agatha had especially suffered from the soldiers garrisoned within its walls between 1793 and 1796.[586] Even when the French had finally left, there was no reason to think these two monasteries had some hope of being spared. But then, and against all expectation, the ceding of the territories of Ravenstein, Megen and Boksmeer to

---

[584] See E. Fontaine, *a.s.c.*, "La Fin de Clairlieu," *Clairlieu* 9 (1951) 6-42. (added as Chapter Eight in this English translation. – Tr.)

[585] Brabant lay to the north and west of the area once governed by the bishops of Liège. – Tr.

[586] Archives of St. Agatha, an account-book of the period.

the Netherlands on January 5, 1800, left the two monasteries under a different law regarding religious houses: St. Agatha and Uden would henceforth be outside the secularizing reach of the First Consul,[587] and therein at last shone a glimmer of salvation.

The situation was complicated, however, by the accidental factor of the Order's internal polity, viz., the disorganization surrounding its central government. The death of Prior General Jacques Dubois on December 21, 1796, coincided with the application of the law suppressing religious congregations, especially in Belgium. The scattered religious were thus faced with a twofold danger: they both lived under the external threat of suppression and had to face internal problems of a hierarchical nature. Did the Order not, in these critical days, need a vigorous, intelligent, loving and therefore forceful Prior General?

There was, of course, another body with jurisdiction on the general level: the definitorium. Under normal circumstances, this consisted of four members elected by the previous general chapter and was able, in case of the death of the Prior General, to provisionally assume his powers. The outbreak of war had prevented a general chapter from meeting in 1792, however, and the sitting definitors were still those who had been elected in 1786: Wilhelmus Jacobs, prior of Schwarzenbroich in the Rhineland; Joseph Leurs, prior of the suppressed monastery at Maastricht; and Lambert Meyers, who had formerly belonged to the monastery in Liège but had been detached from it since 1789 by his incorporation into the canonical chapter of the collegial church of St. Denis. (That had not, however, kept him from functioning as a de-

---

[587] Napoleon's title after his seizure of power in November 1799. – Tr.

finitor several times during the six years which followed; the mandate he had received in 1786 was therefore deemed still to be in force.) The fourth, Wilhelmus Loverix, prior of St. Agatha in the Netherlands, had died in 1793, but the Order's constitutions did make provision for the vacancy caused by his death. Henricus Peters, prior of the German monastery at Briiggen, was the only surviving definitor of those who had bee elected at the second-last chapter[588] and so was entitled to fill the seat of Loverix.

Soon after the death of Prior General, the definitors were called on to end the handicap under which the Order's central government labored and which seemed so dangerous to it in those dark days. The initiative began in Germany, with I. G. Mertens and H. Gossens, the priors of Marienfrede and Emmerich, respectively. They and their supporters would soon make every effort to see that the effort succeeded, viz., a proposal meant to re-establish the Order's central government on foundations which took account of the factors in the new situation. They summarized their position as follows: since the course of events had made it impossible to elect a successor to the deceased Prior General, it was imperative that, as in the case of other orders, an assembly of the sitting definitors and priors name, within three months, a commissioner general who would be invested with the jurisdictional authority of a prior general for the purpose of maintaining discipline and attending to the most pressing matters.[589] To that end, the two priors conferred with several of their peers and with Peters and Meyers, whom they appar-

---

[588] The others elected in 1779 had been Arnold Odendal, prior of Cologne, who died in 1782; Jacques Comely, prior of Hohenbusch, who died in 1785; and Anton ab Oeyen, prior of Venlo, who died in 1794. (Hermans, *Annales*, 3:571 and 577.)

[589] Hermans, *Annales*, 3:598.

ently had soon rallied to their cause. With firm resolution and full knowledge of what was involved, however, Leurs and Jacobs took the opposite position in the debate over this matter. To take such a step, they argued, was premature, and there was even merit in not taking it.

Opinion thus remained divided in the four months after the death of Prior General Dubois. The two Rhineland priors then deemed it necessary to overcome the delay in adopting their proposal. They decided to conduct a referendum among the Dutch and German priors, and so addressed to the latter, on April 10, 1797, a circular letter intended to rally them to their own point of view and so remove the obstacle which Leurs and Jacobs had set in the way of naming a commissioner general. Anticipating effective support in achieving their objective, Mertens and Gossens also took care to note in their letter that the other definitors and several priors did not agree with the opinion advanced by Leurs and Jacobs.[590]

Did the Order in fact not then find itself at the most critical juncture in its history, a time so filled with dangers of every sort that its very existence was threatened? What reason might Leurs and Jacobs have had to delay a step which seemed so urgently required?

The reason was quite simple, although it involved some rather complex considerations. Certain points of law in fact demanded the exercise of special prudence regarding the proposal advanced by Mertens and Gossens. The latter's foundations were the regulations enacted by the Council of Trent regarding canons regular,[591] and we must assume that, in seeking to be guided by them, the two priors were acting

---

[590] Hermans, *Annales*, 3:598.
[591] See Hermans, *Annales*, 3:598.

in the best of faith. Leurs and Jacobs were also worthy men, and too upright to have raised objections to the pressure for adopting this measure without sound motives. What the two more circumspect definitors had taken into account was that Trent's provisions assumed strict adherence to the bulls which Pope Innocent VIII had issued on October 27 and 29, 1489, regulating the election of a Crosier *prior maior* in case of the latter's death or resignation. The norms in these bulls, which had been added to the Order's constitutions, stipulated that (1) the election must take place only in the mother house at Huy and (2) not only did the sitting definitors and those of the preceding general chapter have the right to vote but so did all the conventuals of that house who had been promoted to at least the subdiaconate. Further, were not the Crosiers bound to observe the regulations and procedures established for this traditional practice of election under penalty of excommunication?[592]

When the two German priors circulated their letter of April 10, 1797, Clairlieu still stood (it would not be demolished until the summer of 1798) and its conventuals were still in residence (they would not be expelled until September 11 of that same year). Their claim to the monastery of Clairlieu at Huy was still valid and could not be denied under the law. That was, therefore, the first point of law which had to be considered, but there was a second and even a third which required no less consideration. The second was that, even were they dispersed, the conventuals of Clairlieu could in no way be said to have lost their right to vote in the election. Indeed, because these Crosiers were under perpetual vows, they had in no way been legally separated from their Order; they were still members of it and could at best be said to

---

[592] Hermans, *Annales,* 2:51, 428 and 431.

have been II separated II from it only by a forced secularization. Just as they remained bound to observe the substance of their vows, the dissolution of their monastery in no way abolished their privileges, so long as their secularization was not formally and finally legalized by their voluntary submission to the jurisdiction of a bishop. On the other hand, no one could ignore a further point which Mertens and Gossens had also made, viz., that the Crosiers of Huy, except for De-met, Tilman and Warnotte, had for all practical purposes acquiesced to the misleading theories behind the French regime.[593]

The election of a commissioner general thus involved such delicate questions that one could not avoid the alternative; nor could one ignore the Crosiers of Huy by replacing them with all the priors of the Order as Mertens and Gossens were suggesting, for that would be to risk that the balloting could be challenged as invalid; nor could one ignore the priors of the Order so as to avoid violating the rights of the Crosiers at Clairlieu, for that might block the good intentions behind the proposal. The Crosiers of Huy would, as everyone was aware, form the majority of voters in any election, and that could mean that what resulted from it would be the appearance of leadership instead of the reality: something which had to be avoided by all means and at all costs.

Under such circumstances, and especially because it had been raised in such agitated times, the question of electing a commissioner general seemed not only insoluble but extremely delicate. Recourse to the Holy See would of course have allowed the prompt settlement of the difficulties through an authoritative interpretation of the assumptions

---

[593] Hermans, *Annales*, 3:599.

surrounding the issue, but it was precisely during these years of 1797 through 1799 that the French invaded the Papal States, expelled Pius VI from Rome, and then escorted him to southern France, where he died at Valence in August 1799.

Our brief sketch reveals that Leurs and Jacobs had good reason and more to argue for waiting, and equally that their opinion was founded much more on principle and the constraints imposed from within the Order than on their views about the future course of political events, as the annalist C. R. Hermans thought.[594] Moreover, the two definitors agreed both with their peers and with Mertens and Gossens on the substance of the proposal but were obliged to differ with them on its execution, both in the interests of the Order and for the sake of prudence and of charity as well. We can further assume that the two Rhineland priors came to agree with them and that the disagreement over the question grew noticeably less, for there is no further trace of the sort of pleas which they had at first so energetically put forward.

In the meanwhile, it is true, all attention was turned to the new course which events were taking. On November 9, 1799, the French government suddenly found itself with the office of the Consulate, a coup d'etat which was everywhere greeted with enthusiasm because of the peace and order which it brought to the Republic. Its effects soon made themselves felt in the conditions under which the clergy lived, too. In virtue of the new law of 11 Ventôse, year VIII (March 2, 1800), the benefits issued to former members of the suppressed monasteries and convents were exchanged for a yearly pension, provided that the priests entered the ranks of the diocesan clergy. The situation was further improved when, on July 15,

---

[594] Hermans, *Annales,* 1(2):169.

1801, Napoleon signed the Concordat which re-established the exercise of cult and provided the diocesan clergy with a suitable salary. Finally, after Pius VII, who had been elected at Venice, was able to return to Rome and ratify the Concordat on August 15,1801, all the priests of the diocese of Liège, and the Crosiers of Huy, too, accepted it and made lithe promise of fidelity to the Constitution.[595]

Henceforth we will find these Crosiers of Huy multiplying their efforts to be enrolled on the "list of pensioned priests. II Strictly speaking, however, they had no claim to avail themselves of the law providing for such pensions since all of them, save for Tille, Tilman and Demet, had accepted and profited by the government's retirement benefit when their monastery had been suppressed. Thus they variously encountered numerous difficulties which hindered that process, so that it was only shortly before the fall of 1803 that they were allowed the privilege they sought. There was, however, a condition *sine qua non* attached to it. Cardinal Legate Caprara, who formally erected the new diocese of Liège on April 10, 1802, notified the Crosiers of Huy "that they had to renounce being part of a foreign congregation if they wished to justify their right to the pension. II Seeing themselves thus obliged by the Cardinal's will to change their status, they declared their assent.[596]

This step was of the greatest import and consequence. By it, the Crosiers of Huy radically changed their status as canons

---

[595] Fathers Noiville and Jerosme had done so on February 20, 1800; Father Tilman did so on September 13, 1801; Brother Walth ere Heusquet on June 5, 1802; Father Warnotte on June 9, 1802; Father Demet on July 5, 1802; and Father Tille on September 11, 1802. (State Archives, Liège, French regime, files pertinent to ecclesiastical pensions.)
[596] Hermans, *Annales*, 3:605

regular and the rights attached to their privileges as such. They had that day put an end to everything which, both in fact and in law, bound them to their confreres outside the borders of French-occupied Belgium. Henceforth they were incardinated into the diocese, the first canonical effect of which was to subject them to and make them dependent on the local bishop. The result was the immediate end of their entitlement to voting rights, since the latter were inseparable from their status as conventuals of Huy. The cessation of their status and rights removed any disagreement there might have been regarding one aspect of the election of a new Crosier general superior: hereafter only the sitting definitors would have the legal right to full and complete voice in chapter regarding everything which touched on the governance of the Order.

Did this mean that the Order would now accede to the long-standing wish of the Rhineland priors and move to the election of a commissioner general? No, for the question had another aspect which had to be considered: if all reservations concerning the Crosiers of Huy had fallen by the wayside, there was a further difficulty which recommended continuing the wise delay. What could cause further uneasiness about this problem, which seemed for all intents and purposes to have been solved? A kind of ill-defined discomfort about the definitorium itself. Heretofore, thanks especially to the spirit of moderation and watchful zeal displayed by Leurs and Jacobs, the definitorium had shown itself a rather solid, firm, even efficient entity, but now it was giving signs of disunity. Peters had died in the meanwhile, and one consequence of his death was the unhappy claim, improperly and presumptuously made by one of the Rhineland priors, I.

Mertens, to the prerogatives of a definitor.[597] We have already noted that, should one of its members die, the definitorium could fill the vacancy in its ranks from among those who had been elected to the office at the previous chapter. Unlike Peters, however, Mertens had not been elected to the definitorium in 1779 but in 1773,[598] i.e., at the Order's third-last general chapter. This did not, according to the Order's legislation, entitle him to a seat on the definitorium if a vacancy occurred. And account also had to be taken of Lambert Meyers, a rather enigmatic figure who had increasingly distanced himself from the Order's affairs[599] and whose unstable and questionable past[600] risked the further complication of the juridical questions which had for too long already afflicted the definitorium. Leurs and Jacobs thus determined to attempt nothing which might not please all their confreres: again they waited, and decided to leave things in their provisional state. We must hasten to add, however, that this appears to be more of a suspension of leadership than it actually was, for the two definitors did not cease taking steps which adequately met the chief problems.

We must also now pay homage, at the distance of a century and a half, to both the German and the Dutch monasteries for the insightfulness and the valor which they displayed in these hours of darkness and long years of internal uneasiness.

At the head of the list is Brüggen, the German monastery which, to its immortal honor, dared to elect a new prior on

---

[597] See the letter in Hermans, *Annales,* 3:599, where Mertens signs himself "prior and definitor of the Order."

[598] Hermans, *Annales, 3:575.*

[599] Hermans, *Annales, 3:605.*

[600] See pages 5-6.

September 18, 1797, even though its members had been threatened with suppression since 1796.[601] Leurs and Jacobs presided over the election of Johannes Boetzkes.[602] The monastery at Emmerich maintained the reputation of its school, and its program of study continued without interruption.[603] That at Duisburg remained unbowed, too, holding fast in its resistance despite its extreme poverty. Not one of these monasteries ceased fighting, step by step, against the perils which pursued the Order on both the left and right banks of the Rhine.

There is similar evidence of the fidelity of the two Dutch monasteries. Uden held firm because of the unwearying diligence of J. V. Beek, Henri van Rooy and the learned Wilhelmus Ryken, who were aided by Theodorus van de Leygraaf, a priest from a suppressed Capuchin monastery. In 1802, this community even grew, by the addition of W. Leyten, who was already a priest.

If we judge it by its history during this period, however, it was St. Agatha which gave the most powerful witness of unity and purpose. From June 1794 until 1799, it had no lack of refugees, mostly priests and religious.[604] In those somber days, Willem Wynantz[605] presided over the destiny of his

---

[601] Hermans, *Annales*, 1(2):170.
[602] Hermans, *Annales*, 3:599.
[603] Hermans, *Annales*, 3:621-622.
[604] See L. Emond, O.S.C., "Het Klooster Sint Agatha in den lande van Cuyk," *Kruistriomf* 3 (1923) 147.
[605] The son of Gysbert Wynantz and Sara van Cruchten, he had been born at Venray on February 7, 1736. After completing his studies at Venray and at the major seminary in Roermond, he entered St. Agatha on September 8, 1755, and was professed the next year. Thereafter he served as sacristan, catechist and, from 1767 onward, as the monastery's procurator, an office he would hold for forty years, until his death.

monastery. More than any other, perhaps, he stood out among his confreres of the time for his realism and reasoned optimism. Hardly had St. Agatha once more found itself within the Dutch borders (January 5, 1800) than Wynantz took it upon himself to obtain from the state the renewal of the contract under which the Crosiers leased their monastery for an annual fee of 1,700 florins.[606] On May 6, 1800, it was done, and the Crosiers of St. Agatha were assured a dozen more years of tranquil residence in their ancestral home. Peace without growth, however, was no great prize, so the President[607] promptly undertook efforts, which he carried out well and thoroughly among those in high places, to have his monastery granted, as it had been in the past, the right to admit eight novices. This was conceded on November 23, 1802, but with the restriction that such permission, given two years after the renewal of the lease, would last only for the ten years remaining in it.[608] It was a galling restriction, of course, but what somewhat tempered its bitterness was that such prohibitions had burdened these Crosiers since 1753. Finally, less than a month and half later, Wynantz's keen foresight led him to re-establish the office of prior in his community.

St. Agatha had at the time only four conventuals, of whom Wynantz himself was the oldest, at sixty-eight.[609] His con-

---

[606] The government had usurped ownership of St. Agatha in 1653. Thereafter the Crosiers had had to rent their home by contract with the state.

[607] The title under which Wynantz directed *St. Agatha's* affairs. Wilhelmus Loverix, the monastery's previous prior, had died in 1793 and not yet been replaced. – Tr.

[608] Hermans, *Annales*, 3:600-601.

[609] L. Emond, O.S.C., *Kruisheren Missionarissen*, 56. Father Joannes Kieviets had been incardinated into the church of Heeze as curate in 1798; he afterwards became pastor at Empel (1808) and then at Zevenbergen, where

freres, all of them also nearly in their seventies, were J. A. Schwartz, and H. van Yperen. There was serious need, then, to revivify, indeed to rejuvenate, the little group of religious. When St. Agatha's President informed the definitors of his "priorial project, II Leurs came to preside over the election on January 3, 1803. We do not know if he was surprised by the results of the election, but every vote cast was for him. Without a moment's hesitation, he accepted. On January 6, at the request of the community, definitors Jacobs and then Meyers ratified the election.[610]

It was no small thing for the youngest definitor (he was fifty-four) to accept this new office: resuming his religious habit required him to leave the comfortable and honorable retirement which he had enjoyed among members of his family at Sittard for the past six years.[611] His action appears even more meritorious and courageous in light of Napoleon's suppression, less than a year earlier (June 1802), of the nine Crosier monasteries on the right bank of the Rhine. In his Order's increasingly weakened condition, then, Leurs had joined these four old men and had made his own their resolve to

---

he died on April 17, 1814, at the age of seventy-eight.

[610] Hermans, *Annales*, 3:602-603.

[611] The son of Laurent Leurs and Marie Catherine Schmaekers, Joseph Leurs had been born at Sittard on October 23, 1749, and educated in the Dominican school in his native city. After joining the Order of the Holy Cross, he had been elected prior of Maastricht on March 3, 1786, and a definitor that same year. At the time of the second French invasion of Belgium, he and the members of his monastery fled to Germany. He had returned to Belgium in 1795 and, after the suppression of his monastery in 1796, went back to Sittard, where he requested enrollment on the list of pensioned priests from the French government on 17 Fructidor, year IX (September 4, 1800). (This information was provided through the kindess of Mr. Verzyl, curator of the city archives at Maastricht.) See also *De Maasgouw* (1906) 77.

fight for life until the end.

The actions he took to anticipate the worst eventualities for his community also reflect the unsettled conditions of the time. On May 10 of that same year, 1803, he legally arranged for a trust of 8,000 florins to be established as a pension fund for his confreres in their old age, should their monastery be suppressed or they expelled from it, and afterwards arranged to extend the benefits of this precaution equally to any novice who might be admitted. Although a step taken to guard against the future, was this not also a provision for his monastery's rejuvenation? There was also a contingent stipulation that these Crosiers undertook to return the money if, because of some misfortune, the monastery had need of it or if, by good fortune, they were not prevented from ending their days there.[612]

The opportunity to apply these measures to a new recruit soon presented itself. On September 1, 1803, W. M. Kanters knocked on the gate of St. Agatha and offered himself as a replacement for Father van Yperen, who had just died. Kanters had belonged to the suppressed monastery at Venlo and was a Crosier with a personal history of great merit.[613] A vigorous forty-four, he aspired to share the ancient monastery's distress and to shoulder its holy task. We may assume that his confreres welcomed him with open arms, for a communal petition was that same day sent to Wilhelmus

---

[612] Hermans, *Annales*, 1(2):174.

[613] Willem Mathias Kanters had been born at Venlo on March 8, 1759, professed vows in the Crosier monastery there in 1784, and been ordained a priest the next year. After the suppression of his monastery in 1797, he had taken refuge among the Crosiers at Briiggen, whose monastery was suppressed in its turn in 1802. Returning to his homeland, he had promptly been hired as rector of the Latin school in Grave.

Jacobs. On September 23 and in a trembling hand, the definitor ratified the community's request that Kanters be made a conventual of their monastery.[614]

Here we must also note the presence of two other former Venlo Crosiers at St. Agatha: Godfridus Neerhoven, who lived there until his death, and P. Geusen, who subsequently became pastor at Baarlo in Limburg. The assistance of these two men during those years, especially for the praying of the choral office, was quite appreciable, but neither of them were made conventuals of St. Agatha as Kanters had been.[615] Why not? In all likelihood, because both men may well have been in precarious health: Neerhoven at least died in 1806, only nine years after his monastery's suppression. Nor must we forget that the state had just restricted St. Agatha to the *limited* admission of only *eight* subjects during a *ten-year* period. The future renewal of that permission remained wholly conjectural, so the monastery's continued existence required that it accord preference to young postulants or at least to individuals whose health seemed to promise relative longevity.[616]

The Order had endured too many breaches, especially in the lands where French ideas and policies increasingly predominated or had become established. The Order was obviously growing smaller, indeed, was obviously dying. It was absolutely imperative, therefore, that St. Agatha above all concern itself with insuring its survival: its task would be to become a height which stood above the sea then breaking over all the

---

[614] Hermans, *Annales,* 3:603.

[615] L. Emond, O.S.C., *Kruistriomf3* (1923) 150, note 1.

[616] Such considerations better enable us to understand, too, why the many German Crosiers, whose monasteries were suppressed in 1802, saw no option other than to resign themselves to their fate and seek, there or close by, other priestly work as pastors or vicars.

conquered lands. Indeed, the two Dutch monasteries never gave up hope of turning back that sea which surged around their doors and so ranked themselves more closely than ever around their head, the definitor Leurs, whose calm firmness in the face of the logic of the situation had brought him to the threshold of a decisive stage, viz., the office of commissioner general.

INDEX

A

Aachen, 21, 32, 34, 55, 202
Aldenhoven, 45
Aubée, 3, 4
Augustinians, 103, 160, 182
Aulne, 103

B

Barbaix, 146, 162, 172, 174, 175, 176, 180
Bassenge, J. Nic., 41, 170
Bastin, 140, 141, 142, 143, 145, 148, 159
Beek, 212
beguinage, 150
Bejar, 42
Bellisomi, 10
Berghes, 5
Berlot, 171, 174
Bertho, 1, 6, 38, 47
Bettenhoven, 189
Bettincourt, 189
Beyenburg, 21, 22, 34, 36, 41, 42, 52, 53

Biergans, 46
Bihet, 103, 104, 180
Billard, 37
Billotey, 158
Boetzkes, 212
Boksmeer, 203
Bomba, 70
Bonhoulle, 115, 117, 118, 120, 122, 123, 124
Bougman, 68
Bouquette, 45, 46
Bourgoing, 64
Bouteville, 62, 96, 98, 146, 156
Braives, 194
Brasseur, 101
Brassine, 197, 198
Briiggen, 16, 21, 50, 55, 154, 204, 212, 215
Brou, 141, 146, 147
Brüggen, 49
Brumaire, 62, 85, 86, 89, 90, 91, 92, 93, 114, 135, 158, 168, 170

143, 145, 146, 157, 159,
166, 168, 189, 197, 198,
214

90, 91, 92, 93, 94, 95, 96,
97, 98, 100, 101, 102,
104, 105, 114, 115, 116,
117, 118, 119, 120, 121,
122, 123, 124, 125, 126,
127, 128, 129, 130, 131,
132, 133, 134, 135, 136,
137, 138, 139, 140, 141,
142, 143, 144, 145, 146,
147, 148, 150, 151, 152,
153, 154, 156, 158, 162,
163, 165, 166, 170, 171,
172, 173, 174, 175, 176,
177, 178, 179, 180, 181,
182, 183, 184, 185, 186,
189, 191, 193, 196, 197,
198, 199, 202, 203, 209
Liers, 196
Ligney, 190
Loncin, 124, 131, 158, 165,
  166, 169, 171, 174, 195
Loneux, 134, 135, 140
Looz, 27, 184, 192
Louvain, 4, 135
Loverix, 47, 127, 204, 213

M

Maaseik, 3, 4, 16, 21, 55, 74,
  190, 202
Magnette, 194
Mainée, 63
Maire, 198
Manil, 190
Marck, 5
Mariae Laudes, 4
Marienfrede, 21, 48, 53, 204

Marmion, 94
Mataigne, 176, 178
Mechelen, 13
Megen, 203
Mengold, 59, 78, 169
Mercken, 42
Mertens, 204, 205, 207, 208,
  211
Messidor, 68, 69, 127, 128,
  180, 189
Meuse, 2, 5, 17, 18, 19, 22,
  24, 44, 45, 48, 104, 150,
  184, 191
Moha, 60
Mons, 44
Montfort, 30
Mottet, 24, 172, 173, 180

N

Namur, 6, 21, 25, 31, 48, 84,
  191, 195, 196
Nansuy, 86, 103
Neerhoven, 216
Neerius, 17
Népomucène, 185
Neufmoustier, 58, 98
Nivôse, 159, 174
Noiseux, 191
Noiville, 25, 44, 60, 64, 66,
  68, 70, 80, 84, 86, 94, 97,
  100, 101, 104, 115, 116,
  127, 128, 138, 143, 145,
  147, 148, 158, 164, 165,
  168, 169, 193, 195, 196,
  209
Nondonfaz, 1

176
Séminaire, 184
Servais, 129, 176, 190
Seulen, 3, 6
Sikivie, 183, 186
Sittard, 214
Smets, 187
Sœurs, 150, 151, 158
Soleure, 179
Songis, 165
Spiroux, 169
St. Agatha, 16, 21, 34, 41, 47, 49, 127, 155, 202, 204, 212, 213, 214, 215, 216, 217
Stadhouder, 39
Steeradt, 42
subprior, 4, 24, 25, 44, 84, 195
suffragan, 191
Suxy, 21, 26, 31, 32, 74, 191, 196, 202

T

Theobald, St., 183
Theodorus, S., 212
Thermidor, 59, 60, 67, 69, 73, 105, 126, 128, 135, 138, 139, 140, 141, 142, 145, 166, 178
Thermidorean, 73
Thirifays, 187
Tihange, 11, 196
Tille, 24, 82, 150, 158, 160, 196, 209
Tilman, 67, 105, 120, 122,

158, 160, 197, 207, 209
Tongeren, 3, 26, 190
Tournai, 16, 21, 25, 31, 34
Trent, 14, 15, 16, 206
Trier, 39, 42
Trognée, 27

U

Uden, 15, 16, 21, 32, 155, 202, 212
Ursulines, 103

V

Vanderkam, 70, 71
Vandewane, 1
Vanspauwen, 70, 71
Velbruck, 5, 6, 8, 10, 28, 29
Vendémiaire, 82, 83, 89, 158, 169
Venlo, 11, 16, 21, 202, 204, 215, 216
Ventôse, 64, 100, 162, 175, 193, 196, 208
Verdbois, 128
Villers, 27, 195
Virton, 16, 21, 26, 27, 31, 59, 74, 145, 194, 195, 202
Vlasseloir, 31
Voltairean, 61

W

Wallonia, 72
Walthère, 27, 158
Waremme, 26

POSTSCRIPT

Additional resources about Jacques Dubois, O.S.C. and the Crosiers in the 18th century are available online at the Crosier Generalate website under the menu *"Resources"*:

http://www.oscgeneral.org

Among the resources found online are:

- "Msgr. Jacques Dubois and the End of the Priory of Carignan". A translation of an article from the 1950 edition of *Clairlieu*.

- "A First Crisis at Clairlieu in the 18th Century (1735-1752)". A translation of an article from the 1950 edition of *Clairlieu*.

- "The Crosiers of Liège in face of the 1796 Suppression". A translation of an article from the 1949 edition of *Clairlieu*.

- Additional photos of Jacques Dubois, O.S.C. and related persons and locations.